LIVING LIFE'S CIRCLE

LIVING
LIFE'S CIRCLE :

Mescalero Apache Cosmovision

Claire R. Farrer

ⁿda ʔi bijuuɫ sią́ ʔ

University of New Mexico Press
Albuquerque

Library of Congress
Cataloging-in-Publication Data

Farrer, Claire, R.
Living life's circle: Mescalero Apache cosmovision/
    Claire R. Farrer.—1st ed.
        p.   cm.
Includes bibliographical references (p. 251) and index.
ISBN 0-8263-1560-7 (pbk.)
1. Mescalero Indians—Astronomy.
2. Mescalero Indians—Religion and mythology.
3. Mescalero Indians—Philosophy.
I. Title.
E99.M45F37   1991
299'.72—dc20   91-23668
                                      CIP

Designed by Joanna V. Hill

For Claire G. Greenwalt, my mother; and Suzanne F. Hall, my daughter; and especially for the Mescalero Apache Reservation children: those who are, those who were, and those who will be.

"Put my name in your book so that, when I am gone, they will know that you told the truth."

Bernard Second, 1946–1988

Contents

Illustrations

FIGURES

MAP

Acknowledgments

Bernard Second was my mentor and the one to whom I owe the primary debt of gratitude. As will be apparent, there would be no book without him; truly, this book is as much his as mine. As the earlier epigraph indicates, this book was important to him. My regret is that he did not live to see its publication.

It is embarrassing to most Apachean adults to be named individually and publicly. Yet I feel it necessary to acknowledge the help of those who assisted me move from a stance of total naïveté to one of the glimmerings of understanding. Rather than risk causing personal embarrassment, however, I here list only the surnames of those to whom I have spoken and from whom I have learned through the years. The individuals know who they are and, I trust, also know the high regard and respect in which I hold them. Once again I ask them to indulge my Anglo ways.

Aperiodically since 1964, but intensively since 1974, I have spoken with and learned from somewhat over two hundred people from families with the following surnames: Antonio, Baca, Balatche, Baldonaldo, Blake, Blaylock, Botella, Breuninger, Caje, Chee, Chino, Choneska, Comanche, Cooney, Cooper, Duffy, Enjady, Evans, Fatty, Gaines, Gallerito, Geronimo, Guydelkon, Hosetosavit, Hugar, Kanseah, Kazhe, Kirgan, Klinekole, Little, Magoosh, Martine, Martinez, Mendez, Miller, Morgan, Naiche, Orosco, Ortega, Padilla, Palmer, Peña, Pinto, Platta,

Robinson, Runningwater, Sago, Sampson, Sandoval, Second, Shanta, Shash, Simmons, Tortilla, Williams, Yuzos, and Zuazua.

Fieldwork was serendipitous from 1964 to 1974; it was supported in 1974–75 by the Whitney M. Young, Jr. Memorial Foundation, Inc. and by the Mescalero Apache Tribe. Additional fieldwork through the years has been underwritten by grants from the Phillips Fund of the American Philosophical Society, the American Council of Learned Societies, the Research Board of the University of Illinois, Urbana-Champaign, and the Graduate School of the California State University, Chico. Additional archival work was funded by the National Endowment for the Humanities.

In 1984, while I was seriously mulling over Bernard's demands for this work and my own agenda for it, Rosemary O. Joyce provided precisely the proper support. In large measure, she made the production of the manuscript possible by her positive intervention at a critical time. I trust she knows how truly instrumental she has been both in the physical product and the long telephone talks that allowed me to think aloud.

Portions of what became this book were first written while I was a Weatherhead Resident Fellow at the School of American Research in Santa Fe and while I was a fellow at the University of Illinois Center for Advanced Study. Each scholar should have the luxury of thinking and writing time provided by these institutions.

Interim and trial writing were done while I was a guest of Nate and Judy Claassen of Albuquerque as well as while a guest of Arthur and Nancy Freed of Los Alamos. The entire manuscript, however, was written during a sabbatical granted by the California State University, Chico. I am grateful to each for their interest in, and support of, my work.

Barbara Tedlock and Janice Wygant read drafts of the early chapters as they were produced; each provided me with valuable suggestions and indications where my prose or logic went awry. My appreciation to both of them, even when I did not take their advice, is profound.

Thomas Curtin of Waveland Press provided critical reading and long-distance support when my attention or confidence flagged. His enthusiasm for a book not destined for his company was both exemplary and personally gratifying to me.

Graduate students in seminars at the University of Illinois and California State University helped me clarify and develop ideas, while John

B. Carlson first made me aware of the term "cosmovision." (See also Broda [1982].)

The Belgian National Science Fund, through a grant allowing me to work at the Rijksuniversiteit-Gent for the spring term of 1990, provided the opportunity for field testing the manuscript. Rik Pinxten, of that institution, and I co-taught a graduate seminar in ethnoreligion using the first version of this book as our text. I am grateful to the students in that class, and especially Jan Matthieu, for the careful and critical reading that has allowed me the opportunity of clarifying some points and expanding others. Also, Pinxten's professional reading and stimulating intellectual and theoretical discussions of the material herein honed my thinking in several sections and thus made this a better book. I am indeed grateful to all associated with Rijksuniversiteit-Gent.

Through the past several years I have gained much from mail exchanges with a colleague in Israel, Don Handelman; he read and commented on many drafts of the material on clowns and chiasm.

Finally, my most sincere thanks to two people associated with the University of New Mexico Press: Beth Hadas, director, for her early interest in the manuscript and for her encouragement, which, even during the tough times, helped keep me focused on the task; M. Jane Young, reader for the Press, whose gentle reminder that I do not spell well caused me to reread, dictionary in hand, and whose careful and well-reasoned criticism brought the manuscript to early fruition.

LIVING LIFE'S CIRCLE

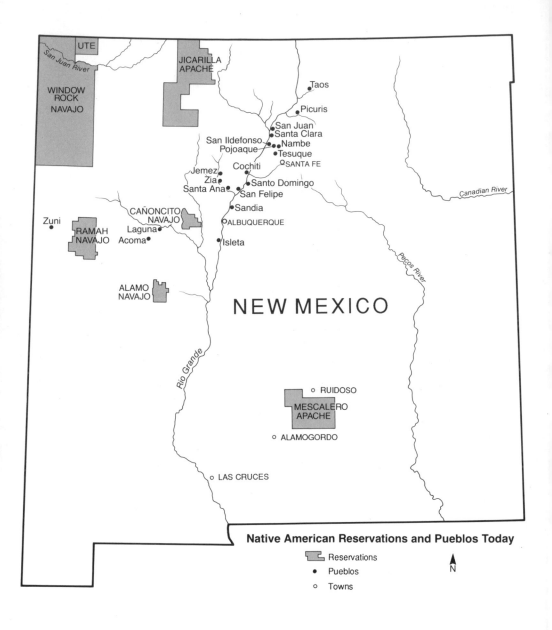

Native American Reservations and Pueblos Today

Reservations
● Pueblos
○ Towns

N

CHAPTER 1

Introduction

What follows is not a complete ethnography of the people of the Mescalero Apache[1] Reservation in southcentral New Mexico; that work, I understand, is being prepared by Morris Opler on the basis of his field experiences in the 1930s. This book is in the interdiscipline of ethnoastronomy, a branch of archaeoastronomy. The nature of the interdiscipline, and indeed of my own interests and training, also demands attention to anthropology and folklore. Yet there is still much that is missing. The picture presented is of only one aspect of everyday reality, that dependent upon religious and philosophical perspectives; they, in turn, are predicated upon a sophisticated understanding of the celestial sphere.

The information upon which this book depends was gathered in the traditional anthropological style of participant–observation, as filtered through the Apachean system of sensibility. It has never been my custom to pay consultants (a term I vastly prefer to the more usual one of informants); no one of the two hundred or so from whom I have learned has received direct compensation. Nor have I ever demanded time or information. Rather, I have spoken to and worked with those who self-selected and volunteered. In return, I have contributed within the bounds of my ability: I have written curriculum materials for children in the reservation grammar school; served as educational liaison with local, county, and state officials when asked by the Tribal Council to do so; designed and initiated in-service teacher training workshops; taught interested people to be literate in Apache; cooked and babysat or otherwise contributed to celebrations; chronicled, photographed and distributed records of significant family or Tribal events; and published popular accounts of contemporary Apachean life to counteract some common stereotypes. On the few occasions when my results of having been at Mescalero have resulted in monetary remuneration, one-half of the profits have been returned to the Tribe through a variety of means. In other words, ours is a relationship based upon reciprocity.

Nowhere is the reciprocity more evident than in the work that Bernard Second and I did together between 1975 and 1988. Here, this cooperation is reflected in a style that is both reflexive and dialogic. The book is very much the work of two people, Bernard Second and me, as he taught and I struggled to learn. It was he who set my research agenda after less than five months of on-reservation fieldwork, an agenda I followed until his death in November 1988. Separating either of us in this book would have made a document with one authoritative voice, a distortion of both the process and the product.

I was taught in the same way that residents of the Mescalero Apache Reservation teach their children. This involves, on the part of the learner, a seven-stage process: observe, see patterns and continuities, wonder, investigate, learn, be corrected, and finally learn how much more there is still to learn. But the book does not follow such a developmental sequence; rather, it takes an omniscient stance by first presenting a case of learning and then moving to examples and results of learning in subsequent chapters.

I do not address the seamier aspects of life, but it is not out of blinded vision. There is jealousy at Mescalero, as there is in any small, closed community. There is alcoholism that exacts a terrible price in family ruptures, fetal-alcohol-syndrome children, road accidents, and violence, all of which have been on the increase since my year 'round residence in 1974–75. There is economic distress amongst the economic strides made by the Tribe as a whole. There is a shortage of adequate housing. There are not enough jobs for those who wish to stay on the reservation, especially for the young and well-educated. There is pressure to acculturate to mainstream American society and contrary pressure to maintain a traditional base. There is all this and more at Mescalero today; although none of it appears here, this book is not a whitewash job. My goal is to present the religious and philosophical systems, rooted in astronomy, that underlie the ideal way of behaving and some examples of that ideal in action. This topic formed the focus of the work Bernard and I did from February 1975 through November 1988.

Bernard had "dreamed" me before I arrived—not in a personal sense but rather in the sense that someone was coming with whom he would work and share much of his knowledge. He was, he told me some considerable time later, greatly disappointed that I, a woman, was the someone of his dream. His knowledge was men's knowledge, not to be taught to or shared with women. While he did not understand why Power would choose a woman, he did not question the choice once he was convinced I was the person of his dream. Nonetheless, it was a problem that plagued us for much of our relationship and upon which I comment below in various chapters. Bernard's agenda for me was one I came to understand as it unfolded.

I went to live on the reservation to do dissertation fieldwork with children's free play, as it could be observed on the elementary school playground, and as entrée into culture-specific communication practices. I was also to work with classroom teachers in the school in an effort to affect positively the communication processes between mainstream American teachers (or those trained in mainstream techniques) and Apache children. I anticipated that the culture-specific communication patterns, readily observable through free play, could be used in the classroom to improve the interaction between teachers and pupils. The Tribal Council and I hoped that the playground work, combined with in-service training workshops for the classroom teachers, would help stem the alarmingly high dropout rate of Apache children. And I did do that work.

However, Bernard insisted I could not understand play without understanding dance, which I could not understand without understanding the girls' puberty ceremonial, which I could not understand without understanding the religion, which I could not understand without understanding the place of the world and its people in the celestial universe. And so I was led to the study of Apachean ethnoastronomy.

Ethnoastronomy is the observational branch of the interdisciplinary field of archaeoastronomy. Archaeoastronomers (and they currently are from the disciplines of anthropology, architecture, art history, astronomy, computer studies, engineering, epigraphy, ethnohistory, folklore, history, iconography, mythology, and symbolism) are concerned primarily with the relationship between celestial phenomena and sites, or the built environment, as well as with the monuments and inscriptions accompanying such locales and with the written record—whenever one is available. Theirs is an interdiscipline where sleuthing and informed deduction are the norms, for the people who produced the sites and documents are no longer alive. Archaeoastronomy has been characterized as "brown" or "green," with the "brown" referring to New World sites that have been dug and the "green" referring to Old World megalithic sites (Aveni 1986; 1989). Be they brown or green, archaeoastronomers dig into the ground and documents. By contrast, ethnoastronomers work with living peoples, usually non-Western, or at least those whose astronomy and perceptions of the celestial sphere and its mechanics differ from the standard Western European derived canon. For these reasons, I characterize us as "blue" archaeoastronomers, or, more accurately, ethnoastronomers involved in observationally verifiable work (Farrer and Williamson 1992).[2] We prefer the terms "ethnoastronomy" and "ethnoastronomers" to those with the archaeo- prefix, since archaeo- refers to the past while our work is with the present, with living people, and with their viable systems of astronomy.

Ethnoastronomers are concerned not only with non-Western perceptions of celestial phenomena but also with how those perceptions organize other behavior, from cognitive structure to values, from timing to enculturation. Ethnoastronomers study the ways in which the sky forms templates for life as seen from particular cultures, or, as I have termed it, "living the sky" (Farrer and Second 1981). So it is not out of an attempt to gloss over the unpleasant aspects of life at Mescalero that I do not discuss much of what would be found in a standard ethnography; rather, my focus is on the sky and its design for living. At Mescalero, much of that design for living is made manifest during the annual public girls' puberty ceremonial.

Particular colors and smells evoke the summer ceremonial time for me: ebony sky blanketed with crystalline stars made fuzzy along the path of the Milky Way; red and orange cinders leaping free as another huge log is added to the eight-foot-diameter fire in the middle of the ceremonial arena; soft white and golden ocher buckskin dresses encrusted with beading and tin cone jingles; Mountain God dancers' bodies painted in high contrast black and white or green and yellow or black and yellow; resinous pine, piñon, mesquite, and juniper woods swirling smoke skyward from cooking fires; afternoon dust dampened by a water truck;

sticky, sweet, cotton candy smells from laughing children's faces. Any of these can transport me instantly to a New Mexican mesa on the Mescalero Apache Indian Reservation, where my mind's eye lingers on tipis, arbors, tents, campers, singing, drumming, the ceremonial lodge, dancers, ceremonial girls, night sky, morning star, visitors. It is summertime and the annual girls' puberty ceremonial at Mescalero.

I first saw the ceremonial in 1964 as the invited guest of my Apachean counterpart, a housewife, she with many children and I with a hip baby. In discussing our lives in common and in difference, I learned one of her ancestors was Naiche, a famous Western Apache warrior. "Funny. I always thought Naiche was a Chiricahua," I said, proud to show off my newly acquired learning gleaned from reading through the Southwest section of our local library in Alamogordo, thirty-five miles from where we sat in the grandstands watching the Mountain Gods dance by bonfire light on a dark and chilly July night. By my statement I inadvertently exercised one of the cultural ways of asking a question: stating what one assumes to be true in a fashion that allows for gentle correction, if needed.

"Most white people think we are all the same. You respect Indians. He *is* Chiricahua," she responded.

While I pondered the use of the present tense for a man long dead, I again demonstrated—albeit unwittingly at the time—a proper interactional stance, that of giving a speaker sufficient time to think and reflect before rushing in to fill a silent space. Anglos are uncomfortable with spaces in conversations; Apaches cherish the quiet times as spaces for reflection and continued thought. She continued, "Maybe you'll be here tomorrow. Maybe you'll come in the afternoon."

I was elated. I had been invited back on my own. She was no longer simply being polite to the wife of her husband's boss. I thought out loud as I responded that I'd have to bring my baby with me and I wouldn't know where to go. And, again unwittingly, I had framed a question in the proper Apachean manner. She, in turn, said that Indians liked babies and she "guess[ed] the camp-out house would be OK," thus responding to my implied question of how to find her.

By the time I returned the next day, it was late afternoon. All the camp-out houses looked alike to me. I had not yet learned to distinguish one from another by the decoration on the tipi covering or by the camp's placement on the mesas surrounding the ceremonial area. But people seemed to know what I was about, since I was passed from one to another until I was once again with my new friend in the midst of a confusion of arbors, tents, and tipis. A cleared space, onto which several structures opened, seemed to be a child care center, for there were several Apache babies sitting in a circle passing fry bread and toys around to one another while babbling confidences.

Saying nothing, my friend looked toward the arbor on one side of the babies' circle. It seemed I was to go in there, but, as I started toward it, a man with his arms folded across his chest appeared in the doorway blocking my entry. In what I was later to learn was ʔinʔchʔindi, or communication without words, he made it clear that my daughter could not enter. Simultaneously an older woman came out of a tent and announced, "I am taking care of the babies."

It is not easy for me to confess what happened next; but I was very young then and undoubtedly made more egregious errors that the Apache people have kindly forgiven. As I sat my daughter in the circle and a child passed her the much-gummed and chewed piece of fry bread, I thought of all the scare stories based on prejudice I had heard of Indians, germs, skin diseases, and infections. With a fleeting rationalization that antibiotics and good physicians were only thirty-five miles away (she required neither, by the way), I heard my daughter say, "Good!" as she eagerly accepted the communal fry bread.

"Shił łika," the babysitter said to Suzanne, "It tastes good to me." Her first lesson in the Apache language had begun as I turned and entered the cool darkness of the arbor with my friend's uncle as my silent, but willing, escort.

I was propelled to a chair to the north of the east-opening doorway. At the south end of the arbor an ancient man picked up a curved willow drumstick and began beating a rubber-topped aluminum pot. His soft singing was almost inaudible, whether because of age or proper singing style I could not then say. His drum accompaniment was augmented by the voices of other men who rose from parts of the arbor to stand behind him and blend their voices with his, while still others began removing their shirts. The ancient man seemed (I had no language tutor, as my daughter did) to be giving instructions to middle-aged men and a young man. Suddenly, it was clear even though they were not speaking English: they were painting and costuming the men who would soon appear as the anonymous Mountain God dancers.

I found it difficult to believe what I was seeing. All I had read insisted that women were not allowed to witness this aspect of the ceremonial; indeed, I was the only woman present and I have never seen it since having been honored that time in 1964.

While I had both notebook and pen with me, each time I started to write, all activity ceased. When I put down the pen and closed the notebook, the activity began again. And I had my first lesson in Apachean decorum. Silently I blessed my mother for her exquisite training of my memory, returned notebook and pen to purse, and concentrated on the pictures and activities in front of me. The words were in a language I did not know, so all the information would have to come through sight. Later that night, after returning home, I typed four pages of single-spaced notes of what I had seen.

When the yellow and green four-pointed star painting had been completed on their chests and backs and just before the men's hoods were put on, it was clear by body action, as well as eye and lip gestures, that I was to leave. I left the tent and stood outside with my friend's uncle, cuddling my sleeping child who, it was apparent as she was handed to me, had been fed and changed into warm clothes against the night chill that is common even in summertime at sixty-five hundred feet. I asked Uncle if there was any meaning to the designs I had just seen painted. He replied, "Au [yes], sure." He paused for a few minutes, looking into the distance, focusing on a particular mountain on the eastern horizon, glancing at the first stars that were just beginning to be visible. When he spoke again, I first thought he had changed the subject: "It is good to live up here. You wake up in the morning. Maybe the crescent moon is still out– – – –and a star.[3] Then the yellow sunlight shines on the green grass. It is good. It is beautiful. Even when it rains, it is good. A man lives a longer time up here."

That was the first of many occasions when I was rewarded with remarkable information after being told, either directly or through *ʔinʔchʔindi,* that I could "keep" anything I could remember but that I could not take notes nor photographs nor make tape recordings. Normally, such admonitions mean that all is safe from Anglos, for few of us have the training my mother gave her children. When I had earlier silently thanked her perspicacity, it was because she had consciously taught my sister and me to observe and remember, gradually bringing us to the point where we could remember long printed or verbal sequences simply by concentrating as we encountered the material. At the time we thought it a game as she would say, "Tell me about everything between here and the corner," or, "I'll time you for three minutes; then close the book and tell me everything that is in the picture." Later she helped us memorize text with similar suggestions.

She gave us hints to help. "Pretend you are going downtown to buy paper dolls. What is the first thing you will see when you leave our property? Then what do you see? Who lives in each house on our side of the street? On the other side of the street?" Or she would ask us to tell her about the color of the water in the West Branch of the Delaware River that ran by our home. Not satisfied with descriptions of the slippery moving water, we would also have to describe the birds and insects we saw.

When we were inside and she had us looking at magazines or books, she would say, "Start in one corner of the picture and go to another; when you finish the corners, do the middle." Or she would say, "Tell me the faintest thing first, then the brighter ones, and finally the brightest."

She trained our eyes and our minds, too, as she made games of memorizing verses, paragraphs, pages, events, pictures, even the action in the Saturday morning serials at the local movie house—always expressing astonishment and pleasure as we verbally drew pictures or recited verses, paragraphs, pages, plots, and dialogue. Long before television, she taught us to associate words and images as mnemonics.[4]

Often people respond with incredulity when they learn that some of the conversations quoted in this book were produced verbatim from my memory. We have grown to accept the mnemonics of pen-and-paper or tape-recorded renderings as substitutes for trained memory; we have even become suspicious of those with excellent memories. Yet we accord memory excellence to others, such as Africans (Vansina 1985), or Burmese (Leach 1965) or, as is rife in our popular literature, American Indians. There is seldom a lack of belief when I tell people that Bernard Second, like all Mescalero Apache Singers of Ceremonies, memorized a complex four-day, four-night ritual with scores of songs each night and intricate ritual actions, and that he went beyond many singers by also memorizing the positions of stars and constellations used for timing within the ceremonial and how those positions change through the course of a year or many lifetimes. Since few Anglo Americans have decent memory training, we are chary when others of us can perform feats we ourselves cannot. Such memorization is not difficult; it only takes practice.

Today, very few of us bother to train our memories; just a generation or so ago, it was commonplace in mainstream American culture. Recitations for entertainment were favored leisure pursuits. And we have but to consider the memory necessary for stage actors and actresses to appreciate what most of us have lost.

Only a generation ago, memorization of data was more common in anthropology as well. Writing of Franc Newcomb, the scholar of Navajo culture, Lyon (1989:139–40) noted,

> Born Frances Johnson in 1887 in Wisconsin, she came to Fort Defiance in 1912 to teach school. Two years later she married the trader at Defiance, Arthur Newcomb, and they moved across the mountain . . . to Blue Mesa . . . to operate their own trading post. Like many other trading families, the Newcombs became acquainted with the Navajo culture of their region, and soon became an agent for its dissemination in the Anglo community . . . She [Franc Newcomb] attended sings and specialized in sandpaintings, and the myths which explained them. *Since she could not take notes during the making of the dry painting, she trained her memory so that she could sketch it out later* [emphasis added].

Newcomb's renderings of Navajo sandpaintings are now considered classics and have been authenticated by Navajos.

Without the kind of training that Newcomb evidently taught herself and that came to me with primary enculturation, my field notes would be slimmer. Yet I am grateful that eventually my note taking—whether with pen and notebook or tape recorder or camera—came to be accepted by most Apache people on the majority of occasions. There were, and still are, times when all are put aside and I may "keep" only what I can remember. At those times, I engage memory and write verbatim records as soon after an event as possible. These notes are later checked with some of the participants and, when possible, with other observers. My notebooks are, and always have been, open to the Mescalero Apache people.

In 1974, ten years after that first field experience watching the painting of the Mountain God dancers, I returned to the reservation with my then twelve-year-old daughter. I was there, with permission and support from the Tribal Council, to live for a year and to do dissertation research for a Ph.D. in anthropology and folklore. It was during this time that Bernard Second began my training, much as he trained children in his care. Truly, I was as a child when it came to things Mescalero.

It was fifteen years after our living on the reservation for twelve months that I wrote what follows. In the interim I have been privileged, in my yearly visits, to share daily life, ceremonial life, birth, death, anger, frustration, joy, and sorrow with friends and fictive family at Mescalero.[5] Although the initial contact with my 1964 friend was a Chiricahua one and many whose surnames appear in the Acknowledgments are also Chiricahua, the majority of those with whom I have worked intensively are Mescalero. This is especially true when considering esoterica such as the ceremonial, religious beliefs and practices, philosophical ideas, and ethnoastronomy, most of which I learned from Bernard.

In 1983 Bernard stated, "It is time to write your book." We began discussing it and designing its structure at that time. It was he who insisted on the gerund in the substantive chapter titles, making the argument that standard academic writing was dead and I was presenting a vital, alive set of beliefs: living beliefs that allowed life. As I roughed out first drafts of the chapters, they were sent to him. The next time I went to the reservation, we would discuss them and, more often than not, he would provide additional information.

When we began working together in 1975, he was impatient with my feeling I needed to publish. He believed it was my task to learn and record, for he always maintained that he would die before me (although he was ten years younger than me), saying, in 1977, "I will not live to see my forty-eighth birthday." He maintained that I would do most of my writing after he was gone and when I "walked on three legs" (that is, with a cane, a situation becoming increasingly necessary due to an arthritic knee). His attitude, combined with the lack of publication enthusiasm on the part of the Tribal Council, led me to an ethical stance that I have not regretted: I have published only with tribal permission or on Bernard's order.

Bernard's death in November 1988 changed the rules. At his funeral Wendell Chino, president of the Mescalero Apache Tribe, recognizing my long association with Bernard, stated that now his people needed the results of those years of conversations. He was unaware that Bernard and I had already begun the process of reproducing those conversations, although not in a conversational format.

In presenting these conversations and learnings from fifteen years of active fieldwork, words are second choice. I would prefer using an interactive videodisk tied to a microcomputer to allow my "readers" to see the complex swirl of an everyday life scene, let alone a ceremonial one. Even that technology would be wanting: I would be unable to present the mingled scent of a wood fire mixed with the smells of coffee and fry bread carried on air so morning crisp that it crackles in your lungs; I'd have no way of expressing the remembered pain of cuddling a perfect, brown-skinned and brown-eyed little girl, who would have called me *shimá* [Mama] in Indian or "Auntie" in English, and who died before she could speak; I'd have no way of communicating the way bones feel brittle, as though made of frozen water, as you stand outside on a windless, bitterly cold winter's night, shock still, bending your neck backward to stare straight up and note with a sudden bone-warming glow that the stars are colored, not white lights, and somehow instantly feeling connected to all creation; I'd have to forgo the almost palpable languor of an eighty-five-degree summer's afternoon with the dust of centuries newly engaged by dancing feet and horses' hooves filling your nostrils and making you think that surely heaven is a cool drink. So I settle instead for words on a page, with a few illustrations and photographs, in an effort to communicate the ineffable, make manifest the sensed, and generate an appreciation for a people who have been so much a part of my life.

Life began, according to Apache religion, with *Bik'égudin̄dé* [According To Whom There Is People/Life], the Creator, bringing the world we know into being in four days. In so doing, Creator also provided a template for people to follow in ordering their lives: ⊕, a quartered circle in its visual form. The template is a base metaphor (Farrer 1980b, 1990) that is transformed verbally and visually and still orders contemporary Apachean life (chapter 2, "Creating the Universe"). Telling time without watches or clocks, as a means of illustrating the base metaphor in depth, shows how knowledge is organized around the sky and how such knowledge is used in a practical way (chapter 3, "Paying Attention"). The transformation of the base metaphor—seen in everyday operation and on a daily basis in activities as varied as picnics, children's play, turns at talk, and basketry—is illustrated in chapter 4, "Seeing the Pattern."

Patterning is fine, but, if allowed to become too rigid, the culture runs the risk of moribundity and consequent death. Cultures must, and do, change in response to the changing swirl of life—whether political, social, or economic—around them. I postulate a theoretical model, which I term "chiasm," for these changes and illustrate the presence and results of chiasm in chapter 5, "Clowning and Chiasm." The stabilizing and transformative principles of chiasm are illustrated and discussed in chapter 6 ("Singing for Life"), where the focus is on the girls' puberty ceremonial, and in chapter 7 ("Crying for Death"), which provides a counterpoint to the previous chapter.

Chapter 8 ("Living Life's Circle") completes the circle begun in chapter 2 by indicating how tradition contributes to the maintenance of self-ascribed identity and everyday life despite the stresses of colonialism and the pressures to accommodate to the larger mainstream American cultural pattern.

For those unfamiliar with Apachean history, I have added an Appendix, "A Brief History of Mescalero Apaches." It contains general historical and contemporary information about location, societal structure, and economics. Some may wish to begin reading here.

In Apachean culture, one must pay for knowledge or it cannot be properly claimed and enacted. Bernard told me my writing would be payment enough, for, he would say, "There will come a day when my people will need what you have written down in your notebooks," or what I taped on my recorders, fixed with my cameras, "or published in the white man's way." But there is another debt that cannot be so easily discharged, a debt I incurred prior to beginning work with Bernard.

In 1974, during the negotiations that preceded my moving to the reservation, I offered to sign a statement of the conditions upon which the then-sitting Tribal Council and I had agreed. Among those conditions was an affirmation that I would share with the tribe any profits that might ever accrue as a result of my being at Mescalero. Wendell Chino, with whom I negotiated rather than meeting with the full council, declined the offer of my signature stating that clever lawyers can destroy whatever is written on paper; therefore, paper agreements are useless. Rather, it is a person's word to which one can be bound, for the Mescalero Apaches believe that "words can come back on you," if a word bond is broken. Words, in coming back, do so in intensified form. So if I were lying to them or they to me, we would in effect "witch" ourselves. So far as I know, such witching is impossible to undo. In the past I most often shared any royalties or compensation for writing with Bernard, since it was primarily his knowledge upon which I drew. On a few occasions the return was in photography or other form. Now, to honor that agreement in word-bond and to pay properly for what I have been taught, I have designated that half of all profits I receive from this book be paid directly to the tribe.

CHAPTER 2

Creating the Universe

For reasons I have never understood, people seem to prefer that there be *a* creation narrative, or *a* version of an event, as with Zolbrod's (1984: 1–29, esp.) beautiful rendering of Navajo creation where an *urform* is assumed. I have critiqued this position sufficiently elsewhere (Farrer 1985); suffice it to say that some scholars seem always to ask for the "truth" and expect that it will come in only one version, despite our experiences of being co-present with others and yet having differing memories of the events. Even should we agree on the content of an event and the remarks within it, there may still be various interpretations of it, as Kirshenblatt-Gimblett (1975) so elegantly demonstrated through the use of a parable that took on different meanings and subtleties depending upon context and the strategic uses to which it was put. Performance theorists (especially Bauman 1984, 1986) and other folklorists (for example, Toelken 1979:30–43) have insisted that folklore and narrative, by their very nature, are variable, though variable within formal constraints.

Similarly, there is no one creation narrative at Mescalero, but several. In their multiplicity there is a powerful elasticity that allows the versions to be called into play for various purposes. Without such elasticity, they might easily become moribund. Ironically, the rendering of oral narrative into the alphabetic format demanded by print is often the first step in the process of morbidity, for literary texts are fixed and quickly become orthodoxy. An oral literature is a living body of information that can change with time, now emphasizing this and later focusing on that. The tellings may be for a variety of purposes: aesthetic, instructional, as a reminiscence, or as history. Yet within the variations, there are common themes and patterns of continuity that allow people to proclaim that they are all "the same thing."

Below there are two dialogues; actually, my part in the dialogues was minimal. I provided only the occasion of telling by my requests, a common practice at Mescalero, and then enacted the part of the audience. The dialogues are separated by eight years; the first was occasioned by a joking comment that was intended and interpreted both ludicly and seriously, while the second was the result of a direct request for a way to begin this book. The dialogues are different but have an important common core, what I have elsewhere called a base metaphor (Farrer 1978, 1980b; Farrer and Second 1981), by which I mean the organizing principles around which Mescalero Apache life is predicated and around which such life is judged. The narratives are the original encoding of the base metaphor, as will become apparent.

DIALOGUE ONE

July 15, 1976 (transcription of tape recording)[1]

> CRF: I wonder how I should begin this "book."[2] Tell me about the beginning time. What happened then?
> BS: When my grandparents started off these stories, they started it off with the Word:

Níaguchilááda?,
> when the world was being made.
At that time there was nothing
> in the universe
> except
> for the Great Spirit, God,
And HE,[3] He made the world in four days.

The first things that He made was the Sun and Mother Earth.
When He made the Sun and the Mother Earth,
> then He made all the elements of the Sky.
He made the clouds, the rainbow, the thunder, lightning

(and,
if you noticed,
I named thunder first because
we call Old Man Thunder and Little Boy Lightning).

And then He made the wind, the rain clouds, fog, mist:
that was on the second day.

On the third day He made all the animals of the world:
those with four legs, those with wings,
those who slither on their belly:
He made all of them.

And then on the fourth day He made Man;
He made Apache.

(Now,
I get into a time in my people's history when
our people were made.)
We were made in a Land of Ever Winter, a House of Ice and
Winter,
which we call in Apache,
Kugha?bikine, House of Winter
or House of Ice—Home, not House,
on the shores of a big lake called *Tuduubits?ǫlidaa,*
Water That You Cannot See Over.
On the shores of that Lake
Mother Earth bore Two Sons;
They were Twins.
She bore them
                                        into this world.
Their Father was the Sun.
The Sun was Their Father.

So when She bore Them,
that land being
The Land of, The Home of, Winter
and The Home of Ice,
She had to keep Them warm.

(Incidentally, Their name was
the First Boy was named *Naayéⁿeskǫne,*
He Killed On Earth.

And
    the Second Son was named *Tubaʔjishʔdiné,*
    He Was Born For Water.
Those were Her Two Sons.)

And
    in order for Her to raise Her Sons on the edge,
      on the banks,
    of that lake,
    She dug a hole
    in the bank
and then put a flat rock on top of there and built fire on it,
    because rock
      heats slowly
        and then it retains its heat a long time.
So She put,
She built,
    a fire on top of that rock,
    that flat rock.
And *under* it,
She placed Her Twin Sons.

And then She nursed Them there
    and
    nursed Them to become Men.
Those were our
    Fathers.
Those
    are who we came from.

Their Father,
the Sun,
    gave Them
    two things:
on one hand He held
    an object that was mysterious and it worked by itself;
    it was deadly.
One,
    one Son took that.
And in His other hand
    He had the bow and arrow.
      And the other Son took that one.

(My people's belief is that the White Man came from the One
    that accepted the strange things that was,
the thing that worked by itself.
And we,
the Apache people,
came from the Son that took the bow and the arrow.)

In that time,
    those Two Twin Brothers are Spirit Warriors,
    who are our Fathers,
    who gave us our beginning.
The Mother Earth and the Father Sun made Them
    Two Wives
    so that
a people could,
could live.
It is from Them that we became a people.

And in those times
    all the animals of the world,
    those that fly and those that are on four legs and those who
        slither
        on their belly,
we all talked the same language then.
We could all understand each others.
And it was a good world then.
    And then something happened.
Something wrong happened
    and we began to have enemies.
And the First,
    the First Born,
    the First Born of the Two,
    of the Two Twin Brothers,
The Two Spirit Warrior Brothers,
the First One was called *Ninaayé^{n}skạn–n,*[4]
He destroyed all,
      all the unpleasant things
    of this world
    for us.
And His,
    His Younger Brother,
    who was born after Him,

(They were Twins but the One that was born after Him.)
who was *Tubaaʔjishʔchʔiⁿé,*
Born of Water,
Born for Water,
   (depends upon what dialect you take it in)
He
made available for us
all the foods of this world.

And all the hardships that we entered when we became a people,
They helped us.
They destroyed our enemy people for us,
  of course, we fought but They helped us.
    And then from there we became a people.

We looked around and we saw all that was around us
  in beauty and in goodness.
We looked around.
  But that there was always something to the south,
  that drew us.
And we started drifting in that way.
    And, as we left
   our birthplace as a people,
  our Spirit Brother Warriors,
They were Twin Brothers,
  They told us,
  They said,
"Go forth as a people.
  You will see many things and do many things.
  And there will be heartaches;
  there will be lonesomeness.
    There will be brutality;
      and there will also be happiness for you.
And remember
  as you travel on your Mother Earth
when you enter the Land of Difficulties
  call on Us,
    CALL on Us,
  for We are your Fathers and your Brothers,
Us Two Brothers;
  call on Us.
Henceforth We will come again

and We will deliver you.
But have faith
  in Us
for Our Father,
the Great Spirit,
God,
    made Us
      that We might protect you,
Our children.
For there is a land that you will enter,
    that you do not know.
You will see the blood of your people spilled.
You will cry, but it will not break your heart.
And henceforth you will be a people.
    And in this world you will call yourselves $^{n}dé$,
    THE PEOPLE."

[The tape recording of this last quoted speech by the Twins was recited in a voice heavy with emotion.]

DIALOGUE TWO

June 15, 1985 (hand-written) [5]

    CRF: I need a complete Creation narrative for the beginning of this book. You know, each time we've talked about this, we keep gettin' interrupted or I ask a silly question that gets us off the track or you remind yourself of something you'd meant to tell me. I put a good story together, but it came from several different times. Tell me the story from the beginning.

    BS: Wait. Let me think. – – – – – – – – – – – We do *not* forget. We remember.

As I told you,
in the beginning of time
  when there was nothing except for the Eternal Power
He decided that He would create.

So on the First Day
  He created the Sun and Mother Earth and the Moon and the
    Stars

and the Wind,
   Rainbow.
On the Second Day
He created all the things that crawl and fly
   like birds, reptiles, worm, insects.
And on the Third Day
He created the four-legged of the world,
   the buffalo, deer, elk, antelope:
   all the ones that walk with hair on them.
And then,
   on the Fourth Day,
He created Man,
   the Apaches.

So
when He created Man,
([Aside to CRF] and by that I mean mankind, women, too),
He told all of His creation,
He spoke to them and
He told them,
   "Because your relative is so weak and fragile, *all* of you are his
   relative and you will help him to live."

And then He,
the Power,
lined up all His creation.
And He told the Sun,
He said,
   "You I have created so that you will be My representative.
      You will be that which Man sees."
And then the Moon,
He told the Moon,
   "You will be their eyesight at night."

And the Stars,
He said,
   "When they travel, by you they will know the directions to
     guide them."

And then the Wind,
He said,
   "You will carry Man's word."

([Aside]: So always be careful what you [head gesture to CRF] say on a
windy day.)

And the Rainbow,
"You will remind Man of My beauty."
And then He goes on to call the Eagle.
He says,
"You who are all-knowing, who is My favored, you who I
have given authority to: Man will have his authority
through you so that when he wears your feathers, when he
wears *your* feathers, it will show to all other of My creation
that I have given Man the authority and autonomy to live
as a people."
(So that's what the [Eagle] feather represents. [Spoken to CRF and
DC.])

Also,
at that time,
God gave the Eagle two names:
the Holy Name, *ʔizhaʔshnantʔą,*
Bird of Authority,
and the two names,
tsełʔlighą-i,
white tail, the bald eagle,
and
tsełʔłitsu,
yellow tail, the golden eagle.

And then He calls up;
He starts off.
God calls the Buffalo, *ʔiyane,*
Eater,
'cause they always spent their day eating, grazing,
"You will be your weak relatives' food, lodging, and clothing."
And the Buffalo accepts
with good grace
his task and chore
in this world.

And then He calls the Elk.
He says,
"You will be food and clothing for your weak relative."

And the Elk also
accepts his chore graciously.

And then the Deer,
He calls the Deer.
    "You will be food and clothing for your weak relatives."
And the Deer also accepts his role graciously.

And then He calls the Antelope
and He tells the Antelope,
    "You will be your weak relatives' food and clothing."
And here the Antelope replied sarcastically
and says,
    "If I am to be eaten by them, if they eat even one hair of my
       body, it will kill them."
So He,
God,
reprimands the Antelope
and says,
    "I created you with generosity and goodness and is this how you
       repay Me? For this I will punish you. Your curiosity will be your
       undoing."

(Have you [to DC] ever hunted antelope? In the old times, they would
get sage and cock the bow with sage and white buckskin on top of a
stick. Once you get their attention, their curiosity, they will not run.
That's their punishment for being mean [selfish].)

([Aside to CRF, recalling an earlier conversation] Now here God calls
an animal that most Apaches would never recognize today; and it
was—though I kept grilling my grandparents and they all agreed it had
to be the horse. And this story was long before we ever met the white
man. Now, *naant'ą–ą* is a slave or someone you order around.)

With you and Man will come love
    and also the Land of Sorrow,
Depredation.

When we were still in the North Country,
    God calls forth the animal who He calls *Nełįįyé*, Beast of Burden,
and He says,
    "You, *Nełįįyé*, will be ^{n}*dé binaant'ą–ą* [the one who people order
       around].

And through your association with each others will come love and
  war, [and] *niu̧ʔyé*," either the Land of Sorrow or of Hardship.
(Now *that* predates Apache-European contact [Aside to CRF].) [6]

And then He goes
  to the Wings of the Air.
And then He calls Owl.
And He tells the Owl,
He says,
  "You are My messenger. So you will be Man's messenger."

(Now people are afraid of owls because they usually bring news of ill
tidings and they associate that with death. If I was to leave here [his
house], I would put a stick across the doorway and I would tell Owl to
let me know if anyone entered my home with ill thought. But today
most people are afraid of it. As I told you [CRF] before, there is nothing
to fear; he is just a messenger.)

And then He calls for the good, ol' boy,
  the Coyote.
He tells Coyote,
  "All of Man's weaknesses and foolishness you will carry—so
  that Man will not be alone in his foolishness and weaknesses.
  And that you will wander on this Earth and in the night you
  will cry in your foolishness, even though nothing bothers you,
  as Man will."

(This Coyote goes on for days. I think that is a good ending right
  there.)

Perhaps the most striking characteristic of these two narratives,
and the primary cornerstone of the base metaphor, is the creation of the
world in four days. By this stroke, four is accorded Apachean significance
tantamount to Western European seven (for the seven days of the Creation) or three (for the Trinity); it is a ritual number with powerful attributes. If, for example, one makes a request of another four times, the
request cannot be denied without acute discomfort or elaborate remedial
rituals. Similarly, when one makes a gift of an important item, especially
if the item has been associated with a ritual event, the item will be prof-
fered four times, with verbal accompaniment, before it actually changes
hands. Or, if one wishes a ritual specialist to perform a particular ceremony, it is appropriate to accompany the request with four gifts. In Dia-

logue One, the first verse/paragraph establishes the primacy of four, while in Dialogue Two it is the second verse/paragraph where the four days of creation are limned.

Invariant order is established within the four days of creation. Creator God, *Bikʔéguindan–n* [Because of Whom There Is Life, or Life-Giver] or *Bikʔégudiⁿdé* [Because of Whom There Are People (and all the other creation supporting people)], first established that which is necessary for life: sun and earth. Contrary to a recent argument (Gill 1987), Father Sun and Mother Earth are not god and goddess, a peculiarly Western European derived notion. Rather, they are seen as progenitors, those responsible for life and upon whom life processes are dependent. "The sun is the physical manifestation of the Creator God," Bernard used to tell me. Father Sun and Mother Earth are understood as a metaphor: just as the sun and the earth are necessary for life as we understand it, so are Father Sun and Mother Earth necessary for people as we understand them to be.

The chain of being established in creation places people not at the apex, as in Western derived civilizations, but rather in a position of vulnerability. Apaches aver that people do not and cannot exist without all that which preceded our coming into being. Parallel to current Western understanding of evolution, as well as having much in common with Genesis, in the beginningtime celestial objects and the earth were first created. These were followed by other natural phenomena, such as wind, rain, cloud, mist, and so on. With the natural world in place, beings, who are dependent upon natural products and processes, could appear. These beings encompassed all things whether insects, fish, birds, or mammals. In other versions of the creation narrative, a feeding order is established, much like our understanding of the food chain. In these versions, plants either come into being with Mother Earth or are created on the next (second) day of creation. While the two accounts differ slightly here, nonetheless finally the stage is set for the appearance of people, beings who are totally dependent upon all other creation before them for their existence. People are inherently weak, because they require the entirety of creation for their lives.

In this creative explosion, there is silence—save for the sound of nature, Old Man Thunder. Old Man Thunder is so named both to accord him respect, since the elderly are revered as sources of wisdom and experience in Apachean social life, and to acknowledge his primacy in the

creative process. Voice is given to thunder and wind but is not an attribute in general of that which is created. Even Creator, *Bikʔégudiⁿdé*, is
silent, not *calling* into being, as with the Christian Genesis, but rather
empowering and bringing forth. The second aspect of the base metaphor,
sound/silence, is thus engendered with silence revered and associated
with Power personified. The most powerful have no need of sound to do
their bidding; as they think, so it is.

Yet ours is not a silent world. We are surrounded by sound, to
which we should attend in order to hear the voice of the universe; but to
hear, we must be silent ourselves and listen. The interplay between sound
and silence is of immense importance throughout Apachean daily and
ritual life. At times Power is manifest through song while simultaneously
being present in silence, as some participating in an event have the role
of voice and others have the role of no-voice. At other times the sound/
silence alternation is nonvocal, produced by costuming or movement
(Farrer 1978). Proper Apachean speech is characterized by periods of
quiet, perhaps interspersed with an occasional "au" (meaning "yes" and
pronounced like English "ooh"]. A proper person leaves spaces in
speech—times of no sound for listening to the universe and one's own
inner voice, times of no sound for contemplation, times of no sound for
framing the next utterance, times of no sound to allow wisdom to descend upon one.

The third aspect of the base metaphor, directionality, is apparent
to Apaches whether hearing the creation narratives in Apache or in English. It is perhaps most apparent to English speakers in the creation of
the Apache people in the north, Land of Ever Winter, and their subsequent movement to the south. There are many other narratives of creation. In the two versions quoted in the dialogues, only two directions
are mentioned specifically, the north and south. However, these narratives encode directionality other than overtly.

Dialogue Two contains embedded symbolic directionality in its
enumeration of natural forces and of animals who have specific jobs in
supporting the existence of their weak relative, people. Each of the natural objects and animals mentioned has a symbolic association known to
Apache people but requiring explanation for non-Apaches. Sun is associated with East, while Moon is associated with South. Stars, though
visibly overhead, are associated with West, as is Wind. Rainbow and
Eagle are associated with North, while also providing the segue between

inanimate and animate. Buffalo is associated with East, Elk with South, Deer with West, and Antelope with North. This is not to say that the earth-surface animal buffalo was found only in the east nor antelopes found only in the north, but rather it is to aver that there is a symbolic association of the animals mentioned with a cardinal direction.

Intercardinal directions are also important, although they do not appear specifically in either of the two creation narratives presented above as dialogues. The following is a transcription of Bernard's response (June 23, 1975) to questions I had about Dialogue One.

> *Nishjaa* [Owl] and Wind are the messengers. West is the Power where Thunder and Lightning lives. And those – – – that – – – [indicating the space between east and south] this two directions on this side represents God's love for us and His ability to give . . . This direction [from the west towards north] represents the Powers . . . represents God's Power to destroy . . . That's where our salvation will come from . . . and, also from these two ways, bad Wind, bad people will come to us – – bad experiences. From the North represents our . . . pride and . . . the ability to harden our faces to live in this world because this world is a tragic and hard world . . . [but] also refreshing and cleansing Power that comes from that [indicating north] side . . . that's the Snow – – – And it is also our ancestral home, when . . . bad Powers come to us . . . then we have, we will retreat back up that way – – – – 'cause that is our ancestral home and we will return to it, until all the bad Winds have battled and we shall come back to our second home.
>   . . . There is another direction that few people know about now; [it] is Northwest, between North and West . . . In the old days it was called *ʔiłchibighą*, meaning the Home of Wind.

I will return to a consideration of directionality shortly. But before doing so, I wish to comment upon the final aspect of the base metaphor: balance/harmony as expressed in circularity.

The two dialogues are perceived by Apaches as being inherently in balance and completing a circle. The first two days of creation bring forth earth, wind, water, sky and those that belong in them; the second two days of creation bring forth animals and people who live on the surface of the earth and depend upon the sky, or celestial sphere, as well: balance. Father Sun and Mother Earth, Moon and Stars, Thunder and Lightning, Wind and Rainbow, Birds and Reptiles, Worms and Insects, Buffalo and Deer, Elk and Antelope—all are in balance. Balanced on the

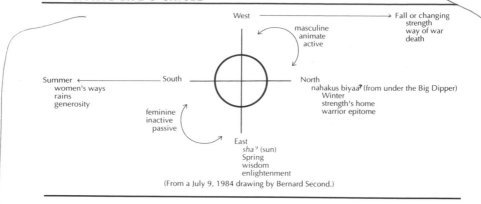

(From a July 9, 1984 drawing by Bernard Second.)

Fig. 2.1   The symbolic association of the base metaphor, readily recognized by most Apaches, had to be explained to me.

other side of them is *ⁿdé,* The People, Apaches. When each retains its proper place and lives in accordance with the plan of Creator, harmonious relationships exist among and between them. Upset any one and the exquisite rightness of the universe is thrown out of kilter. To restore the balance and harmony, a ceremony must be performed, costly in terms of both time and resources.

On July 9, 1984, when Bernard was discussing how I should explain to readers unfamiliar with Apache life the interrelationships between ethnoastronomy and the base metaphor (a term with which he was familiar both from reading my publications and through our discussions of the term), he said, "ⁿdaʔi bijuuł siá̜ʔ" (life's/creation's circleness/completion sits there [or, as I have termed it, both life's living circle and living life's circle]). He spoke the sentence as he drew ⊕ in my notebook. He began by labeling the portions of the cross bars, beginning with the east and gradually filling in the rest of the drawing (fig. 2.1) to illustrate how the base metaphor organizes life and is a reflection of the perfection of creation as generated so long ago by Creator, the Eternal Power: how all is balanced and in harmony, how all is intimately tied to directionality, how all is dependent upon a quadripartite view of reality, all is circular—thus leading back to balance and harmony.

To summarize the associations, East is symbolically linked with *sha?* (the sun) with the spring of the year, with wisdom, and with enlightenment. South is symbolically linked with women's ways and the moon, with summer, with rains, and with generosity. West is symbolically linked with men's ways and the way of the warrior, with the fall season or changing, with strength, with death, and with stars. North is symbolically linked with *nahakus biyaa'* [from under the Big Dipper], with winter, with the original home of strength, with the height of a warrior's life, as well as with Rainbow and Eagle. Taking the east and south together, the primary associations include qualities suggesting femininity, passivity, and inactive nature, while taking west and north together, one finds a masculine, active, animate nature.[7] But each set of associations must be co-present for there to be harmony and balance in the social world or in the universe. Neither set is complete in isolation; rather, it is within the interactions that each assumes its rightful meaning. As Bernard stated in a tape recording of June 28, 1975,

> . . . and to us a cross is the four directions of the universe coming together, converging; that's the cross to us. And then the circle, . . . that means all the Powers of the universe encircled makes God, for all His Powers are spread out but you put that all together again and there's one God. So that's why they bless it [i.e., perform a pollen blessing sequence] like that [sprinkling pollen to the east, to the south, to the west, to the north, and then from south to north and from west to east, forming a quartered circle anchored at the cardinal points].

In Western European derived societies, metaphors are considered to be rather simple statements that provide information about the unknown, or about a poorly understood concept, by linking it to something well known, as in the example, "A mighty fortress is our God" (from the definition of "metaphor" in the 1980 *Random House College Dictionary*). We do not pretend that any of us in our society knows or understands God, but we do believe we can limn a portion of Him through a comparison of God with something we do know and can understand, a fortress. So God stands in relation to us as a bulwark protecting us (or, as some might have it, imprisoning us), just as a physical fortress protects us (or imprisons us).

Metaphors in English are usually verbal ones. But, until very recently, most Apaches were aliterate, relying instead on verbal and graphic representations of that which we usually write. Thus, in its essence and in its simplest form, the Apachean base metaphor is visual—the quartered circle, ⊕. Yet that simple symbol is packed with an encyclopedia's worth of information and association, some richly symbolic itself and some straightforwardly informational or instructional. Contemporary Apache life is built upon the foundation of the base metaphor, which in turn had its genesis in the very acts of creation.[8] The base metaphor's visual representation as a quartered circle is transformed in many different ways, both verbally and graphically. But in its essence, it always refers to the celestial sphere as the residence of the physical manifestations of that which is given verbal currency in creation narratives. It is to a consideration of the base metaphor in the celestial sphere that I shall turn next.

CHAPTER 3

Paying Attention

Ethnographic fieldwork is a little like putting together a two-thousand-piece jigsaw puzzle bought at a garage sale without its box: colors, shapes, bits, and pieces are all there, but you don't know where they go or how they are supposed to fit together to form an integrated whole. You don't even know if you have all that you need when you begin to work nor do you usually know whether or not, and when, you have all the pieces necessary to construct the picture. Gradually recognizable images emerge. The joy recognition brings quickly fades as you accidentally kick the table, upsetting it and the puzzle you have worked so hard to piece together. Or, just as you think you have a clue for the whole picture, someone comes along and rearranges your work, declaring their vision is better. While you might argue with better, you must agree that it is as plausible. Ever so slowly, the patterns and colors repeat in ways that lend unequivocal assurance to a particular interpretation. The puzzle process fades into the background as you eagerly fill in the missing bits to form a coherent whole.

In this chapter I discuss two such ethnographic puzzles that I worked on, literally for years, until finally all the pieces fit and the picture that emerged was both valid and correct.[1] One puzzle concerned the timing of the ceremonial while the other involved the singers of the ceremony moving their positions, sometimes in ways that made it more difficult for them to accomplish the ritual actions accompanying their singing. It seems now that I was very slow not to have apprehended the picture earlier. At the time, however, these aspects of the ceremonial were great puzzlements indeed as I tried various patterns that were upset or rejected by the Apache people. Both puzzles were solved ultimately with the same data. The solution is simple—or it would have been, if only I had been capable of "paying attention," as I had been admonished to do on so very many occasions.

The puzzles were solved through ethnoastronomy and the base metaphor. In retrospect, I should have realized the importance of ethno-astronomy in 1964 as I watched the body painting of the Mountain Gods and heard it described with reference to the stars, moon, and other natural phenomena. Instead, I assumed Uncle was giving me a poetic and metaphoric explanation engendered by our being outside on a lovely summer's night as the stars rose. His statement *was* poetic and metaphoric, but I missed the proper referent: the natural universe and especially the celestial sphere. In 1975, Bernard told me for the first time that, for the Mescalero Apache, *everything* is based upon the natural universe and the way it operates. Again, I should have been more perceptive—but, then, that is always what we say when the boxless jigsaw puzzle finally begins to make sense.

I noted aloud one day, while Bernard and I were talking, that the outline form created by the four main tipi poles of the ceremonial tipi used in the girls' puberty rites, along with the ceremonial tipi itself, replicated the visual representation of the base metaphor ⊕. The four main tipi poles are called the Four Grandfathers, and each one stands for a day of creation and a cardinal direction. While in fact the Four Grandfathers do not stand in the precise cardinal directions, given the exigencies of having the tipi doorway open due east, symbolically the base metaphor is given visual presence. I was rather elated at my startling discovery but was quickly brought back to proper perspective by Bernard's matter-of-fact comment, "It's the same thing." Soon, I found that narratives, visual representations of many kinds, structures, and even politeness and decorum were also said to be "the same thing." All of the sameness, I was told, comes from the natural order of the universe. It was clear I needed to learn more about that natural order, as it is perceived and constructed by the Mescalero Apache. I needed to learn Apachean ethnoastronomy, but how was it to be done when such knowledge is the province of men rather than women?

Mescalero Apache men say that women have all the power.[2] In traditional times, and to a significant extent now as well, women owned houses and all the goods within them except for a man's hunting gear and his personal clothing, jewelry, and other minor possessions. Although it is technically no longer legally possible, women could divorce their husbands merely by placing the husband's goods outside the house. Apache women enjoyed freedom in other areas as well and were never restricted to the hearth or home; they could even be warriors or hunters, if they so chose. Indeed, there are many Apachean stories of women who were superb warriors, hunters, peace emissaries, and diplomats— especially during the times of harassment by the Spanish, Mexican, or American armies.[3] Women seldom held political authority,[4] but nonetheless made—and make—their political views known both in public and in private. There are those who maintain that today no man is ever elected to the Tribal Council at Mescalero without a coalition of matrilineages backing him and his position. Should he fail to represent the interests of those matrilineages, and especially if it is perceived that his actions may redound to the detriment of either the matrilineages or the tribe as a whole, he will not be supported for reelection. Mescalero Apache women have power and importance in life in general; they certainly are not second class or the second sex, as is common in Western European—derived cultures.

Nor is the term "elder" reserved only for *men* of wisdom. Elderly women are considered repositories of cultural knowledge and folklore today, as they were in the past.[5] The place of women in Mescalero social life was, and is, important (see Flannery 1932). Because this is so, Bernard averred that men invented religion and kept it to themselves; for, if women had that, too, they would be in total control. So the religion is the province of men, as is the ritual language with which so much of religion is put into praxis.

Sometimes women do learn the ritual language, simply from being around it so much of their lives. This is especially true of the women who themselves are ceremonial practitioners and is particularly true for the *naaikish* [godmothers or sponsors] who shepherd girls through their puberty ceremonials. These women learn some of the ritual language not only from cognates in context, but also they learn it from the men who conduct the puberty ceremonial. The *gutą́ą́ł* [singer; literally, one who sings, i.e., a ritual specialist who sings ceremonies][6] will instruct the *naaikish* in the meaning of that which he sings as well as the appropriate behavioral responses of both *naaikish* and girls having their ceremonial, even if he does not directly provide a word-for-word translation of the text of the songs. When a women does learn the ritual language, in whole or in part, she teaches it to her own apprentices. I do not know of any women, however, who set out specifically to learn the ritual language, nor do I know of any singers who would purposefully teach women the language of the ritual songs. Men teach this language, that is said to be an archaic form of Apache, only to other men, just as they teach religious practice and rituals only to other males.

Because women do have power in Apachean culture, my own life at Mescalero was easier. Yet the inappropriateness of women being taught or learning the ritual language complicated my understanding of that which Bernard termed "the same thing." It is relatively easy to associate a visual representation, such as the quartered circle, with the floor plan of a tipi having a tetrapod as the basis of the structure. It is quite another thing to understand the association between that quartered circle and a complex of songs sung over several nights, with their associated ritual actions, when one is of the wrong sex to be instructed. It often seemed language was the key to what I was trying to learn.

Language had been a focus of my interactions from the very beginning—partially because I, like any anthropologist, was convinced of the importance of learning the local language and partially because of Bernard's own insatiable curiosity about "whiteman's scholarship." Then, too, my dissertation work at the school and on the playground included a goodly portion of language; children spoke Apache on the playground and (all too often, from their teachers' perspectives) in the classroom as well. Plus, both the Title IV and Title VII programs at the Bent-Mescalero Elementary School on the reservation were heavily involved with the Apache language.[7] And, since a large part of my reason for being at Mescalero was the elementary school and keeping Apache children in it, I spent much of my time in the school on the hill behind (to the south of) the Tribal Center at Agency. At the school, my headquarters was in the Title VII workshop that, fortuitously, was also the center for language instruction.

In 1974 Elaine Clark, a Summer Institute of Linguistics/Wycliffe Bible Translator, had been working at Mescalero for about five years. She had developed an orthography, based on the Roman alphabet, that was in process of being accepted, with slight modifications, by the tribal language committee, the members of which represented each of the three linguistic groups on the reservation (Mescalero, Chiricahua, and Lipan). Clark was also teaching Apache literacy classes both to native Apache-speaking teaching assistants, who were doing the classroom language training for children, and to the few Anglos associated with the school's Title VII Bilingual Program of cultural retention and training. As I sat in on Clark's classes in writing and reading a language that is still primarily an oral one, the Apache participants insisted that, if I really wanted to learn the language properly, I should work with Bernard Second, since he was the one to whom they went when they themselves had questions about Apache, whether it was Mescalero, Chiricahua, Lipan, Jicarilla, Western Apache, or even Navajo. When Bernard and I did begin to work together in 1975, we struck a mutually beneficial bargain: he would teach me colloquial Apache and I would teach him structural and descriptive linguistics.[8] Despite Clark's classes, my pronunciation of Mescalero with its many glottalizations and its four tones was abominable.[9] This led Bernard, during our early sessions, to admonish me, rather sharply, "Pay attention! Pay attention!" This became almost a litany in many contexts through the years.

Sometimes, even when deemed to be paying proper attention, I still could not grasp a sound, or perhaps the meaning of a word, Bernard would explain it to me using what he called the "roots," the etymology from the ritual language. The ritual, or root, language is replete with allusion and metaphor, well suited to poetry. It is believed that the ritual language was once the language of all the people, but, while the everyday language changed, the ritual language remained constant, so that now only specialists understand it fully. It is a situation parallel to Latin, Greek, or Old High German as they relate to the spoken English of today. Of course, since I am a woman, it was inappropriate for Bernard to teach me the ritual language itself; instead, I learned only a word or two when it became necessary for me to access a root in order to comprehend. Whatever I could remember from having paid attention, I could keep—and that included root words that might provide additional keys to the base metaphor.

During the course of our linguistic work, we became good friends and eventually fictive kin. The fictive relationships opened new opportunities that made paying attention much easier, for I acquired sisters to help me learn what things women ask and what things are improper for us to ask. I learned what one may expect from one's brothers and the persuasive power of invoking a kin term to realize goals or desires. And I learned that, to pay attention properly, one must observe quietly and constantly.

Apache children are socialized from birth to pay attention to their surroundings, to observe what goes on around them, to learn through such observation, to absorb quietly without questioning. It is quite sobering to be an adult but also to be just learning what even two-year-old children already know. Through observation and through a sincere effort to pay proper attention, I realized with chagrin that I had made naive errors on the basis of limited previous visits. And, as Wendell Chino said, confirming what Bernard and others had hinted at, "Now that you've been here, you won't make those mistakes again."

"Those mistakes" concerned an elegant, and even replicable, analysis in my master's thesis on Mescalero clowning that unfortunately was published (Farrer 1973). While elegant and replicable, the analysis was wrong, by Apachean perceptions. Rather than being upset at my naïveté, I was told simply to "pay attention," especially in matters of ritual, religion, ritual language, and the meanings of each. While I was not to be instructed, it was assumed that I would reach a correct understanding in the way that Apache children do: by observing. Once believing I understood, I could discuss matters and be corrected, if necessary. But paying attention was crucial.

Paying attention raised as many questions as it answered, especially when the topic was the girls' puberty ceremony or other religious or ritual activities. And asking direct questions is not polite at Mescalero, even when it is in an area to which one reasonably might expect access. When an Anglo person persists in asking direct questions of an Apache person, an answer will be given to quiet the Anglo's persistence, if the Anglo and the questioning cannot be ignored altogether. The answerer is under no obligation to answer truthfully and usually will say almost anything plausible in order to escape what to an Apache is an acutely embarrassing situation. Proper adults do not question other adults; for that matter, proper children question adults only in private, usually in the confines of the family, nuclear or extended. When Anglos insist on asking questions in ways they feel are acceptable to gain information, a situation arises for which Anglos and Apaches have very different definitions.

Apaches do not wish to be embarrassed by having to respond to what even children do not ask in public. But, if an Apache person indicates impatience or anger at the inappropriate Anglo behavior, it is the Apache who loses face. Similarly, if the Apache were to cause the Anglo to become embarrassed, it is again the Apache who loses face. One simply does not place another adult in an embarrassing position; to do so is to diminish one's own self. Oftentimes, when placed in such acutely uncomfortable positions, Apaches will provide an answer they assume the Anglo wishes to hear. Or sometimes people will say, "I don't know," and, if at all possible, leave the situation immediately.

The preferred method of asking questions is by indirection, especially if one is asking about things that may be sensitive in nature. A proper person asks questions using frames such as, "Somebody said . . . ," or, "Maybe they do that because . . . ," or, "I wonder if . . . ," or simply by making a statement that can be corrected if it is wrong. It is a breach of decorum for an adult to correct or instruct another adult in public. An Apache overheard doing so, even to a persistent Anglo, is likely to be chastised, either directly or by pointed teasing, for one must always avoid a potentially embarrassing situation, especially in public. By contrast, private teasing and joking is an exquisite art at Mescalero.

Having long understood and exploited proper questioning procedure, I felt confident to broach the two questions about which I had puzzled for some time. Even though the questions concerned ritual activity, I felt I had assimilated enough decorum to ask politely. One question had to do with the timing of the girls' puberty ceremonial, particularly on the last night and final morning. The other question concerned why the singers conducting the ceremonial reversed their positions—relative to each other and the girls for whom they were singing—depending upon whether it was night or day.

The first question was likely to be a delicate one, since it dealt with obviously intricate ritual actions. On the last morning of the girls' ceremonial, a ritual event is performed: *haighá* [sun pulling; in slow speech—*shaighá*]. The sun is "pulled" up over the eastern horizon by the singers so that, if it is timed properly, the last line of the last song is sung just as the complete disk of the sun fully clears the mountains to strike the sun symbols painted on the upraised left hands of the singers. In order for the singers to perform all the songs that must be sung as well as the ritual actions necessary to complete the ceremonial, the timing for the sun pulling must begin by about ten o'clock of the previous night. If this careful timing does not occur, and there have been years when it has not, then there is insufficient time to sing all that must be sung and to perform all the necessary ritual actions in time to greet the rising sun properly. It was obvious to me that timing was crucial to the proper unfolding of the ceremonial, but I had never seen Bernard wearing a watch inside the Holy Lodge—or anywhere else, for that matter. Yet, when he was the Head Singer of the ceremonial, the timing was exquisite, with the sun seeming to rise on his command to strike the sun symbols on the singers' palms.

When, after several years of watching, I finally did ask (using the appropriate indirection, of course) how this exquisitely contrived control over the sun was accomplished, I was told, "Pay attention!" This obviously was not women's business and I was not going to have even properly phrased questions answered, other than by being told to do what I thought I was already doing—paying attention.

The other question did not seem to be quite so sensitive. When singing inside the Holy Lodge at night during the ceremonial, the singers face west and face the girls for whom they are singing. The Head Singer is in a position farthest to the north or right, while the other singers are arrayed in descending order (according to the length of time each has been singing) to the Head Singer's left—despite a verbal insistence that the position of honor is in the south. The only exception to this arrangement when facing west at night is when a singer is training an apprentice; then, the apprentice will sit immediately to the left (to the south) of the singer from whom he is learning and thus will be in line ahead of men who are full-fledged singers.

To further deepen the enigma, all movement in the Holy Lodge is sunwise. Upon entering from the eastern opening, one must proceed to the south, then west, then north—never would a person turn right, to the north, nor cross the center to go immediately to the west. Thus the positioning of the singers is awkward: to reach the girl for whom he is singing, a singer must make a circuit that is sometimes difficult to manage when several girls are having their ceremonial at the same time and hence sharing the Holy Lodge (fig. 3.1).

However, when it is daytime and the singers are outside the Holy Lodge, as they are on the first and last mornings, the Head Singer is in the south, in the putative position of honor, with the others in rank order to the north of him. It also seemed significant that during the day, when

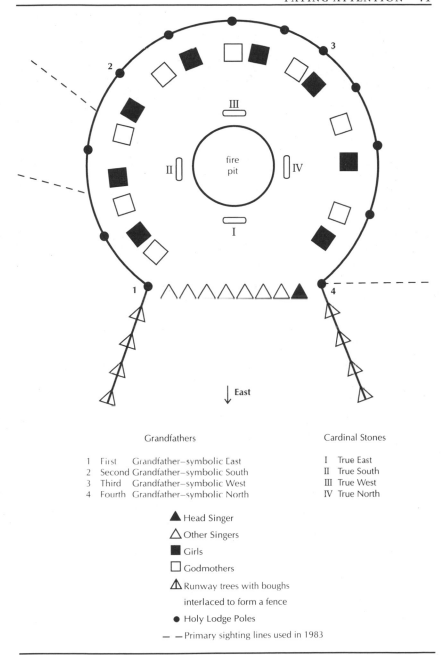

East

Grandfathers

1 First   Grandfather–symbolic East
2 Second Grandfather–symbolic South
3 Third   Grandfather–symbolic West
4 Fourth Grandfather–symbolic North

Cardinal Stones

I   True East
II   True South
III True West
IV   True North

▲ Head Singer

△ Other Singers

■ Girls

□ Godmothers

⚠ Runway trees with boughs
   interlaced to form a fence

● Holy Lodge Poles

— — Primary sighting lines used in 1983

Fig. 3.1   Holy Lodge 1983

lined up in rank order from south to north, the singers stand up; at night, they sit down inside the Holy Lodge. For a portion of the last morning, however, the singers sit and face east, again with the Head Singer in the south. These movements were too deliberate and too consistent to have been simply chance. The movements between positions in the south and north, as well as between facing east and west, obviously carried import; reversals of positions are not to be taken lightly in ceremonial contexts. But again my carefully phrased questions were answered with the by now familiar, and at times totally exasperating, demand to "pay attention."

I tried various hypotheses about why these reversals occurred. Sometimes my speculations were greeted with, "Bah!" That was clearly an indication that my ideas were so ridiculous as to be unworthy of serious comment. Sometimes my tentative explanations were countered with, "Interesting. I never thought of it that way." That is a much more polite way of saying, "Bah!" Sometimes my explanations were met with laughter. That was perhaps the worst reaction of all; but at least it was always done in the privacy of the home of one of my fictive family members, rather than out in the open, in public. More and more frequently I was simply, if somewhat petulantly, told, "Pay attention!"

The unanswered questions had to be set aside for, while I was sure I was paying attention to everything possible, there was something I could not ken to which I still needed to attend. I continued to work at Mescalero whenever possible and to bring Bernard to my teaching sites when I could not be at Mescalero. While other questions received answers in a variety of ways, my two ceremonial questions remained frustrating enigmas, despite my rigorous attention paying.

During the years that my questions were unanswered, and many times unasked, I toyed with the notion that I may have been misinterpreting what was being presented to me. Perhaps the sky was not so important; after all, as late as 1873 the Mescalero were hunters and foragers. Conventional wisdom holds that calendars and seasons and time and stars are important considerations for agriculturalists but of little consequence for others. Yet I could not sustain such heretical thoughts for very long when I recalled that the Mescalero had names for seasons as well as for months. It is of vital importance for nonagriculturalists to know when to expect to be able to harvest which foods, when animals are in rut and their meat tastes terrible, when bad weather is to be expected and it might be impossible to gather sufficient food to sustain a population. Not knowing such things—and they do require intimate knowledge of seasonal rounds—could well mean starvation. It seemed I had no choice but to modify my position to a belief that celestial phenomena and the sky were important only in gross metaphoric terms and as a loose calendar. After all, I reasoned with myself, there are no stonehenges or medicine wheels associated with Apaches, nor any for which they claim ownership. Yet, even as those thoughts meandered through my head, which ached from paying attention and yet still missed what I was supposed to be attending, I had to consider Chamberlain's (1982) Pawnee work. He demonstrated that the very structures in which the Pawnee lived were astronomically important. And the Pawnee, like the Apache, relied for a goodly portion of their sustenance on hunting. I also had to consider the concept of "the same thing," which seemed clearly to be linked to celestial phenomena and Creation. I could not begin to count the times I had been told that the base metaphor was "the same thing" as Creation, which was "the same thing" as the Holy Lodge, which was "the same thing" as politeness—and on, and on. No, I finally had to reject the idea that astronomy was unimportant and instead had to admit that I needed to learn what its importance was and how properly to pay attention to whatever it was I should have been attending as I went about my disparate chores at Mescalero.

In some years I went to Mescalero a few days or weeks early for the summer ceremonial. This provided time to visit with fictive family and friends, as well as to fill in notes and attempt to provide answers to questions that arose during the time I was gone.[10] The time immediately before a ceremonial was always busy, for there was always someone to see, some event to attend, cooking to do, errands to run, new babies to meet and to hold and snuggle, a lexicon to be worked on, or time to be spent with Bernard learning the next items on his agenda for me. Each year as ceremonial time nears, the pace of life intensifies and everyone becomes extremely busy.

Thus, when I was told for a couple of years in a row to awaken Bernard at 3:30 or 4:00 A.M., or some other predawn hour, I did so begrudgingly, feeling my head had just hit the pillow, after hastily scribbling rough field notes, when I had to get up once again. At those hours, I could never match Bernard's wide awake stride and clear-headedness. After he offered prayers, what I came to call the sky watch would begin.

He stood, always first facing east, craned his neck and assessed the sky from various places and angles around the house, and spoke to me only to ask the time. Before replying, I almost invariably looked at my watch—not an easy procedure, since it was still dark outside and I would have to fumble in the backpack for my flashlight, examine my watch, replace the flashlight, reshoulder the backpack, and grump silently about being outside when I wanted to be asleep. I knew better than to query him during times such as those and so simply had to endure silently having each of my digitally precise hours and minutes ignored and commented on only by a rather sharp, "Pay attention!"

I, too, looked up to be surprised at the vast canopy of stars that are so very clear and seemingly so close in the desert Southwest, and to be delighted to find the shimmering colors of stars that I had previously assumed to be white lights. But I was not sure to what I was supposed to be paying attention—the sky is vast.

Sometimes we would not go outside until around 6 A.M. and we would look only to the east. At these times I was sure he was ascertaining precisely when the sun would rise so that his timing would be proper on the last morning. I was especially convinced of this when he would again ask me the time. Yet my reasoning was difficult to sustain; his house was a couple of hundred feet lower than the ceremonial mesa and the horizon line was very different. Again my questions went unasked, for they would have received no answers, and again, after each tolling of the time by my very Anglo watch, I was told to pay attention.

During our early morning forays, whether before or after dawn, I found my thoughts hovering around the matter of timing. Perhaps, I thought, if timing *is* as critical as I suspected it was, we should be three miles up canyon, even though at Bernard's house we were in a direct line with the ceremonial mesa. If timing is so critical, it should be practiced on the mesa itself rather than at a house miles down canyon—or so I thought. During another year's musings I thought that perhaps he was taking cues from the sky but was focusing on Anglo time from a watch. Yet, if that was so, then I should have seen or heard him ask others what time it was, since he never asked me the time before or during a ceremonial.

If all this early morning rising and star watching did have to do with the ceremonial, then did it also have to do with pulling the sun? There is a picture of Bernard in a National Geographic Society publication (Billard 1974:190) as he performed the sun pulling; in that photograph, he was shown standing, although in the late 1970s and 1980s he sat to perform those actions. I told myself that the photograph had been taken several years previously, before Bernard was Head Singer and when the ceremonial was being sung on a lower mesa.[11] Perhaps, I thought, details of the ceremonial, like colors and their symbolism and like directional quality, depend upon the individual singer's vision. Maybe some singers like to sit while others like to stand, or maybe changing the mesa also changes the posture. Of course, the two mesas have different horizon lines with different apparent angles, depending upon whether a person sits or stands. Maybe I should concentrate more on horizon lines. Or maybe the physical location of the ceremony has something to do with the timing. That thought was difficult to sustain, for singers will sing a ceremony almost anywhere on the reservation, providing there is sufficient flat space for the pitching of the ceremonial tipi and dance grounds for the Mountain God dancers. It was a nice hypothesis that I reluctantly put aside, for it simply did not work.

Many times I felt it would all make sense if only I could stay on the ceremonial grounds all night, something I was not able to do between 1975, when I left the reservation, and 1983. There is a midnight curfew for Anglos at Mescalero, from which only resident Anglos are exempt. Since I could not observe and since I am a woman—and therefore not allowed to ask salient questions on this subject—I paid attention whenever possible, while knowing I was missing a great deal.

During the summer ceremonial in 1983, Bernard insisted that I remain behind him inside the Holy Lodge throughout the night's singing, regardless of the Anglo curfew. While I felt uncomfortable, he assured me that inside the Holy Lodge he was in charge and, therefore, if he said I stayed, I stayed. For the last night, as with the previous nights, we entered the Holy Lodge around 10 P.M. in a strict order. Bernard, as Head Singer, walked in first, followed by the girl for whom he was singing, me, the godmother for the girl, and then the other singers, girls, and godmothers in order of rank of the singers. My placement between the girl for whom he was singing and her godmother made a powerful symbolic statement of my belonging. I was not challenged by the civil authorities either that night or any other night in subsequent years. At last I was in proper position to pay attention throughout the night.

The Holy Lodge (fig. 3.1) is like no other tipi. It is predicated on a tetrapod, rather than on a tripod as with everyday tipis. The lower two-thirds of the framework is interlaced with oak boughs with leaves intact, while the upper third is covered with white canvas, leaving a smoke hole free at the apex. The only night light comes from the fire pit in the middle of the Holy Lodge. The pit is marked at ground level by four large stones, each placed at a true cardinal point, rather than at an intercardinal as for the Four Grandfathers, the four primary poles of the tetrapod. Each Grandfather is associated with a cardinal direction, and with a day of Creation. However, because of the necessity of having the Holy Lodge open directly to the east, the Grandfathers are displaced from true cardinals. With the singers sitting with their backs to the east just at the dividing line between the eight-treed runway and the Holy Lodge, the circle of the Holy Lodge is completed. A bird's eye view shows the quartered circle, with the cross lines defined by the four cardinal rocks surrounding the fire pit. But the Holy Lodge is not a completely closed circle; the east is opened to the rising sun and is framed by the runway consisting of four small evergreen trees on its north side and four on the south.

On the fourth and last night of the ceremonial, the singers arranged themselves at the eastern entry of the tipi while the girls took their places on cow skins on the ground around the inner periphery of the Holy Lodge and their godmothers settled next to them on blankets placed on the ground. In 1983 I stood immediately behind the Head Singer, and thus was next to North Grandfather. Since this position was also perceived to be the beginning of the runway area, people crowded in and pressed from behind in order to get a better view and to hear the singers better, for there is substantial aural competition from the singing and drumming for the dancing of the Mountain Gods that takes place in the arena proper (see fig. 3.2). In order to hold my place, I sometimes had to cling rather tenaciously to North Grandfather. The Holy Lodge is not arranged for the convenience of spectators but rather with regard to holy canon.

Before the night's singing began, Bernard kept bending down to look to the south-southwest through boughs and between poles of the lower portion of the Holy Lodge. Suddenly, although one girl and her godmother had still not come in (her singer was present, however), he signaled the beginning of the night's singing by the rhythmic shaking of his deer hoof rattle. After only a few sets of songs, he abandoned his looking between the boughs and looked straight up through the smoke hole. The singing continued with occasional breaks to allow the girls to

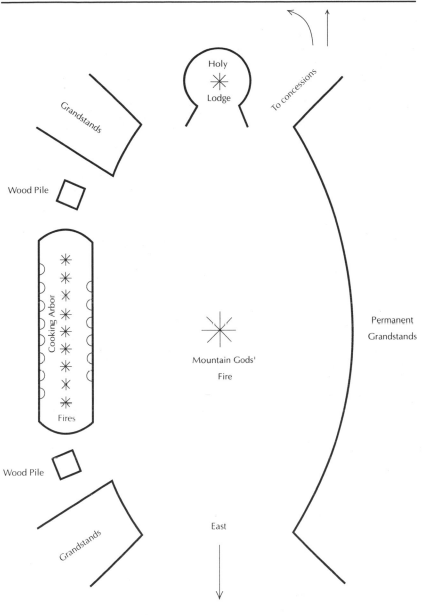

Fig. 3.2   1983 Ceremonial Site Plan

sit and rest for short periods of time, since they must dance whenever the singers sing.

A break was called around 1 A.M. Mountain Daylight Time (MDT), but not until after Bernard had asked a Navajo man, who had been standing behind me, to step aside a couple of times while Bernard looked up between the North Grandfather and the first runway pole. Each time the Navajo was moved aside, Bernard murmured a polite, "Excuse me."

From all the before-dawn mornings when I had awakened Bernard for a sky watch, I had learned to look up at the sky when he did. So each time he moved aside the Navajo man, I, too, looked upward, but could see little of significance other than the familiar stars of the Big Dipper outlined against the north ridge behind the ceremonial mesa. By 1 A.M. MDT in the summer at Mescalero, much of the Big Dipper has disappeared behind the mountains of the ridge to the north of the ceremonial arena; I was again left to wonder to what I was supposed to be paying attention.

As we, too, went to rest, moving from the ceremonial arena to our tipi on the south periphery of the ceremonial grounds, I asked Bernard, "Did you find it?" I was too tired to invoke proper canons of questioning. "Uhm," he replied, "nahakus." My startled "Oh!" was heard as "au," signifying agreement or yes. And finally it did make sense; I was supposed to be paying attention to the Big Dipper, for *nahakus* is its Apache name.

Nahakus is difficult to translate into English and has nothing to do with dippers or largeness or bears of the larger constellation we term Ursa Major, of which the Big Dipper is a portion. Rather, *nahakus* means that which revolves around a pivot point or around itself and also connotes falling. Indeed, given the mountainous horizon surrounding the ceremonial mesa, the Big Dipper does seem to fall into the north ridge as the night progresses. Even without the north ridge of mountains, the Big Dipper can be observed to pivot throughout the night.

It was the Big Dipper that was the ceremonial clock, or at least a portion of it, for the last night's singing. Finally, I had paid sufficient attention to understand that my checking the Big Dipper was indeed what I was supposed to be seeing; finally I understood why Bernard had been so impatient with me when he asked for the time during the pre-dawn sky watching. He was trying to teach me to tell time from the stars,

Fig. 3.3a Big Dipper's rotation on July 6, 1984, as photographed by Gene
Ammarell at 11:00 p.m.

Fig. 3.3b   Big Dipper's rotation on July 6–7, 1984, as photographed by Gene Ammarell at midnight.

Fig. 3.3c Big Dipper's rotation on July 7, 1984, as photographed by Gene Ammarell at 12:56 A.M.

Fig. 3.3d   Big Dipper's rotation on July 7, 1984, as photographed by Gene Ammarell at 2:17 A.M.

Fig. 3.3e   Big Dipper's rotation on July 7, 1984, as photographed by Gene Ammarell at 2:42 A.M.

trying to alert me to the importance of star clocks. And that instantly led to the realization that other stars were being attended to earlier in the night's singing when sight lines were utilized through the poles of the Holy Lodge. I was quite relieved to realize that I *had* been paying attention, even if I had inappropriately been integrating the resultant data.

With one of those flashes of insight that cartoonists illustrate with light bulbs going on over a person's head, I saw many previous ceremonials I had witnessed where Bernard, although all might have been present inside the Holy Lodge, delayed the first shaking of his deer hoof rattle while he looked several times along the East Grandfather or between some of the south and southwestern poles forming the Holy Lodge. And I saw a sleepy, yawning, fumbling me, awkwardly searching for a flashlight and looking down when I should have been looking up. I was glad it was dark so Bernard could not see my blush of embarrassment. Then I was again at sea, albeit in a sea of stars, for I still did not know to which stars I should be paying attention, other than those of *nahakus*.

He continued talking as we left the ceremonial arena, for, once having demonstrated that I understood the problem at hand without his having directly taught me, he could correct my probable misapprehensions. He said he must begin singing when all the color is gone from the sky and as the stars become visible on the western horizon. To delay beyond that time on the first three nights is not a problem, for there are only relatively short sequences of songs to be sung and all can be easily accommodated. But to delay beyond that time on the fourth and final night is to insure that not all the songs can be fitted in before the girls have to leave the ceremonial arena for a brief rest and to be bathed and have their hair washed. That, in turn, will insure that the sun cannot be pulled on time. By watching stars in the south-southwest early in the evening, Bernard could tell the time with a very high degree of accuracy. Around midnight, he switched his star gazing to the north-northwest and the Big Dipper.[12]

Thus, in 1983 he kept watch between the positions of the second and third girls (see fig. 3.1). The way in which the ceremonial mesa is situated prevents one from looking due west, for concession stands and an intervening ridge occlude the view of the horizon. But by looking south-southwest, there is a clear vantage across the White Sands to the horizon line formed by the San Andres Mountains near Las Cruces, approximately seventy-five miles from the ceremonial mesa. Bernard stated that, although all the stars are important, he timed primarily by *nahakus* and *suus biné* [morning star]. Singing must begin when stars can be clearly seen in the west and south. The last of the singing must be accomplished before *nahakus* fully sets behind the northern ridge in order to have sufficient time for rest and ritual bathing before the girls must be called back onto the ceremonial arena and into the Holy Lodge.

When we returned to the ceremonial arena around 3 A.M. MDT and once again had to ask the Navajo man to stand aside, Bernard, in a double entendre that both teased me and moved the Navajo man, said in mock exasperation, "You're standing on my Indian watch!" My reliance on Anglo watches had prevented me from seeing the Indian ones being paraded before me for years. Now, though, even I could laugh.

The next summer, in 1984, with funding from the American Council of Learned Societies, Gene Ammarell, then education officer of the Fiske Planetarium at the University of Colorado in Boulder, accompanied me to Mescalero to photograph and to check my findings as well as to provide precise identifications of the stars being used to time the ceremonial. Spica and Arcturus, both bright stars and both clearly visible in the south-southwest in the summertime sky shortly after full dark, were the primary stars used in the early part of the evening. Sighting and timing also utilized Saturn and Mars that year. As the stars and planets appear to move westward and to set during the night, a star first sighted on tipi pole 4, for example, will, about ninety minutes later, have transited between poles 4 and 5, thus providing a measure of time that can be correlated with the singing of the songs. This timing allows the Head Singer to increase or decrease the time between songs or, if necessary, to cancel or truncate the songs themselves. Despite my elegant hypotheses to the contrary, the apparent sighting straight up through the smoke hole was not a sighting line at all. As it developed in subsequent conversation, when Bernard looked in that direction he was praying rather than sighting.

In contrast to the south-southwest observations through the tipi poles, which provide a rough ninety-minute clock, the movement of the Big Dipper in the north-northwest allows for a more precise clock marking both thirty minute and one hour intervals. These intervals are clearly apparent by observing the movement of Alkaid, the first star in the handle of the Big Dipper, furthest from the bowl. At 11 P.M. MDT, Alkaid is 55° above a flat horizon; by 12 midnight, it is 45° above a flat horizon line:

this 10°/hour movement continues throughout the night. However, 5° shifts in the constellation pattern of the Big Dipper are clearly visible to the naked eye; thus, half-hour intervals are readily determined. At Mescalero, by 2:42 A.M. MDT the only stars of the Big Dipper still visible are Alkaid, Mizar/Alcor—the double star most of us using naked-eye observation see as only one star—and Alioth, the handle stars of the Big Dipper. These stars sit on the north ridge of mountains at that time. Two hours later, no Dipper stars are visible at all; but, by this hour, timing attention has shifted to the east and morning star.

Ammarell identified *suus biné*, or morning star, as Capella, a star that Western astronomy assigns both to the constellation Auriga and to the zodiacal constellation of Taurus. In Mescalero astronomy, Capella, along with the stars Auriga Eta and Auriga Iota, is part of a three-star constellation called *taanashka?da* [Three Who Went Together, meaning three who died at the same time].[13] Of these, Capella is by far the brightest, and, of course, makes excellent sense as a morning star.

While technically Capella has risen by 2:30 A.M. MDT in July at Mescalero's latitude, the surrounding mountains preclude its being seen until 3:00 A.M. MDT at the earliest. Observation of Capella as morning star may begin as early as 3:00 A.M. MDT; however, observation becomes critical two hours later, at 5:00 A.M. MDT when Capella is "two hand-spans," or approximately 20°, above the local horizon.[14] It is at this point that all must move quickly and smoothly, for the coming dawn rapidly obliterates all vestiges of stars, and only ninety minutes remain before the full disk of the sun will have completely cleared East Mountain and beamed across the ceremonial arena, lighting the center of the runway and shining directly into the center of the Holy Lodge.

Thus, the pulling of the sun actually begins around 10 P.M. MDT of the previous night, when the first sightings are taken through the poles of the Holy Lodge. The timing continues through observations of the Big Dipper; this timing includes the attendant songs and ritual actions that must be accomplished through the night. Finally the timing culminates in a flurry of action around 5 A.M. MDT. If the singing is not finished in consonance with the Big Dipper's time and extends beyond the setting of *nahakus*, then *suus biné* will be more than two palms' width above the eastern horizon before the girls can be brought back into the Holy Lodge—or they will get no break at all. That means there will be insufficient time to bathe the girls, wash their hair, re-dress them, paint them, paint the hands of the singers, sing, and pull the sun. This, in turn, means that the sun will shine fully into the Holy Lodge and onto the girls prematurely—perhaps without even having been pulled by the singers. While the ceremony will not be invalidated, it will not be considered quite proper. It will be lacking in aesthetic appeal and will leave the many onlookers with a vague feeling, sometimes stated aloud, that all was not as it should have been.

When, however, all is timed properly, then the circle of Creation is once again recapitulated and the world rewound, as it were, for its continued existence. Sophisticated star watching and its attendant interpretation will have re-validated the essential correctness of the base metaphor.

The base metaphor operates on many levels during this time. The girls enter into their ceremony as unformed as was the universe before Creator initiated order. While each girl becomes a physiological woman upon initial menstruation, she becomes a fully social woman and one who understands that she is truly "the mother of a people" as she participates in, or even watches, the full cycle of the ceremonial. Each of the four nights of the ceremonial represents one of the four days of Creation; the songs and actions of each of those four nights recapitulate the structuring of the world and its natural and social relationships.

All ceremonial movement is as it would be from the perspective of *Bik'égudi^{n}dé*. Creator is first visible in the east with the appearance of Creator's physical representative, the Sun. Utilizing a bodily image, with Father Sun facing His Children and with emphasis on the left-hand side, "the side closest to the heart"—which is the seat of life in people, as the Sun is the seat of life in the universe—Creator's vision sweeps sunward, to the left, toward the south. It is here, in the south, that the Head Singer stands or sits when facing east—in the place of honor and in position to address Creator as representative of ^{n}dé, all the people.

The sun moves during the year between southerly and northerly extremes. We mark a solstice at each extreme, with the winter solstice coming when the sun rises and sets in its most southerly position and the summer solstice coming when the sun rises and sets in its most northerly position. On a daily basis, of course, the sun rises and sets east to west, moving through the south in the course of a day. Quite obviously and logically, if it is to reappear in the east the next day, it must pass through the north during the night. Therefore, the base metaphor's visual representation is created linearly through a combination of yearly motion south to north (————) with daily motion east to west (|); it is enclosed by the repetitive cycling of life and seasons and time and even the position of the sun itself: ⊕.

The Head Singer reverses his position and sits in the north in the evening, when the sun is not visible, and then only so he is in better position to monitor one of Creator's clocks: the Big Dipper. It has nothing to do with symbolic reversals; it is purely practical. No wonder some of my earlier speculations had been dismissed with laughter, mock serious introspection, or with "Bah!"

The base metaphor's existence is also alluded to with blessing sequences that the singers and girls both bestow and receive. Pollen is first sprinkled to the four directions (east, south, west, north), always in a sunwise and circular movement; thus the circle of life is established. Then pollen is applied across the nose, from south to north; finally, cascading from fingertips, it is sprinkled from the crown of the head to the forehead—and the visual representation of the base metaphor has again been created, with the person blessed by being enclosed within it, literally by being enclosed within life's living circle.

A further manifestation of the base metaphor is in the movement of the stars. I have concentrated on the summer position of the stars but, as any star watcher knows, the stars and their constellation patterns appear to move throughout the year as our own earth moves against the backdrop of the celestial sphere. If Arcturus is in the south-southwest in July shortly after sundown in the 1980s, it will be there in the 1990s as well; our life spans are not sufficiently long to watch precession at work, so through the years of our lives we see a relatively static sky. That very perspective lends credence to the essential correctness of the formulations given presence in the base metaphor and its visual representation, for we see a great circle of movement throughout the span of each year. Obviously, the universe is not only circular, but it is also in exquisite balance, from which it achieves a harmony that humans hope to emulate in their own lives. The base metaphor and Creation itself are visible in the apparent movements of the celestial sphere. We can each attempt to live out life's circle as it is dictated in the stars and interpreted by the singers for us.

Singers must be aware of celestial phenomena for the entire year, not just for the summer, since a girl's family can request that a ceremony be sung at any time of the year and in any place on the reservation. Therefore, a competent singer must be familiar with the appearance of the sky from a vast variety of perspectives and a plethora of sites.[15]

Consider a simple phenomenon: sunrise. Depending upon the configuration of the mountains and canyons in the portion of the reservation where the ceremony is being sung, "sunrise" can vary by more than an hour.[16] Similarly, the appearance of constellations and their visibility depend not only upon the site but also on the time of year. Any given constellation will, through the course of a year, be initially seen sometimes just after dark; at other times it will rise just before sunrise; and at still other times it will rise an hour, or two, or more after sunset.

Further, while the Mescalero are now sedentary, their ceremonial grounds are not. The primary (summer) grounds have been moved several times in this century. Such movements of sites and seasons are not of consequence to competent singers, for theirs is knowledge based upon years of observation. No wonder there were so many of the 4 A.M. calls; no wonder Bernard spent so many nights awake, walking and looking at the stars! And no wonder he constantly told me to pay attention, for I committed the usual Anglo sin of not attending to the natural universe. My learning was from books, not from observation, and I stubbornly (from his perspective) clung to my own culture's method despite his doing his best to show me that I must observe the sky to understand and to have my two puzzles solved. In retrospect, I am amazed by his constant patience with his slow student and now fully understand why he was sometimes so sharp in his insistence that I pay attention.

A fixed stonehenge or a fixed medicine wheel or a fixed building is of little use when the critical factor is the sun washing over you and your party at the particular site where you happen to be whatever the time of year. It is far better to make a clock of the poles of a tipi that can be placed anywhere at any time, or to use the natural rhythm of the created universe, to time events. One's clock, whether of short term of a few moments or long term of a year or more, need not be left behind nor need it tie people to a particular location, if one has learned to tell time by the stars. It is not a simple procedure that can be learned in a few nights. Rather, it takes long hours over many years to become thoroughly intimate with the harmonious balance of the universe as set in the stars.[17] Somehow, it is a comfort to know that it is not only anthropologists who must properly attend; singers, too, must constantly, and consciously, be paying attention.

CHAPTER 4

Seeing the Pattern

The base metaphor establishes the importance of sunwise directionality, of circularity (beginning in the east), of the number four, of sound and silence, and of balance and harmony. While some of these qualities have been noted by other scholars who worked with the Mescalero, understanding the genesis of the base metaphor allows understanding of why these qualities are considered important. That, in turn, leads to an understanding of why patterning is consistent through time for the Mescalero.

Morris Opler, the anthropologist most readily identified with Apache scholarship, first went to Mescalero in 1931 as one of the graduate students on Dr. Ruth Benedict's Field Training Project. He had already written about the Apaches and has remained the most prolific of those interested in Southern Athabaskans. Some years ago Opler (1969: 44–45) wrote,

> The Chiricahua-Mescalero color directional ceremonial circuit begins with the east, the most important ritual direction, and moves clockwise, or sunwise, around the cardinal directions . . . Four is the most important Apache ritual number . . .

By understanding the genesis of directionality, sunwise movement, and the ritual number, it is much easier to understand the value placed on them and the concomitant behavioral patterns that evolve from them. For example, it is not arbitrary choice that demands four is an important number. Rather, four is the number of days it took *Bikʼégudiⁿdé* to bring the world into being—this is Power, indeed. We, as humans, would be foolish not to accord significance to four, once we understand the import of that number to Creation and Creator.

Understanding the genesis of, and consequent value placed on, the base metaphor illuminates aspects of behavior and practice of other Athabaskans, especially the Navajo, whom most Apaches consider to be "like cousins: once we were the same people, now we are like cousins." Toelken, who has worked with Navajo people for most of his adult life, speaks of some interesting practices among the Navajo for which there are analogues among the Apache. He (1979:241) states, for example,

> . . . in spinning the yarn [for proper Navajo weaving], the spindle must be turned in a sunwise direction (we call it clockwise), for since it represents the direction of the sun's movements, to spin the yarn by turning the spindle "backward" would be to produce yarn that represents the reverse of the normal state, yarn that will "come unraveled," "won't stay in the rugs," and "might cause sickness . . ."

Again, there is the importance of sunwise movement for proper harmony and balance. The unraveling and sickness that are believed to occur if spinning is antisunwise are ritual in nature and are due to the inherent order and balance of the world that would be upset by reversal. Once things are inharmonious and out of balance, disaster is likely to occur—disaster that can only be put to rights by ritual means.

Because ritual and its practices are inherently interesting to human beings and because the ritual and practices of others usually strike us as exotic and hence fascinating, those who have written about Navajos and Apaches have concentrated much of their investigation on ritual or folklore or other aspects of expressive culture. I confess to a similar fascination with expressive culture and will, in both this and subsequent chapters, explore expressive culture in relation to the base metaphor. But does the base metaphor influence daily life? It seems logical that it should or I should term it something other than a base—that is *basic*—metaphor. No sooner had I asked the question of myself than it seemed that evidence of the base metaphor was everywhere.

In this chapter I shall first examine some of the less esoteric aspects of life, those everyday and periodic practices that are nonceremonial in nature. Then I shall turn to a consideration of two regular, but not daily, events: a tribal meeting and formal speech style. Finally, I shall consider the base metaphor in one of its expressive-culture aspects: design, especially that on basketry. In these meanderings, I shall show how the base metaphor is an integral part of life, even when lived in mundane fashion, and how it is essential to the organization of all life at Mescalero today.

The adherence to principles established in the base metaphor is so ingrained that deviation from them causes Mescalero people to feel uncomfortable. Small activities, ones that each of us takes very much for granted, are also structured along lines consistent with the base metaphor. The ubiquity of the base metaphor and its many transformations is manifest even in such a mundane activity as salting food.

Whenever there is a public meal, for a homecoming or a girl's puberty ceremonial or a funeral or a tribal picnic, salt is set out on serving tables in cups. While helping serve food at a meal many years ago, I learned the "proper" way to salt food. My Anglo sensibilities were violated by seeing person after person put thumb and forefinger into the salt in order to obtain enough to sprinkle, almost always in a circle, on the plate of food. So I put a small plastic spoon into the cup on the table, only to find that the very next person in line removed the spoon, carefully placing it to the side of the cup, and daintily dipped his thumb and forefinger into the salt cup. He then, equally carefully, sprinkled the salt around his plate, first from the east and then around in a circle, ending again in the east. Then, in an apparent second thought, he quickly crossed the circle with two neat lines perpendicular to each other—the visual representation of the base metaphor, the quartered circle: ⊕. Intrigued by his behavior, I watched several others in line. Some of the younger people, teenagers and children, used a haphazard salting approach, but even most of them salted their food in a circular manner. I did not see any middle aged or elderly people salt their food other than in a circular, sunwise pattern—and most of them also provided the cross arms of the visual representation of the base metaphor as well.

Making a mental note to ask about this later, I turned to bring out another salad only to be handed more plastic plates, since the stack on the table was precariously low while the line for those yet to eat was quite long. The new plates I was to lay out were rectangular and had divisions rather than being open and round as was the first set on the

serving table. But the shape of the plate did not alter the pattern of salting. Nor did it alter the precise use of thumb and forefinger—that I tested
by aperiodically replacing the spoon in the cup of salt. Each time I did
so, the very next person in line, even if it was a small child, would carefully remove the spoon and instead carefully insert thumb and forefinger
into the salt. Never did I see anyone make two passes at the salt—only
as much as could be held between thumb and forefinger was sprinkled
on the food. Again, almost everyone used a circular, sunwise salting pattern, and a goodly number recapitulated the visual representation of the
base metaphor.

Later, sitting with some of the ladies who had cooked the meal, I
mentioned that I had done a "carrots" again with the spoon in the salt.[1]
We all had a good laugh about how difficult it was for a woman to learn
another culture's way of preparing, cooking, presenting, and clearing
food. Then, after a rather lengthy time and with some intervening conversation, a woman within our little group mused that not so long ago
salt was very difficult to obtain. She continued by saying that men had to
go to New Mexican salines—which, unfortunately, were the property of
other Indians, and therefore they had to steal the salt or barter for it. In
later years, they would try to barter with Mexicans or Anglos, or even go
to Baja California or the Gulf of Mexico to obtain salt. After another
pause, she murmured that valuable things should never be wasted. Now
that I was properly instructed about salt, our conversation turned to
other matters.

Somewhat later I checked my newly learned politeness at table
with Bernard. He confirmed that only a selfish person would be so rude
as to use a spoon to bring salt to food, while properly brought up and
polite people would never take more than their share: that which can be
held between thumb and forefinger. He underscored what the woman
had said about salt and the difficulty in obtaining it. He also said that a
holy blessing should be performed while salting food; even in meals at
home, where a saltshaker could be expected to be on the table, he believed that most people would still use a sunwise circuit. So a proper
person both salts and blesses food simultaneously, "like Catholics bless
with Father, Son, and Holy Ghost before they eat." Apaches perform
with salt the same actions they use for a pollen blessing. Once again, the
base metaphor, rendered in salt, reminds people of their being held inside
the blessings of the created universe, within the created circle of life.

That created universe, that circle of life, exists everywhere, not just in ritual actions. For example, school areas abound with sunwise circles. On the playground or on inside play areas, children move in sunwise circuits in their play. Tag at Mescalero is a circular game, usually played on a jungle gym. Children in the Head Start class ride their tricycles in a sunwise circle around a room; disruptive children purposefully turn their trikes around to establish an antisunwise track. Such movement first shocks the other children and then irritates them, while teachers tell the offender to be a "proper" person and to go around in a sunwise way (Farrer 1990).

Tables in the Day Care and Head Start rooms are round or semi-circular, rather than rectangular or square as they are in the elementary school.[2] The elementary school is administered by an independent school district in a town fourteen miles from Agency; elementary school class-rooms were furnished through decisions made by Anglo and Hispanic administrators. The Day Care and Head Start workers themselves, most of whom are Apaches, made the decisions on the furnishings in the Day Care and Head Start portions of the educational facility housed in the Tribal Center, separate from the elementary school building. Apaches prefer circles, while Anglos and Hispanics prefer squares and rectangles. These preferences can be seen in microcosm as well; the reservation class-rooms in which Anglos teach have the children arranged in lines and rows, while those few classrooms with Indian teachers are usually ar-ranged in circles. The elementary school, under the control of the County Board of Education, conforms to the Anglo American pattern of squares and rectangles, while the Apache controlled class spaces of Day Care and Head Start conform to the Apachean pattern of circles.

The Tribal Museum conforms to the prevailing Apache pattern as well. It is constructed of four interlocking circles and, from a bird's-eye view, resembles a stemless four-leaf clover. In a historical exhibit of Apa-chean culture that was a permanent exhibit for many years, one gained the proper time perspective only by entering the building and turning *left*, sunwise, to proceed through the four interlocking circles that form the rooms of the Museum. When that direction was chosen, not only were the exhibits in order chronologically but also the slide-tape show began as one entered the third room, where an electric eye triggered the tape player and the projectors. However, most Anglo tourists to the Museum entered the doorway and immediately turned right, seeing the latest developments first and moving backward in time through the other displays. What was supposed to be the third room was, for them, the second, and they triggered the slide-tape show as they were leaving what had appeared to be an empty room with nothing in it but large, round, carpeted shapes. Upon hearing a disembodied voice begin a narration, most of them turned around, looked up and saw the synchronized projectors displaying images keyed to the voice track. Then the meaning and function of the carpeted shapes became obvious—they were clearly for sitting on while watching and listening to Apachean history from an Apachean perspective. Most Anglos making the directional mistake laughed nervously. A few were irritated and voiced their anger to the Apache director, who responded by having signs made indicating the proper direction. The signs helped very few, for they were ignored.

In the original display, there were no signs stating, "Begin here." Yet Apaches made no mistake when entering; nor, for that matter, did Western Apaches or Navajos. Even after an arrow-pointing sign was installed indicating one should turn left upon entering the Museum, the majority of Anglo tourists still persisted in moving to the right in their proper cultural direction, in which traffic of whatever variety moves to the right, rather than following the instructions and moving to the left, in the proper Apachean direction. For Apaches, sunwise circuits yield properness; antisunwise circuits yield chaos, and, in this case, many embarrassed giggles from tourists.

Many everyday activities, and all important ones, must adhere to the sunwise principle. Powwow and other social dancing, as well as the ritual dancing of the Mountain Gods, always follows a sunwise circuit. And, it is said, if one wishes to witch another, it can be accomplished by doing a blessing sequence backward, beginning in the west and going antisunwise. This recalls the Navajo injunction to spin only sunwise or else sickness and unraveling will result.

While it may be relatively easy to insist upon sunwise directionality in small matters, is it also possible when large ones are considered? A Tribal Meeting is a large occasion, since it is intended to bring together all the members of the Mescalero Apache Tribe at one time and place.

Tribal meetings are called for a number of reasons: to decide issues bearing on the entire community, to present progress reports on the litigation between the tribe and the United States government, and to distribute the dividend checks to each member of the tribe as a member of the corporate entity that is the Mescalero Apache Tribe. These meetings present interesting spatial and speech patterns that can be seen as transformations of the base metaphor.

The meetings I witnessed were held in the auditorium of the Community Center building, a space sufficiently large to accommodate the entire tribal membership and still leave room for movement around the room. Usually people entered the auditorium through a west door that opened off an interior corridor of the Community Center building. It was possible, however, to enter directly from the east side parking lot, an entry that some preferred. There were entrances on each of the other sides as well, but they were seldom, if ever, used when a tribal meeting was the center of business.

The Tribal Council sat on a slightly raised platform in the south end of the auditorium; it will be recalled that the south position is the one of honor. The council members were seated in two sections divided by a small center aisle, at the front of which was a microphone to assure that the council members' voices could be heard well. Tribal members were seated on the north side of the auditorium, facing the raised dais. They, too, had two sections divided by a center aisle. There were two microphones on the floor for tribal members to use to address their fellows and the council. Balance was created and maintained in this structural opposition of council and tribe.

A meeting usually opened with the tribal president stating the purpose of the meeting and then announcing the position of the council on the issues to be discussed. If, as rarely happened, there was an unresolved difference of opinion among members of the council, this too was announced.

In a practice that seemed strange to the Anglos who learned of it, the council had (and has) ten members. In the Apachean view, odd numbers are inherently unbalanced and thus not conducive to harmony. The Euroamerican pattern of uneven numbers so that majority votes are more easily accomplished is not a pattern in keeping with Apachean sensibility. It is unnecessary to have an uneven number when majority votes are unimportant but consensus is imperative. The goal of all decision making in tribal meetings was to achieve consensus, or as close to it as was possible within certain time constraints. Even numbers on the council, then, created no difficulty and were felt to be more proper. No member's vote was weighted more heavily than any other in the council, just as no one opinion in the tribal meeting could be assumed to hold sway until all who chose to speak had done so. Evenness led to balance and harmony.

After the tribal president spoke, the statements made and position taken were either supported or countered by the other council members in a rank-ordered hierarchy of speakers: council officers first, then regular council members. Council officers spoke according to rank (i.e., vice-president, secretary, treasurer), while regular council members spoke according to seniority, eldest first. However, when there was a particularly old person on the council, that person spoke after officers but before younger members, regardless of the length of time the very old person had been on the council. After each council member had spoken, the president recapped the council's position(s) and closed the council's initial portion of the program by requesting statements from the floor. Council members remained on the platform while statements from the floor were heard.

Speakers from the floor followed a pattern of oldest first. The elders, whether men or women, moved to the floor microphones first; very old or infirm people occasionally had a microphone brought to them, if moving to the speaking area would have caused them difficulty. Younger people, even when they had a strongly held opinion they wished to present, did not move from their seats to speak until after all the elders had spoken. When all from the audience who wished to speak had done so, the president and other council members had another turn to rebut or support what had been said from the floor. Further rebuttal was expected from the floor after the council's second turn at speech making. Harmony and balance were evident in the movement between council and floor, as well as within the positions presented on each side. The pattern continued until all who had opinions they wished to present in public had spoken. By that time, a clear consensus was expected to have emerged, and, if all went as it was supposed to, gradually those who had been in opposition to the majority opinion would rise, move to a microphone, and voice their willingness to support the clearly preferred position.[3]

While individual members of the tribe spoke, there was often much movement in the auditorium. Some people's positions were so well known that their opinions really had no need of being repeated in public. However, no one ever considered suggesting that it was, therefore, unnecessary for any particular person to speak. If a person's position was not only well known but also had been heard many times, there sometimes was a rather loud buzz of talk while the predictable speaker had the floor. Nonetheless, when any person was finished speaking, there was always a silence, during which no one spoke above a modulated whisper and no one advanced to the microphone to claim the floor. Even when the silence was kept, though, it did not mean that all noise was absent: people moved about, whispered to each other, discussed what had just been said, mustered their own arguments, or tried to determine who was likely to rise to be the next speaker. The kind of silence maintained during the no-speech time was a silence of no formal speech making, while people reflected upon what had been said and those still to speak had a chance both to ponder what had been said and to form their own words. Thus, the silences between speeches were busy times, even if not busy in the formal speech making sense.

Young people wishing to speak used the silent time to locate older people who had not spoken and who usually spoke in public gatherings, trying to read whether or not the older people would speak on that occasion. When it appeared that no others from a particular age range would speak, a person recognized as a good speaker from the next younger age group would move toward the microphone in an unhurried fashion, all the while scanning the older people to be sure that they were indeed finished and not just taking a bit more time to frame their thoughts or move to the speaking area. Young people who were just beginning to speak in public might not even take the microphone, but instead might rise where they had been sitting and speak for a short period of time. It seemed that one had to earn the right to a long speech at a microphone in the center of the room or at a side aisle.

The proper circle of wisdom had been upheld, with the eldest in the tribe speaking first, followed in descending age order by those others wishing to participate, and ending with the youngest speakers—those with little wisdom, for that must be garnered through years of living proper lives.

While both men and women speak in tribal meetings, it was usual for only one member of an extended family to speak for the group. When that occurred, the speaker was almost invariably the eldest member of the family present in the auditorium. That eldest member could, of course, be female or male. Any family members who disagreed might also speak at this time, if they so chose.[4] A person's performance on any one speech occasion would help determine the order in which a turn at speaking might be expected on the next occasion.

When all who wished to be heard had spoken, a balanced picture had usually been presented; all sides of an issue had been explored rhetorically. If it appeared that there was a substantial division of opinion in the tribe, the president, another council member, or someone from the floor could suggest reconsideration of the issue at another time rather than risk a divisive vote. If there could be no consensus, there would be no firm decision.

It was when the council's position was not supported by the speakers from the floor that the balance between council and tribe, which was so graphically enacted on the placement of positions on the floor of the auditorium, could best be seen in operation. Were it not for the spatial separation, there would be few clues to where the supposed power lay. Indeed, council members did not claim power for themselves, but rather insisted that they were there to serve the people and to do the people's will. The people subscribed to this statement and had no qualms about calling a council member to task, in public or in private. Then, too, each council member, including the president, had to stand for election every other year. One either reflected the will of the people, swayed them to one's own position, or lost council membership.

The tenor of the speeches, especially by the second, third, or fourth round of speech making, allowed those present to know the outcome with a good degree of certainty before the vote was taken. Nonetheless, at the conclusion of the speech making, the president, or another council member, called for the vote. People voted by standing in place rather than raising hands or using ballots. Voting by standing seemed to be a powerful incentive to join the majority, if a person was one of only a few left seated on a vote. For some, however, to remain steadfast despite overwhelming social pressure could be an advantage, provided it was made clear that the arguments, no matter how well reasoned, simply were not persuasive enough and that one remained sitting as a matter of principle rather than as a matter of pique. Outsiders were surprised at the number of times consensus was reached even in spite of the vehemence with which some positions were propounded. In those meetings I observed, consensus gradually emerged through the speech making process, so that by the time a vote was taken, if unanimity had not achieved, at least there were very few dissenters.

The base metaphor could easily be seen in operation in the tribal meeting. A striking aspect of the meeting was the segregation of people into the four proper positions: south for dais, north for floor, west for speakers, east for young. Harmonious balance was seen in seating areas, as well as in turns for speaking and the oppositions of older and younger, leaders and followers. Circularity was apparent in the spheres of activity moving from council to elders to middle-aged to younger and back to council once again, with repeats as necessary. Silence, or periods of no formal talk, alternated with sound or formal talking. The base metaphor was enacted in dynamic fashion during the tribal meetings I observed.

Using a perspective grounded in directionality, the council was sitting in the south facing north, while the audience had their backs to the north. Audience speakers moved to the west to use a microphone. If they were sitting on the east side of the auditorium, they moved to the center aisle microphone; if they were sitting on the west side of the auditorium, they usually moved to a microphone near the west entrance to be recognized as potential speakers. Children, too young to be in school and yet not old enough to be playing outside with their peers free from adult supervision, almost always found ways to break away from their adult caretakers to mill about between the north and east positions. Again balanced opposition was presented with leaders and followers opposite one another and with older and younger also opposite each other. Council leaders were in the south, followers in the north, older in the west and younger in the east. It presented a pattern repeated in the lineup of singers for the girls' ceremonial and also brought to mind the association of age with the west and youth with the east, as with the story of White Painted Woman, who was an old woman in the west and a young one again each time she appeared in the east.[5] Balance that produced harmony, sound and silence, the use of the number four, circularity, and directionality: all were present and important in the tribal meeting.

The tribal meeting generated grand presentations of the base metaphor writ large that orchestrated the entire event. But, within the event, there was an even more striking manifestation of the base metaphor in the way in which formal speeches were constructed. I do not mean that calls for points of order or for the vote followed the base metaphor. Rather, I refer to the structural organization of formal speeches that replicated the essential aspects of the base metaphor: quadripartite form, circularity, balance and harmony, and—for those who were elegant speakers—sophisticated use of sound and silence to make or reinforce points.[6] The base metaphor's use also provided closure for each speaker's remarks.

Formal speeches adhered to the primal balance in that they were carefully structured into four parts. To use more than four divisions was to be like an Anglo and "talk all the time," while to use fewer than four divisions was to leave one's Apachean audience unsatisfied and waiting for closure, feeling as though there was, or should have been, more to come. The customary speech pattern during formal events, and especially during tribal meetings (or when people were relating stories that were true or cosmological), began with a preamble, was followed by a statement, then a restatement, and finished with a formal closing.[7] The formula, preamble-statement-restatement-closing, was so much a part of Apachean life that I even heard it on the playgrounds when children were recapitulating school experiences or other life events.

During the preamble, the speaker's right to speak was affirmed by recourse to what ancestors, usually termed "grandparents" or "grandfathers," had said or what the individual had learned during a long life or a particular course of study, whether in the Indian or Anglo world. A younger speaker would use a preamble that was more heavily weighted toward ancestors, while usually also offering an acknowledgment that the speaker was young and therefore might be uninformed or might have misinterpreted what had been taught. Phrases that were used after this initial one included the possibility that the speaker might not be in possession of all the relevant facts or that misinterpretation of the facts might have occurred. The speaker would continue with a statement similar to "Nonetheless, it appears that . . ." and give voice to what that speaker thought must be considered. After these obligatory opening remarks, the speaker would proceed to the argument formulated in his or her own mind or to the narration of a story pertinent to the item under consideration.

The statement phase was the story proper or, if the speaker was presenting original thoughts, an argument as clear and as well reasoned as the person was capable of producing. Oftentimes a speaker became emotional during this phase, even though good speakers were supposed to argue from logic and not from emotion. It was also common, during this phase of formal speech presentation, to recap briefly arguments heard before the speaker's own, whether from people of import (such as elders or council members) or one's own peers. When relating a story to make a point, speakers sometimes made reference to stories related by others. If appropriate, agreement was expressed with previous statements or stories; or the faulty logic of the previously presented statements or stories was pointed out. At times amplification was offered; or, after recapping previous arguments, the speaker could challenge the conclusion(s) reached. Verbal accolades could be awarded to other speakers, both to those with whom the speaker agreed and to those with whom there was disagreement. Every effort was made to praise individual expressions even while trying to destroy that same individual's argument. A speaker did not gain by humiliating the opposition; rather, a speaker gained prestige by presenting such a forceful and logical argument that opponents were swayed to one's own position. Only rhetorical skill and memory limited the presentation in this phase.

People sometimes became bored or tired listening to speakers who spent what was perceived as being too much time in this phase, but no one ever cut short another without receiving condemnation from the others present.[8] Statements were as long as the speaker thought necessary to make the point sufficiently and well.

Having once presented the statement (argument or story), it was considered mandatory to restate, succinctly. The restatement was always brief and summarized the point, or points, made—usually just by the present speaker, but occasionally by other speakers as well. People always paid particular attention during this restatement phase, for it contained the essence of what the speaker intended.

Finally, a brief closing statement was made. The closing usually recalled the appeal to the ancestors, or grandparents, and included a standard disclaimer that the speaker might have spoken from ignorance or misinformation, though that which preceded represented the speaker's understanding and preference. Older people especially often ended with a formal term, *daaiinaa* [this/here it ends].

The quadripartite pattern of speech making or storytelling was considered to be in balance even when the individual parts were of vastly varying lengths. It was the number of parts, not their length, that was key to the aesthetic judgment. Of course, the parts had to be in proper order and presented with proper modesty as well. Balance was further enhanced by brevity of the preamble and closing statements; especially in storytelling, these were often only a sentence or two that indicated the kind of story to be told, as in, "They say Coyote was walking one day . . . ," or as in, "We do not forget, we remember . . . ," while the ending could be as brief as "That's what they say" or "Daaiinaa." The statement, or primary story segment, was supposed to be considerably longer than the recapitulation that followed it; when this pattern was adhered to, it was said that the middle sections were in balance. When the middles balanced and the outer segments balanced, too, then the entire speech or storytelling was considered harmonious and proper. A circle had been opened and closed when all four phases were properly presented. Proper decorum had been maintained and the speech had operated as speeches should.

Speech, of course, makes use of sound and hearing; salting food and playground circles involve the whole body, while circular tables help define the space in which people move. The base metaphor's patterns extend beyond these areas of environment and the senses to form templates for aesthetic constructions and judgments, as Apachean basketry illustrates. The principles established in the base metaphor are so ingrained that to deviate from them causes Mescalero people to feel uncomfortable, to judge things as being "not right" or, as is often heard, "someway," meaning out of the ordinary and unexpected, as well as meaning improper. But to follow the invisible injunctions of the base metaphor is to create *nzhúne*, or *hnzhúne*, a word that means good, proper, harmonious, beautiful, balanced.[9] A lovely child is *hnzhúne*, as is a well-told story, or a morning sunrise, or a basket.

Mescalero Apache basketry has been of interest to scholars for a considerable period of time.[10] Writing in the early 1900s and pondering the question of whether or not Mescaleros retained their designs and construction techniques from their earlier sojourn in the north, Mason (1904:363–64) queried, "Did they bring with them and preserve uncontaminated the stitches and patterns of their priscan basketry and keep the ancient models unchanged?" His question was motivated by noting the similarity between Mescalero basketry and that from other Athabaskan speakers "on the lower Yukon" (ibid.:251). He concluded that the Mescaleros did not remain pristine pure in their basketry and turned to a consideration of similarities in Athabaskan basketry in general, as well as to tribal differences.

Questions of purity are not in vogue today, as most scholars agree that it is very seldom, if ever, that a group of people remains pristine. Each of us is in contact with others and is influenced by—as well as influences—others. Today, when we consider people's interactions in the remote past, we base our speculation upon citations of archaeologically demonstrated trade routes or linguistic affiliations and discontinuities. So, while our questions are different today, Mason nonetheless focused attention on concerns that are still active, such as the similarities between Northern and Southern Athabaskan material culture—especially basketry—and we still quote him. Were I trying to explain the similarities, I would assign great time depth to the base metaphor and cite it as reason enough for the observed similarities between Northern and Southern Athabaskan styles.

While Mason was charitable, James (1972) had little good to say of Mescalero basketry, preferring that of the Western Apache. James, a contemporary of Mason, found Mescalero baskets to be crude in manufacture and uninteresting in design—this just a scant generation after the Mescalero were on their reservation and no longer being harassed nor harassing others. Personal preference is certainly legitimate, but James seems to have used it inappropriately as a scholarly measure.

A generation later Douglas (1934, 1935), writing for those interested in diagnostic features of basketry as well as its classification by tribal groups, indicated that a vertically stacked three-rod bundle, or a bundle of two rods with grasses, formed the basis of Mescalero Apache basketry. He contrasted this vertical stacking with the three rod triangular base of the Western Apaches and noted that Mescalero basketry was limited to simple designs because of the technique of manufacture, beginning with the stacked bundle. Douglas continued by noting that the bundling, or vertical stacking, provided an easily identifiable contrast with what is sometimes very similar looking Western Apache basketry. Where Douglas saw simplicity by constraints of materials and technique, I would argue for design by adherence to the base metaphor, perhaps even going so far as to say the techniques may well have been chosen to allow easy transformation of the base metaphor. However, such speculation is not meant to diminish the fine service Douglas rendered by his meticulous description of technique and materials, as well as his mention of design regularities.

Working shortly after Douglas, Chabot commented that Mescalero baskets were of coil or twill manufacture. Of the twilled burden baskets, she noted that they were "so very adaptable to our waste papers needs" (1936:26), echoing a statement made earlier by James (1972: 107). When Chabot did her work, the basketry at Mescalero was being produced for trade and sale in the nascent tourist industry.

Opler (1965:380–82) detailed the plants used in basketry, their preparation for use, and parts of the construction processes, while Whiteford (1970:39, 53; 1988:55–61) commented particularly on the stacked rod and bundle base for the coiling technique, and presented lucid illustrations of construction. The Turnbaughs (1986:222–23) devoted less than a column, with one illustration, to all of Mescalero basketry. Perhaps this was because they were discussing Native North American basketry in general, but it is for me nonetheless a disappointment—not only because I am an Apache scholar but also because so many museums have Apachean baskets.

Both Tanner (1968) and Josephy (1973) commented upon the general Southern Athabaskan habit of borrowing from each other and from neighbors. Mescalero do indeed freely acknowledge taking what is pleasing from others. However, they also rework such loans to fit their own aesthetic sense and, in the process, produce an item that is recognizably Mescalero and usually one that adheres to the base metaphor.

Current Southwestern basketry scholarship in anthropology is led by Whiteford (1988:193), who states,

> Unless noted otherwise, these [Mescalero Apache] baskets are coiled with two sumac rods stacked above each other and topped with a bundle of yucca or grass fibers. Each stitch of yucca splits the stitch below and interlocks with half of it. They are decorated with yucca of various shades and deep red yucca root.

Prior to Whiteford's work, statements made by Evans and Campbell provided the most succinct characterization of Mescalero basketry. Their work, especially when coupled with Douglas's earlier work on construction techniques and with more recent examinations by Whiteford, allows easy recognition of Mescalero Apache baskets, for Evans and Campbell (1970:17) note that

> The Mescalero Apache . . . make baskets so distinctive . . . they cannot be confused with the baskets of any other American Indian group. This coiled basketry is marked by thin, flat, and loose coils with coarse, irregular stitching, and bold designs featuring large single stars, terraced pyramids, diamonds, and squares. As the stitching is done with split yucca leaves and yucca root bark, which are bleached, partially bleached or left natural, these baskets have a mottled surface of soft greens, yellows, creams and browns. The most common form is a large tray-like bowl . . . .

In the illustration that follows their description, they picture a four-pointed star [*suus,* star] with what they call triangles at each intercardinal position, assuming the points of the star indicate cardinal points. I shall turn later to their designations of stars, pyramids, diamonds, and squares. But first I want to consider the most complete description and illustration of Apachean basketry available to date, the work of Tanner (1982).

In a full consideration of both Western and Eastern Apachean basketry, Tanner provides synthesis and detail not previously available. While I have great admiration for her fine eye, attention to detail, and scholarship, nonetheless I am in disagreement with some of her assumptions based upon Western, Euroamerican art notions of space, symbolism, design, and design name. This is not too surprising, since she works from an art historian's perspective while I work from the stance of an ethnographer.

Despite quoting Goddard, who worked among the Apache during the early part of this century and who indicated that designs are sometimes symbolic and named, Tanner wrote, "As to design symbolism, one never knows to what extent the Indian is attempting to please the white questioner. Certainly as these baskets were commercialized they lost any symbolic meaning—that is, if they ever had any" (1982:161). However, by following the base metaphor and by asking (in culturally appropriate ways, of course) Mescalero Apache names for designs, I demonstrate here that it is indeed possible to know which designs are symbolic and what their meanings are. Indeed, if Tanner had had the advantage of the reservation experiences I have had, I am confident she, too, would note the importance of design names and their symbolism. An outsider, whether superb art historian like Tanner or folklorist/anthropologist/ethnographer like me, may never achieve native competency in understanding the full range of meanings of any one design, but a great deal can be learned that can lead to an understanding of at least a portion of the meaning a design has for an Apache person. In so doing, it is also possible to set aside Euroamerican based criteria for judgment and begin to approach an Apachean perspective that is far more productive.

The base metaphor alerts expectations of finding certain things in the designs worked into Mescalero Apache basketry. First, the baskets probably will be balanced in design placement per se as well as in design/

no-design areas. There is likely to be an emphasis on four—perhaps as cardinal points with intercardinal elaboration as well, if the assumption is that there is a standard directional orientation as in Creation narratives or tribal meetings. This directional orientation should hold no matter in what manner the basket is viewed. Additionally, quadrilateral symmetry should be present and, therefore, design motifs will likely be repeated in fours, eights, or twelves and sixteens. All these items are expected because the base metaphor indicates there is a cultural emphasis on balance, harmony, four, and directionality. It seems a bit farfetched to expect sound and silence in a nonliving object, but perhaps instead there will be both filled and unfilled spaces (what art historians often refer to as positive and negative spaces) as the analogue of sound and silence. The base metaphor can provide the means of making hypotheses about Mescalero Apache baskets that can be readily tested against a collection, thus providing ways of assessing basketry that were not available to previous scholars.

By far the most common motif on Mescalero Apache baskets is *sųųs*, [star], usually with four points; such a design inherently produces balance. In basketry, the Mescalero say that "it is the center that speaks," meaning that the basket's center design is used for the characteristic name of the basket, regardless of any motifs which may be on the periphery or interwoven in other places.

Although not a spectacular example of basket weaving skill, a basket belonging to the Laboratory of Anthropology in Santa Fe shows a characteristic design typical of pieces intended for everyday use as well as for the tourist trade(fig. 4.1). Some Apache people consider the triangular-shaped motifs on the basket's rim as separate designs and name them, but most people say that they are just designs to fill space, since the star motif does not fill the basket. Tanner (1982:167, 186, and passim) refers to this design motif as flower or star and frequently refers to its radial extensions as petals. But whether these designs are simple, or a bit more complex as in a basket from the School of American Research's collection (fig. 4.2), or very elaborate (fig. 4.3), they are all considered *sųųs* by Mescalero Apaches.

The *sųųs* design always tapers from the center of the motif to the arms of the star, and usually the tapered extensions meet. Designs with tapered extensions that do not meet may still be called *sųųs*, although

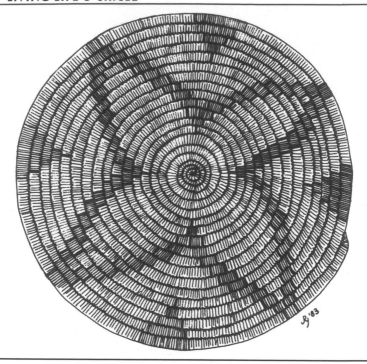

Fig. 4.1 Sųųs [Star] design. (Museum of New Mexico, Laboratory of Anthropology #48105/12. All basketry drawings by James R. Yingst.)

they are not considered to be very good renditions of the star motif, as in figure 4.4.[11] When Bernard and I examined this basket in 1981 at the School of American Research, he believed it to be a Mescalero Apache basket, as it is so cataloged, on the basis of the construction and materials. However, he maintained that the five-pointed star was "unusual" and speculated that the basket was made on order for a tourist, or at least for a non-Indian.

Similarly, he found an example of a basket with a six-pointed star motif from the School's Indian Arts Fund collection to be a "better" design, because it had an even number of points on the star. Still, it was not a good design, in his opinion, and not one a proper Apache person would want to use, as indeed the base metaphor would indicate.

Not every quadripartite design is *sųųs*. *Sha*ʔ [sun] is another common four-part design; it is usually distinguished by projections, seen as rays, at the ends of the arms of the primary design (see fig. 4.5).

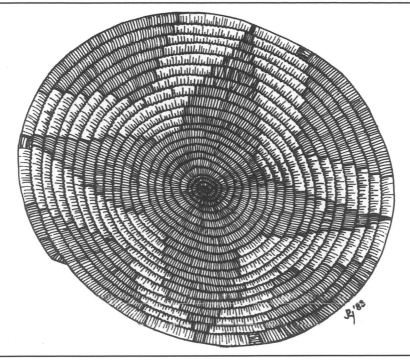

Fig. 4.2 Sụụs [Star] design. (School of American Research, Amelia E. White Collection #SAR 1978-1-53.)

Tanner sees a similar sun design as the result of negative space produced by the "triangles" between the arms, rather than seeing it as a legitimate, purposeful design motif; she calls it a "negative cross" or "flower with squared-off petals" (1982:169, fig. 6.8a). When the arms of the central, quadripartite motif do not curve in toward each other, most Mescalero Apache maintain that the design represents the sun rather than a star—never a flower. Such a design is always called sun when it has straight lines projecting from the arms, since those lines are seen as forming sun rays. The roundness of the sun is in the middle of the design, with the "arms" being the primary rays, one for each of the four cardinal directions or the four days of creation, etc. Sometimes secondary rays are also depicted, as in figure 4.5.

　　While I cannot accept the sun design as being a flower or a cross, this is not to say that crosses are not used. What we call a cross does often appear in designs, although it is usually termed *intin* [road] and

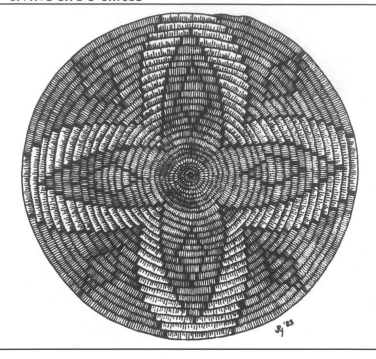

Fig. 4.3   Suus [Star] design. (Museum of New Mexico, Laboratory of Anthropology #48103/12.)

usually is said to represent the cross-arms of the base metaphor with all its symbolic associations. The sun, on the other hand, is usually depicted with four or eight rays, whether woven in basketry, stitched on clothing, beaded on moccasins, or painted on tipi covers. The difference lies in shaping. A cross—whether referring to roads, directions, or Christianity (as it does sometimes, if rarely)—is always rendered with straight cross arms (+). By contrast, the sun is always rendered with slightly curved extensions from the center circle and stars are always shown with pronounced curved extensions.

By using knowledge of construction techniques and materials, combined with expectations derived from the base metaphor, those who must classify basketry (such as anthropologists, art historians, collectors, folklorists, and museum curators) no longer need to rely upon setting up Euroamerican culturally biased criteria by which specific items are assigned to a particular group of people and to a particular point in time. Reliance upon outsiders' criteria, rather than native ones, can lead to

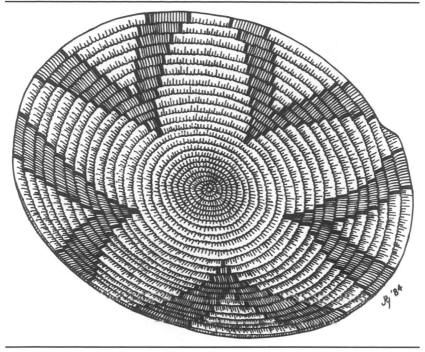

Fig. 4.4 Sųųs [Star] design. This is not considered to be a proper or skilled rendition of sųųs. (School of American Research, II. P. Mera Collection #B.161.)

mistakes that may be avoided by using the base metaphor. For example, often these outside criteria are "proven" correct by an item purchased in a particular place at a specified time. Such an item is likely to become a type piece, since it is believed that provenience has been well controlled. There is, however, real danger in this method of operation, without also having good ethnographic control, both of the item and of the situations giving rise to the item. By that I mean that merely acquiring an item in a particular place and at a particular time is no guarantee that the item is of that place or time.[12] As an example of the possible pitfalls in such thinking about basketry, consider my only Apachean basket, a bowl-shaped one (fig. 4.6).

The base metaphor should cause immediate suspicion about this basket because of the six-element design motif, even though in technique of manufacture the basket could be Mescalero, since it has a three rod foundation. But it does not have a design of two, four, or eight motifs, as is expected from projecting the base metaphor. Nonetheless, Mescalero

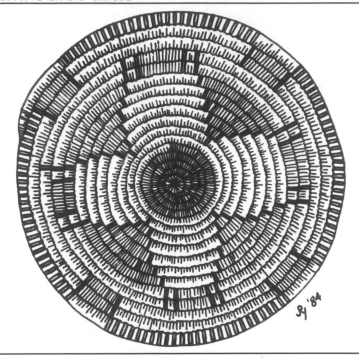

Fig. 4.5   Sha⁷ [Sun] design. Note how the arms do not taper but have extensions [called "rays"]. (Museum of New Mexico, Laboratory of Anthropology #48104/12.)

Apaches report a six element motif is allowable, since it is balanced and thus "all right," although a four or eight element motif "would be better." Following provenience, it is tempting to conclude the basket is Mescalero Apache, for it was used in the Mescalero girls' puberty ceremonial in 1974 and can be seen in that context in photographs, both still and moving (Farrer field data). It also appears on a painting made by a tribal artist, the late Ignatius Palmer. Given its ritual context, it could easily be assumed to be Mescalero. But when my field notebook data are considered, it becomes obvious it is not a Mescalero basket. Bernard received the basket as a gift after having sung a girls' ceremony for a young Jicarilla woman. It is a Jicarilla basket that he then continued to use for a period of time at Mescalero when singing ceremonies there; he also used it domestically until he presented it to me in 1975. In other words, one has to be very chary indeed of assigning place of manufacture based upon

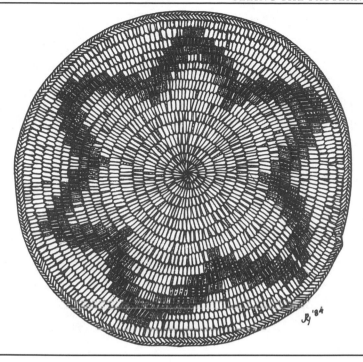

Fig. 4.6 Suus [Star] design. (Claire R. Farrer Collection, Jicarilla Apache basket.)

place of purchase or receipt. Had the base metaphor been given greater credence, this basket would have been listed as a suspect piece from the very beginning, despite its having been "collected" at Mescalero. It is rare, unfortunately, for those responsible for museum exhibits to have the ethnographer's notes. Much too often items are donated from collectors with no provenience, no notes (other than sometimes the place of purchase and price), and no good documentation. It is no wonder there are misattributions.

Tourist items, or those baskets made specifically for sale rather than for domestic or ritual Mescalero use, also present some problems, base metaphor notwithstanding. Most of us like to think our purchases of Indian baskets are authentic and designed for native uses rather than for contemporary mainstream American uses. What we often fail to consider is that most contemporary Indians use the same kinds of utensils mainstream Americans do and that, at least for the Mescalero Apache,

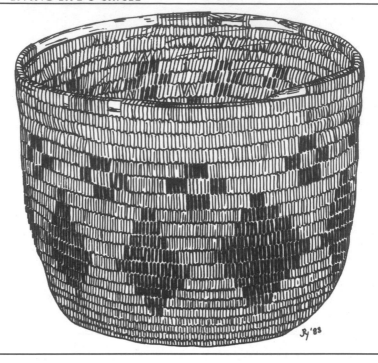

Fig. 4.7   Sizi [Standing] design. (School of American Research, H. P. Mera Collection #B.158.)

basketry is not a common practice anymore. Nonetheless, some items are produced for local and tourist trade. Wastebaskets are examples of such tourist baskets.[13]

A wastebasket (fig. 4.7), although made for the tourist trade, is nonetheless an excellent demonstration of the value of the base metaphor in assigning probable Mescalero manufacture to the item. Whiteford correctly identified this basket as being Mescalero even though it was constructed using a split rod plus a bundle. However, he incorrectly called the design "terraced diamonds and small crosses" (1988:194). Tanner (1982:166, fig. 6.5b), as well as Evans and Campbell (1970) refer to the larger design motifs on this basket as diamonds, as indeed they are in Euroamerican culture. Tanner terms the smaller design motif "coyote tracks" (1982:passim), a misnomer unfortunately perpetuated by Whiteford (1988:5.8) in another context. "Coyote tracks" is not a term I have ever heard at Mescalero in any context. But what we call diamonds Mes-

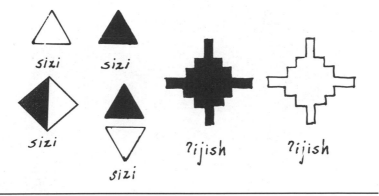

Fig. 4.8   Sizi appear in a number of orientations.

calero Apache people call *sizi* [standing, △]. *Sizi* can be singular or re-duplicated with bases attached, as in figure 4.8 (two colors are used in order to differentiate the two *sizi*).

These *sizi* are interspersed not with "coyote tracks" but with *ʔijish*. It is unimportant whether or not the center is filled in on *ʔijish*, nor is it important whether *ʔijish* is dark on light ground or light on dark ground—it is still *ʔijish*. The *ʔijish* motifs are said to "fill up" the spaces. Which motifs carry significance and which are decorative cannot be as-sumed. Using a term such as coyote tracks, especially one so richly evoca-tive in Euroamerican culture, can be very misleading to an understanding from the perspective of the producing culture. This small design that to Tanner seems equal in importance to the primary design is simply a filler to Mescalero Apaches; it is used to fill up the spaces so the total design "looks right." Spatially, *ʔijish* fulfills the perceived need for balance to produce a harmonious design. But note that while *ʔijish* is not considered of the same importance as *sizi*, it nonetheless conforms to "proper" pat-terning by being quadripartite.

Not all so-called triangles are *sizi*. Those with stepped sides, as in figure 4.7, especially when drawn on bodies or worked into clothing, are often termed *dził* [mountains]. *Dził* can be doubled as well as joined at their bases for variation. Or, in outline form and oriented on a slant, they are termed lightning; in another incarnation, they can be perceived as outlines of mountains (see Farrer and Second 1981:148). Or consider the design in figure 4.9, that at first glance seems to be *sizi* connected a

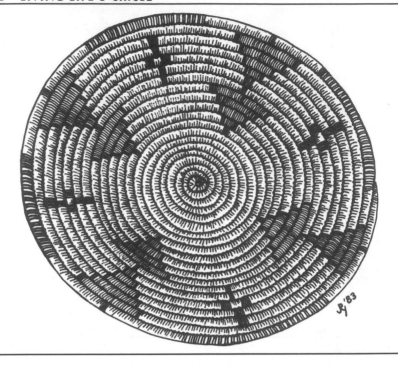

Fig. 4.9   ʔindidé sąą ʔigish [Old Man Thunder and Little Boy Lightning] design. (School of American Research, Indian Arts Fund #B.286.)

little differently and with *ʔijish* as spacers. They are neither triangles nor *sizi* to Mescaleros, however; rather, these linked triangle motifs, or terraced triangles in Whiteford's (1988:193) terms, are called *ʔindidé sąą ʔigish*, a term used to denote two Power people, Old Man Thunder and Little Boy Lightning.

Identifying a named design motif and associating it with a referent does not necessarily insure recognition of its variations, as can be seen with the *sizi* shape. Euroamericans see diamonds formed by base linked triangles in figure 4.7, while Mescalero Apaches see *sizi*. Euroamericans see linked triangles in figure 4.9, while Mescalero Apaches see evocations of myth and the powerful Twin Warrior Gods as represented by Thunder and Lightning.

It is not surprising to find myth encoded in basketry designs, for the base metaphor itself has a mythological basis that is replicated in the natural workings of the universe and that can be observed in the celestial

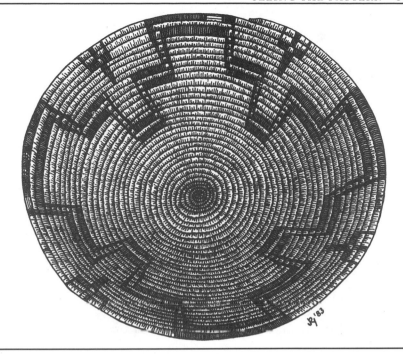

Fig. 4.10 Dii ⁿdá [Four-Stages-of-Life] design. This design is also called dii ji-dighạ [four traveling]. (School of American Research, Indian Arts Fund #B.291.)

sphere. Another example of myth in basketry is the four-stages-of-life design. When the world had been made and White Painted Woman had lived her life, the basis for *dii ⁿdá* [four-stages-of-life] was set. If a person is fortunate enough to live a normal span of years, each of the four stages (infancy, childhood, adulthood, and old age) will be experienced. The four-stages-of-life are beautifully worked into the design in figure 4.10. Not only did the Mescalero Apache basket maker encode myth and reference to the four stages of life that repeat infinitely, as White Painted Woman demonstrated, but also she (almost all basket makers were women among the Mescalero) included a very unusual feature for a Mescalero Apache basket: a human figure.

Those commenting on this design do not agree when they assign Euroamerican names, and they view the basket with a Western perspective. What for the Mescalero Apache is a primary design motif, the four-stages-of-life, becomes "meander" with "odd crosses" for Tanner (1982: 170, fig. 6.9) or "four-armed terraced cross" for Whiteford (1988:193), rather than being identified for what it is: a powerful and elegant mnemonic for both ritual and everyday life and a visual representation of a mythic event combined with the expectation of one's own life course. Apachean people who have no ritual responsibilities identify the "odd crosses" as human beings who will each experience the four-stages-of-life. Bernard, whose singing responsibilities brought to his mind a different set of associations, saw the four figures as being two depictions each of the Twin Warrior Gods, reduplicated so that they would be represented in association with each of the four motifs necessary for *dii ⁿdá*. Further, he noted that East is associated with birth and early childhood, South with puberty and sexual maturity, West with adulthood, and North with old age. He perceived the design as being *guzhuguja,* everything in order/in balance, just as life itself is in balance. East and North balance each other, for both infants and old people must rely upon others to meet many of their needs, while South and West balance each other, for young people and adults are expected to be responsible for themselves as well as for the aged and the recently born. When I told Bernard that several others had seen the figures as simply people, he agreed that they could be termed *dii jidighą* [four traveling], but that such a term carried the connotation of continuously traveling through life: through infancy, childhood, adulthood, old age, infancy, childhood, adulthood, old age, and around and around again; or from east, to south, to west, to north, back to east, south, and so on.

Once having identified the four-stages-of-life design, one is tempted to see it everywhere, even in a basket such as that in figure 4.11, with its four groups of three lines linked together. However, no one to whom I have shown this design has recognized it. It is rejected as a four-stages-of-life design because the motifs are separate; they are not linked, as they should be in a proper four-stages-of-life design. Most people seeing the basket, or an image of it, believed it could have been a Mescalero design but that it was probably a personal one with meaning only for the one who made it. While people accord the basket respectability as a properly made Mescalero Apache one, they maintain the design has no meaning for them. Whiteford may well have solved this problem by changing the attribution of the basket and listing it as Jicarilla, rather

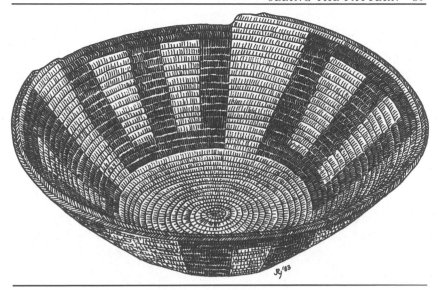

Fig. 4.11 *This design is not Mescalero; they have no name for it and do not consider it either dii ⁿdá or dii jidigha. (School of American Research, H. P. Mera Collection #B.167.)*

than Mescalero Apache. He describes the design as "four large rectangles in vegetal brown . . ." (1988:191). I find it interesting that he sees this design as four rectangles, focusing on the dark areas, rather than as twelve light rectangles, four of which are large and eight of which are small and all of which are outlined by dark areas. Further, it is interesting that they are described as rectangles rather than parallelograms. At any rate, he is probably correct in moving this basket out of the Mescalero category, where it was when Bernard and I examined it at the School of American Research.

In order for a basket to be termed *dii ⁿdá*, the four-stages-of- life, it must have each of the four motifs linked or connected to each of the adjacent motifs. So the linked-stepped design showing interconnections and, thus, having a sense of neverendingness, even without the human figure, "speaks" its name as four-stages-of-life (as in fig. 4.12).

The four-stages-of-life design recalls to Mescalero Apache minds a panoply of associations—with four seasons, four winds, four cardinal directions, four intercardinal directions, and the four days of Creation,

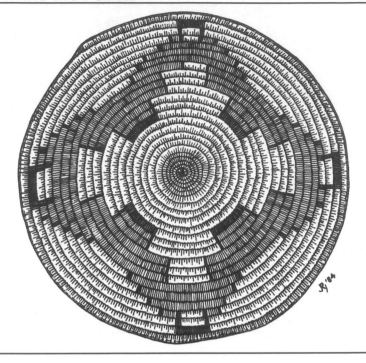

Fig. 4.12   Dii ⁿdá [Four-Stages-Of-Life] design. (Museum of New Mexico, Laboratory of Anthropology #36736/12.) '

in addition to association with the proper life course. It is a peaceful and satisfying design and always drew the comment of "hⁿzhúne" [harmonious/good/beautiful/proper] when people saw an image of it.

It is important to remember that there is differential access to knowledge and different knowledge bases among people in any culture. And, of course, there are idiosyncratic designs; yet what I find fascinating is that even the idiosyncratic designs usually conform to the canons set forth in the base metaphor. While the base metaphor channels expectations for specific elements in Mescalero Apache basketry, it can neither predict what will be on any one basket nor provide esoteric information, such as is woven in a highly stylized manner into the basket in figure 4.13. Whiteford captioned this basket as "an open four-pointed star with . . . diamonds and . . . coyote tracks" (1988:58). But Bernard saw this basket as being holy and was upset that it was not woven sunwise (about which I shall have more to say shortly). In his view, the basket

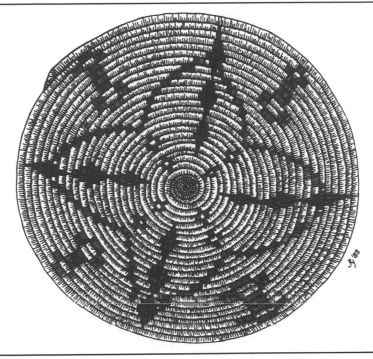

Fig. 4.13 While Bernard thought this design symbolic of Little Boy Lightning, other Apaches see only a pleasing, but unnamed, design. (School of American Research, Indian Arts Fund #B.323.)

contained representations of Little Boy Lightning moving inward in the arms of the central star motif, and he suspected that what he could only label as ʔijish had specific meaning to the maker. Individuals, of course, are free to name their own designs and assign symbolic associations to them; others are under no obligation to accept these idiosyncratic designations, however. Usually people will name designs based on their general associations.

Design names may also change as contexts change. Sometimes, especially in a ritual context, linked "triangles" are associated with the Twin War Gods. Or, as mentioned already, what is perceived as a mountain in one instance may be perceived as lightning in another context. Even more confusing for an outsider, these may all be said to be "the same thing" (e.g., see Farrer and Second 1981:146, 148, figs. 13.7, 13.8, 13.9). Design symbols—whether on basketry, clothing, tipi covers, or wherever—are multivocalic, as is the base metaphor itself; the realization

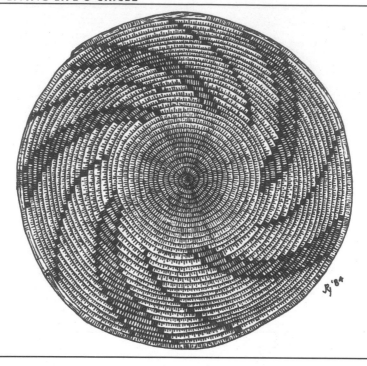

*Fig. 4.14   Ņubił [Whirling/Whirlwind/Chaos] design. This is at times termed a
"violent" basket, because the swirls suggest antisunwise movement. (Museum of
New Mexico, Laboratory of Anthropology #36735/12.)*

of their many voices can be understood only by examining the designs in
many contexts.

When working with a limited palette, as Evans and Campbell
noted the Mescalero Apache do, the contrast between light and dark
fields must be a focus of attention. Euroamericans have a tendency to see
dark as primary, perhaps because of associations of print on paper. Mescalero Apache people begin to describe designs with the central motif
first, gradually moving outward to the edge of the design field. This is
also the way in which the design—and the entire basket, for that matter—is created. It follows, then, that the central design is usually the most
important one and the one by which a piece is characterized.

With a basket such as that in figure 4.9, where the center is empty,
it is the largest motif that "speaks" the name of the basket design. Or, as
in the case of figure 4.14, the center is seen as the pivot point for the

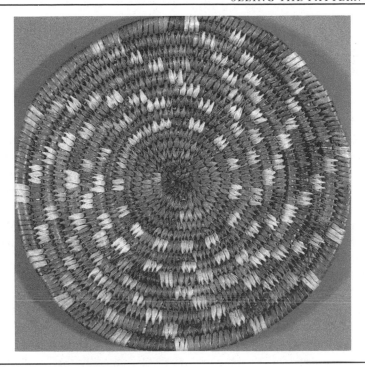

Fig. 4.15   Nubił [Whirling/Whirlwind/Chaos] design. (School of American Research, Mabel Morrow Estate #SAR 1979/6/71.)

design that is called *nųʔbił* [whirling/whirlwind/chaos]. *nųʔbił* is a word that can be used to characterize the visible movement of wind in a dust devil, those mini-tornadoes that frequently skip across the New Mexican desert. The term is also sometimes applied to the design that Euroamericans call a swastika, a design Apaches used until negative World War II Nazi connotations. Some Apaches saw in figure 4.14 a "violent basket" and thought it depicted an ill or destructive wind, because it went "backwards"—that is, it went antisunwise. Others, though, maintained it was just "whirling around," as with the basket in figure 4.15, another example of *nųʔbił*. Regardless of the goodness or badness imputed to the design, it was seen as being in motion from the center outward. Where Mescalero Apaches move from the center outward, Euroamericans tend to focus on the outside, examining first the frame and then what it encloses.

In each of the baskets discussed, the frame, or the edge of the basket, indicates that the basket was woven counterclockwise, or, as the Apaches would say, antisunwise—against the movement of the sun. The antisunwise construction indicates that the item was not made for a ritual purpose, but rather that it was intended for an everyday, nonritual use. In order for these baskets to be used in ritual contexts, a singer would have to bless them, as Bernard did with my Jicarilla basket.

When a basket is intended for ritual use, and is made only for that purpose, it is constructed with sunwise coiling. Unfortunately for a researcher trying to document them, ritual items tend to be destroyed ritually when they are no longer to be used for the purposes for which they were made or when they are no longer serviceable. I have found only one ritual Mescalero Apache basket in the collections I have examined to date; it is housed in the Wheelwright Museum in Santa Fe. Its lack of good documentation precluded its inclusion here; it had even lost its identification tag. The rim of the basket is sufficiently worn to show construction details, thus allowing confirmation that it is Mescalero Apache from the three rod, vertical stack foundation. However, its time of manufacture, place of collection, and other data are simply unavailable at this time, although I trust sometime the Wheelwright will once again locate these data. With no design and no provenience, even the base metaphor cannot be of assistance; while authentically Mescalero in manufacture, final judgment must await better documentation. Nonetheless, sunwise coiling does exist, even though many people believe otherwise, since such coiling is more difficult for right-handed persons to do and since most people are right-handed. Difficulty, however, is often a part of ritual. It is difficult to spin sunwise, but the Navajo do it routinely, as Toelken noted above. For the Mescalero Apache, antisunwise movement or coiling deritualizes, desacralizes. In fact, if one is interested in witching, one (among other actions) reverses blessing sequences so that the movement is antisunwise. If a Mescalero Apache basket is being made for ritual and if the basketmaker is skilled enough, the basket will be coiled sunwise.

The Mescalero are not alone in this practice of reversal to signify a difference between the ritual and the everyday. Wilbert (1974:29) [14] clearly states the importance of directionality and also quotes Rowe in discussing a similar situation with South American Indians, whose spinning is differentiated on the basis of its intended ritual or non-ritual use.

Yarns may be spun in two directions, the spiral formed by twisting upward to the left being called the S-twist and that to the right the Z-twist by contemporary weavers . . . Peruvian Indians right-spun thread "except in manufacturing articles to be used in sorcery" (Rowe 1946:241). An Inca sorcerer who wanted to visit harm, sickness, and death on an enemy would "spin a thread of black and white wool, twisting it to the left (the reverse of the customary direction), and then place a noose of it on a path where the enemy might pass so that it would catch his foot" (Rowe 1946:314).

The analogy between S-twist and Z-twist spinning with sunwise and antisunwise basketry coiling is obvious. Power can be controlled and manipulated through ritual means, including the reversal of normal directionality.

An earlier publication of Goodell's (1969:6–7) also discusses the S-twist and Z-twist of the Peruvian Indians. Her discussion is even more specific with regard to the clockwise/counterclockwise or sunwise/ antisunwise motions and handedness:

> In some areas, however, there are many distinctions that clearly govern the direction of the spin or twist of the yarn. These are based on faith in the magical properties of yarn spun "clockwise" (with an S twist), called *lloq'e,* in contrast to the normal everyday product made with a Z twist. The Quechua word *lloq'e* means left and also "something different." In this case it would mean "the left-spun yarn" . . . Sometimes only *brujos* (Medicine men) can spin *lloq'e,* in which case everyone else, *even left-handed spinners, must produce Z twist yarn* . . . [emphasis added].

Goodell continues her discussion by noting that usually everyone, regardless of handedness, must spin clockwise when the thread is to be used for a special, ritual purpose. Such spinning is protective and curative, as well as appropriate for offerings. Euroamerican cultures are not exempt from the power inherent in reversals. Mainstream Americans are as apt as Peruvians to give symbolic import to reversals, as both Halloween and Mardi Gras practices illustrate.

Even though there may not be numbers of lovely museum examples of sunwise coiling on Mescalero baskets and even though prevailing opinions of handedness and ease of coiling would have us believe that sunwise coiling is unlikely to occur, nonetheless there is excellent reason to believe what the Mescalero aver: namely, that sunwise coiling

Fig. 4.16   *A visual representation of the base metaphor. (All geometric drawings by Linda Kling.)*

of basketry is for ritual only while antisunwise coiling frees a basket for everyday use. Perhaps a difference between Peruvians or Navajos and Apaches is that the Apaches are willing to sacralize an object by blessing it, even when it was not constructed according to ritual canon. Even without extensive examples, the base metaphor suggests that the highest positive value would be placed on baskets with sunwise coils. Their designs would speak with voices of ritual and holy authority and, of course, would make exquisite statements when used in ritual.

Curiously, "speaking" designs that were all said to be "the same thing" were easier to understand than other aspects of Mescalero Apache cognitive culture. Rather early on it was apparent that the base metaphor's visual representation could easily be geometrically transformed into a variety of other visual representations that abound on Apachean clothing, tipi designs, body painting, and, of course, basketry.

The base metaphor has two common visual representations: the one in figure 4.16 and another that is the same except that the cross arms go beyond the bounds of the circle; it is shown on the title page as well as in figure 4.17. It is this latter figure that is used to provide most of the geometric transformations.

Fig. 4.17   *A visual representation of the base metaphor.*

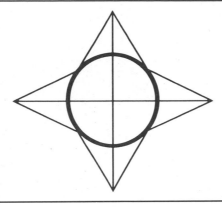

Fig. 4.18   ⁿdaʔi bijuuɬ siáʔgenerates a 4-pointed star.

In order to begin the transformations, it is necessary to draw eight more lines, or a continuous one linking the end, the cardinal, points of the figure (see fig. 4.18). This first transformation produces the four-pointed star that is so common on Mescalero Apache basketry, for, when the depiction of the base metaphor is removed, all that is left is the four-pointed star (see fig. 4.19). It is no wonder that the *sųųs* design is almost ubiquitous on basketry. It is found on body painting as well, as will be seen in chapter 6, and can also be found on clothing and worked in beads.

By taking any one of the segments of the four-pointed star, *sizi*

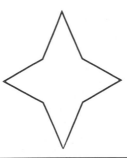

Fig. 4.19   The four-pointed star.

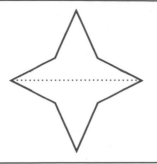

Fig. 4.20   Cut line to produce mountains.

($\triangle$) is generated. The orientation is unimportant—even standing on end (∇), it is still *sizi*. Cutting apart the four-pointed star (fig. 4.20) yields mountains (fig. 4.21). Rotating the mountains and reduplicating them produces a design that is also seen as an elaboration of the cross arms of the base metaphor (see fig. 4.22). The design thus suggests the quadripartite symbols and the number four itself, with which the base metaphor abounds. (The cross lines indicated on the drawing in figure 4.22 are meant to suggest other designs that appear on clothing and on some baskets, although not on baskets discussed in this chapter.)

It no longer seems quixotic to suggest that the base metaphor is "the same thing" as a four-pointed star, or the four-stages-of-life, or mountains, or the floor plan of the girls' ceremonial tipi, or the way in which food is salted or speeches are made.

Yet the simple design and its transformations also suggest more subtle aspects of Mescalero Apache life and society. Women, for example, are associated with the moon, since the moon changes, as did White Painted Woman when she walked the surface of the earth. As the

Fig. 4.21   Mountains produced from the four-pointed star.

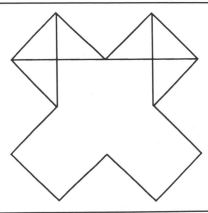

Fig. 4.22   Other geometric transformations generated from ⁿda²i bijuuł siá. *The cross lines indicate designs that appear on clothing, body painting, and some baskets, although not on baskets discussed in this chapter (but see fig. 6.1).*

dotted line in figure 4.23 illustrates, the crescent moon is easily generated from the base metaphor. The darkly outlined circle can be seen as a full or new moon, as well as the circle of life, the circle of the universe, or the form that the stars and constellations describe as they move through the seasons of the year. Crescent moons beaded onto or cut into the top fabric of *tsąął* [cradles, or cradleboards as they are usually termed in

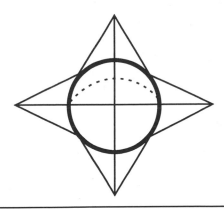

Fig. 4.23   ⁿda²i bijuuł siá² *also generates moon designs.*

English] indicate that there is a girl baby in the cradle; if the baby is a boy, the design will be of four-pointed stars.

Life, as we know it, requires sexuality in order to continue. That, too, is encoded into the base metaphor and constitutes a part of its balance. There must be male and female or life ceases. The Mescalero Apache believe that each needs the other and neither should dominate the other. Rather, they must be in balance and harmony, or the inherent order of the universe and life itself will be out of balance—and then surely catastrophe will result.

Non-Indian people find it easier to see the pattern engendered by the base metaphor in a concrete item, such as a basket or in drawings showing what is essentially a cognitive process. Mescalero Apaches "see" the pattern not only in basketry or body painting or on tipis and clothing, but also in games, furniture arrangement, formal speeches, seating, salting food, and so on. The base metaphor does indeed impinge on almost every aspect of life whether ritual, ceremonial, everyday, or secular. Its ubiquity is not a burden, however; rather, it is partially what makes life worth living, what gives organization and beauty to the mundane. Enacting the base metaphor—and seeing its enactment all around, whether in one's own life, in those of one's fellows, or in the very universe and its celestial sphere—helps Apaches to live in accordance with *hⁿzhúne*, in beauty, harmony, balance, and grace.

The pattern is so ingrained for them that often it is recalled only when it is breached—when a child deliberately rides a trike in an anti-sunwise circle or when an Anglo gives a speech with only three parts to it. The base metaphor provides simply, and profoundly, the right way to live. It provides a template by which to order experience and even to perceive experience. The pattern for living a proper life can be seen all around, whether in interpersonal actions, in the shape of the round corrals that dot the reservation, in the idea of four-stages-of-life, or on baskets in the cases holding Mescalero Apache artifacts in Anglo museums. The pattern is *hⁿzhúne*, and it is the base metaphor that generates what is perceived as being *hⁿzhúne* and even generates *hⁿzhúne* itself. The pattern is there in the sky and there on the ground, where it is lived and enacted daily. Held within its ordering confines, the pattern that is, and that produces, the base metaphor also holds the key to the possibility for change. It is to change, but change within ordered bounds, that I next turn.

CHAPTER 5

Clowning and Chiasm

CRF: "Bernard, why am I here?"
BS: "To make some rhyme or reason out of chaos."
(From a tape recording of June 28, 1975.)

Pattern, with its derived and associated structures of sociocultural life, provides welcome consistency.[1] None of us seems too comfortable with constantly changing situations or perspectives; adjustments to change are difficult for most of us, even when such adjustments are welcome.

A contemporary case in point is the restructuring of the Iron Curtain countries that began in the U.S.S.R. and had important consequences in divided Germany: while we applauded the opening of the Berlin Wall, we also worried over the ramifications of German reunification. As a nation, we had grown used to, and therefore comfortable with, the world as it was with Communists on one side and Capitalists on the other. We may have argued with or grumbled about massive defense spending, but at least we knew the face of the enemy. Perestroika and glasnost quickly blurred the enemy's face and even called into question whether or not there was an enemy. Then the Wall began to crumble, and we had to face the possibility of a Germany united, a Germany that had twice in this century plunged the Western European world into horrid, devastating wars of such cataclysmic magnitude that we termed them World Wars. While we watched our nightly television news in fascination as one then another Communist nation swayed to the demands of its citizenry for freedom, those of us old enough to recall one or both of the World Wars found old fears of vulnerability ready to surface. We in the United States had grown comfortable with the patterns of the post—World War II period and could not see the direction of new patterns nor the eventual shape they would assume, let alone what our role might be and whether or not we would remain a primary world power. Altered patterns and structures can easily lead to social chaos and the usurpation of power and authority by yet another dictator or megalomanic leader.

The threat of chaos and the threat of the unknown blend readily into each other. Almost all of us, whatever our country, make nostalgic noises, ignoring the undesirable aspects of past times that we seek currently to glorify. Yet, when viewed diachronically, most of us can see changes that did improve life, as well as ones that made everyday living more difficult. When in the throes of change, however, very few of us have the necessary vision to predict the direction of change, or luck to envision them. With no solid perspective, we must rely upon old patterns recast into new structures and new, daring thoughts as we seek to forge new means of adjusting to a changing world. And underneath it all is the very real threat of social chaos while the old is being set aside and the new is not yet born.

During the years that I have observed Mescalero Apache lifeways and society, I have seen many changes and many adjustments to the mainstream American way of life. Yet the essential character of what it means to be Mescalero Apache has remained intact. The base metaphor's underlying organizing principles have continued to shape new ways of life, new behavior, so that change within established values has been possible. Such a balancing act demands more than applause; it also requires explanation. How can things change yet remain the same? In order to answer the question on a level other than mere reference to the base metaphor, in this chapter I postulate a mechanism of cultural change, termed chiasm (Farrer 1979, 1980a, 1983, 1987d). I think graphically of chiasm as being a series of chis, χs, suspended and intertwined in metaphysical space. I use the concept of chi to indicate the complex interplay of cultural life, whether it is the culturally proper way to dress, eat, behave, think, or act. The nexus, or crossing points of the chis, provide entry into potentialities for culture change; it is the potentialities for change or affirmation of cultural norms that are the most prominent features of chiasms. Certain events and individuals function as chiasms, opening the way to the underlying behavior symbolized by the chi figures. Once opened, the figures themselves—the culturally appropriate ways to be—are subject to change, affirmation, redefinition, or validation.

It is also at the chiasm point that rituals and some festivals coalesce. Since everything is possible or potential at chiasm, then everything is impossible as well; the power of possibilities is part of the magnetism of ritual and festival events. The sun may not begin its reversal at solstices—it may go too far and burn up or freeze the world; so there were, and are, midwinter and midsummer festivals. In ancient Mesoamerica, there was a huge festival every fifty-two years at the point where the 260 and 365 day calendars cycled back into their positions of over a half century previously; it was at this time that it was believed that the world could end. The world, as it is known and understood, can as easily end as change or be affirmed during the events of chiasms. Examples of times and activities of chiasms are replete in anthropological literature but are difficult to envisage in the abstract. I find it productive to view chiasms as those instances where the members of a society confront themselves and their cultural institutions.

Chiasm's visual format evolved from my first encounter with a semiotic square in the work of Greimas and Rastier (1971:87ff).[2] The semiotic square, however, is a two-dimensional figure. I wished to suggest a model of n-dimensionality such that time, space, fantasy, cognition, imagination, behavior, custom, habit, belief, ritual and horror—among other things—could be equally conceived and equally accessed. Initially I visualized the chiasm model as separate chis existing in a cultural field, as X X X X. Then I saw the model as a series of interconnected chis, as xxxx. The cursive and hooked aspects of the interconnected chis were structures for thinking, since it seemed to me that when a chiasm was in existence, as in a ritual event, there were all kinds of behavior and thought patterns that were catching hold of each other and influencing each other, rather than there being separate and singular instances of behavior or thought.

Each of these models suggested linearity, however, and called to mind the literary use of "chiasmus," an inverted relationship between syntactic elements of parallel phrases; or they brought to mind the biological use of "chiasma," when paired chromatids form the X shape in a portion of the meiotic prophase in the cellular equivalent of genetic crossing. There is yet another physiological chiasma: the optic chiasma, that switchpoint where stimulus to the eyes is received, inverted, switched to the opposite side, and passed to the brain for sense-making. Our visual perception depends upon the complete process; action cannot stop at the optic chiasma nor can perception be what is registered only at the retina. Neither is "reality." Perception is a combination of all the elements: sensory input, crossover, inversion, sensory reception, and integration for meaning. But the term optic chiasma describes only the switchpoint, not the entire process. Process and nonlinearity are crucial to my conception; thus, the term chiasma was inappropriate and would, I feared, lead thinking into static models for what is a series of complex processes.

There was another disadvantage with the term chiasma; there is a strong cultural element in what is perceived and what such perceptions mean, as Hall (1983, for example) demonstrates. While the crossing-over idea was useful, the idea of an inverse relationship in a static field was misleading for what I was trying to describe—namely the fruits of analyses of on-going processes.

Needing something more dynamic but wishing to retain the core of the base metaphor, I began using the term chiasm. In my mind's eye I saw chis, of various sizes and meanings and taking differing amounts of time to form, whirling around each other in several planes simultaneously. While the chis—discrete events or thoughts in a cultural context—whirl and move, they sometimes intersect, crossing each other simultaneously in every possible plane. Further, I thought of chis as being multidimensional in particular ways, incorporating not just space and time or height and depth, but also thought and action. Wherever a crossing or intersection occurs—whether of an entire chi or a segment of it—there is a chiasm and the potential for creativity and reordering. As I envision it, a chiasm does not sit on a boundary; it melts boundaries, so that each melds into the other such that there is union between the extensions of the arms of the chis at unpredictable places. (See Begley, Carey, and Kahn [1983:53] for a similar discussion regarding chaos theory.)

Chiasm may most graphically and easily be seen at Mescalero during performances of the ritual clown, Łibayé, one of the cultural institutions that Mescalero Apaches themselves use to contemplate and chart changes in their society.

BS When the world began and the [Mountain Gods] came out, the first
    one to come out³ was the Clown and he sings for himself, as he
    dances. The first one out was Łibayé [the dust/dirt/gray-colored
    one]; he sang for himself, because he was so powerful.

Me, me, the Gray One.
I am the first one to be on this land.
I am the first one to be on this land.
I am the first one to be on this land.

(From a September 1976 tape.)

Łibayé is said to be first among the Mountain God dancers seen
today, although he dances last in their line. He is first ontologically as
well, for Łibayé is a boy among men, one clothed in motley to their elegance, an inept dancer counterposed to their virile, postured movements,
unformed potentiality to their fully realized manliness. Like any child, he
gloats over his superior position, but unlike any proper man, his power,
while greater than that of the Mountain God dancers, is uncontrolled,
unchecked, unbridled, almost unbearable. Yet he is a boy who cannot
even dance properly. He is painted to resemble the color of cold ashes,
that in themselves have the power to repel ghosts and other evil. When
the Mountain Gods dance, the bells on their costumes produce music
that is stridently mocked and interrupted by the clank of a cowbell dangling over Łibayé's derierre. He is paradox incarnate, with his antics
simultaneously holding up for public scrutiny the potentiality of unchecked chaos and the promise of continued ordered, patterned life as
danced by the Mountain Gods themselves. Łibayé's order is that of wait-
ing-in-the-wings chaos; it is the kind of order that each moment taunts
with its implicit message that, when least expected, it will dissolve
into . . . and the statement is left unfinished for fertile human minds to
contemplate precisely what kind of chaos will ensue.

Chaos theory, which recently came of age in the so-called hard
sciences, was initially stimulated by the thoughts and mathematical work
of Jules Henri Poincaré, the nineteenth-century French mathematical ge-
nius, who noted in his demonstration of the importance of nonlinear,
non-Newtonian mathematics that that which cannot be predicted can
only be described (from Poincaré's *Science and Method*, as quoted in
Gleick 1987:321). Poincaré thus set the stage for the emergence of quan-
tum mechanics, with its reliance on probability predictions rather than

upon deterministic predictions as in Newtonian physics. In this century, a seemingly minor player, climate (with its notorious unpredictable nature), created a revolution for the major players—physics and the other hard sciences—and is now influencing the cameo parts played by anthropology and folklore. The elegantly simple but profound equations of Edward Lorenz (1963a, 1963b, 1964), who worked with models to understand and improve weather prediction, have had a salutary effect on diverse disciplines seemingly quite far removed from Lorenz's meteorological interests. Contemporary chaos theorists (Bass 1985; Feigenbaum 1981; Mandelbrot 1977; Prigogine 1984; Smale 1980; Sparrow 1982)—whether they characterize themselves as physicists, mathematicians, astronomers, or, more recently, chaos specialists—describe and quantify what Mescalero Apaches have known for time beyond their reckoning: that is, apparently disorderly behavior is creative (Gleick 1987:43) and is isomorphically patterned within certain limits. While isomorphic patterning is *not* the same as congruence or equivalence, it nevertheless remains within certain constraints. It is "locally unpredictable, globally stable" (Gleick 1987:48); or, in Apachean terms, the specific action or behavior, whatever its present shape now or whatever it was in the past, will nonetheless be consistent with the base metaphor. The base metaphor provides the stability of form and values within which specifics may vary.

Chaos theorists needed terms to describe the appearance of the graphed computer printout that resulted from the input of the simple equations Lorenz used to model climatic conditions, equations describing bounded chaos or the "sensitive dependence upon initial conditions" (Gleick 1987:20ff). Originally called the "strange attractor," this ordered chaos pattern has come to be known as the "Lorenz attractor"; Lorenz himself prefers the term "butterfly effect" (Gleick 1987:44ff). Whether strange attractors or butterfly effects, the essential point is that there are patterns within apparent disorder; there is iteration, or repetition, within chaos. That iteration is not necessarily isomorphic, but rather conforms to an overall pattern. The butterfly effect, especially when modeled through computer computations, readily displays how very minor changes produce different tracings, albeit within a stable pattern—hence the sensitive dependence upon initial conditions. A base metaphor is an initial condition; cultural and social life unfolds within

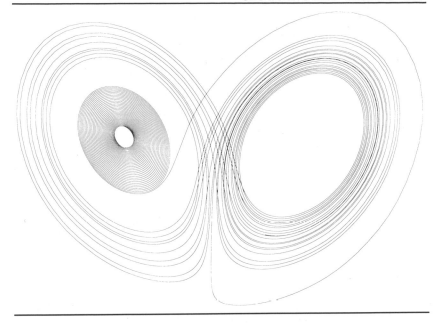

Fig. 5.1   Lorenz attractor, or "butterfly effect" (Paul Haeberli, Silicon Graphics, Inc.)

that primary condition and is, as long as the culture is intact, dependent upon it while not being its slave.

When I first saw a photograph of the butterfly effect (fig. 5.1), I was stunned, for there, in gorgeous color and lacking only dimensionality, was my mind's eye vision. Embedded within it, at the middle crossing point, is the figure, χ, I had been using for chiasm. It was comforting to know others had also visualized and brought into view chis and chiasms, since they were analytic terms for me, having no ethnographic, tangible reality. Just as Lorenz's butterfly effect models were produced from mathematical models of portions of ongoing processes, my chiasms were the result of trying to model the complexities of ongoing cultural change or those items of culture change to be contemplated, if not accomplished.

The butterfly effect is an excellent visual analogue of a Mescalero mental construct concerning time, or, to be more accurate, times.[4] Since Lee's (1950) perceptive essay on non-lineal time, it has been canonical in anthropology to state that Anglos, or those participating in Western

European—derived cultures, have a lineal model of time while many other people have a cyclical model. It is more accurate, with respect to Mescalero Apache abstract constructions, to think instead of the butterfly effect, for the Mescalero Apache do not see time as cycling 'round and 'round but rather conceive of time*s* as being in effect simultaneously: parallel, overlapping, merging, or in opposition—but always within specific confines and always conforming to the base metaphor. In like manner, the Lorenz butterfly effect, or strange attractor, is constrained, even while being nonreplicating and nonperiodic. Its tracings show parallel, overlapping, merging oppositions within the confines of the butterfly pattern. The pattern repeats in recognizable form even if it does not provide precisely identical tracings; it is "locally unpredictable, globally stable"—the scientific equivalent to the base metaphor. Or, as some might prefer, the base metaphor is the Apachean equivalent of the butterfly effect. Both butterfly effect and base metaphor allow for the unpredictability of the immediate present, or very soon to be, while maintaining chaos at bay through the stability of form over the long term. Today's behavior may well change, but it will change within the pattern dictated by the base metaphor. The base metaphor, predicated upon observational analyses of the natural universe, is unchanging—it is globally stable. While precession alters the stars, planets, and constellations through very long periods of time, the basic and unchanging facts are that there is still the earth below, the sky above, and the lights in the sky. Chiasm is to precession as the base metaphor is to the natural universe.

I deliberately chose the word "time*s*" above, although it is rather awkward, to focus on properties of the two Mescalero Apache coexisting universes. There is The Shadow World (which is our own world) and The Real World, to use Bernard Second's felicitous phrases (Farrer and Second 1986). This World, the one in which we live, is the shadowed one, the transient one, the illusionary and illusory one, mirroring aspects of The Real World of Power, Potential, Spacetime, and Truth. See-ers (a term I borrow from Pinxten and vanDooren, [1992])—or shamans or medicine people or singers—have the capacity to traverse the two times and Worlds, but not with impunity. Their point of entry/exit is a chiasm, a point Gleick (1987:160) describes as being where there is a phase transition or a boundary "between two realms of existence."[5] Times of This World and times of The Real World may meet each other in a chiasm; whether or not anyone is aware of them at any given moment, the times of The Two Worlds are always in association—now crossing each other, then moving parallel to each other.

Multiple times are perhaps more easily understood in relationship to Western use of parallel times, as with Greenwich Mean Time (GMT) and local time (LT). GMT is in the realm of specialists—such as astronomers, pilots, navigators, meteorologists—who enter and leave it at will. Those of us in LT seldom attend to GMT, even if we happen to be aware of it—that is, unless we are fans of something like BBC international radio where time checks or upcoming programs are often referred to in GMT. In a similar manner, Mescalero Apaches acknowledge that there is the time that living people structure and experience, as well as the time that is of Power and Creation. These times are coexistent for Apaches. While people may well speak of something as having occurred when the world was being made, there is also a simultaneous understanding that the time in which such actions took place is also accessible by certain few people who, like pilots or navigators, enter and leave it at will.

Without careful preparation and planning, those traversing the times and chiasm from This Shadow World to The Real World risk being caught in the crossing—forever suspended between illusion and reality. But for those who can successfully endure the strictures and remain out of their own proper spacetime long enough to find an answer or effect a cure, for such individuals there is great power and satisfaction, as well, for they assist their people in reaching a greater understanding by healing, or even by changing the course of cultural practices. The power for change is not bought cheaply, however.

Only a certain few individuals can withstand the tremendous psychological and physical pressure of continued crossings. Only a certain few individuals can bring new order to the group or reestablish an old order, thus forestalling imminent chaos. Only a certain few individuals can live with the knowledge of the depth of our illusions after having glimpsed times in concerted action, after having seen Truth in The Real World. Gleick (1987:5) notes, "To some . . . chaos is a science of *process* rather than a state, of becoming rather than being" [emphasis added]. It is extremely difficult for humans when this process of becoming is a constant. Only a certain few individuals are empowered to dance on the thin ice of times in motion. For these few individuals the illogic of Euclidean space or Newtonian time is ludicrous. Even relativistic time is too simplistic to describe the Truth they witness in The Real World—a World, it must be remembered, that coexists with our own even if we are unaware of it or the chiasms open to reach it, let alone of how to visualize it.

Linear relations are graphed with straight lines on x-axes and y-axes. Nonlinear relations are very difficult to graph, with a result that "means that the act of playing the game has a way of changing the rules" (Gleick 1987:24), of engendering creativity, or of what has elsewhere been called "contesting" (Farrer 1981), that kind of gaming in which the only rule is that there are no rules. At the chiasm of the intersections of The Shadow and The Real Worlds, the ruleless game is the deadly serious one of cultural survival; without change to meet differing conditions, a culture becomes moribund. Yet change itself can hasten the death process of a culture and the conjoint lives of the people making up its society. How is change to be accommodated yet controlled? How is culture to survive when established traditions have no answers, no rules of behavior or action or thought or belief that make sense in light of contemporary conditions? Chiasms provide the means of sustaining the base metaphor while changing surface behavior, of sustaining the values of a culture while adjusting to new circumstances, of being globally stable while being locally unpredictable.

Truth, and solutions, may be apprehended in The Real World, according to Mescalero Apache philosophy. Or stated another way, "Those studying chaotic dynamics discovered that the disorderly behavior of simple systems acted as a creative process. It generated complexity: richly organized patterns, sometimes stable and sometimes unstable, sometimes finite and sometimes infinite . . . ." (Gleick 1987:43). Creativity has never been easy for Western minds to encompass; it becomes even more problematic when its essence can only be slid around rather than firmly grasped.

The seemingly chaotic behavior of certain Mescalero Apache clowns (or singers, or medicine people, or even politicians) often results in, or is suggestive of, a creative restructuring of present conditions. A small perturbation in the system may have very large consequences, as Poincaré himself noted. But how is one, even a see-er or singer, to establish credibility? How is one to convince others that his, or hers, is a message to be attended to and acted upon? How can one demonstrate one's ability to suggest viable alternatives? One answer is to show to others the substance of times, a substance from The Real World. How better than to show The Real World in operation in This Shadow World? How better than to demonstrate control over spacetime itself?

One way of establishing the immutable existence of times and the Two Worlds is in the consonance sung and enacted through placing people's events in harmony with sky events, as when singers time by the stars throughout the night and then end their night's singing with the performative pulling of the sun.[6] This demonstration is carried out each time a girls' puberty ceremonial is sung. Our World's insipid reflection of The Real World of Power, Song, Creator, and Spacetime is accessible in its full panoply to those with a fluid perception, those whose success in manipulating Power is recognized, those who own songs, those who sing the people into existence—constantly creating and re-creating the world (Farrer 1980b). They are the ones who understand and can demonstrate the workings of times. And they show it to the rest of us as they match song to space and both to times.

During a girls' puberty ceremonial, The Shadow and Real Worlds open to each other, liberating properties such as time. There time's assumption of substance can be seen, and each of us, if we so choose, can begin to grasp the complexity and subtlety of both Creator and Creation. Turner noted that an important part of the meaning of a symbol is in its "union of ecology and intellect that results in the materialization of an idea . . . ." (1969:26). Such a materialization, in the dimension of time, is manifest with each singing of a girls' puberty ceremonial at Mescalero, as the singers symbolically re-create, through song, the universe and the Apaches' place within it.

And it is also during a ceremonial that *Libayé*, the clown, is most readily accessible and his role as chiasm most easily played out on the impressive stage of the ceremonial arena, lit only by a bonfire. *Libayé* dances a chiasm, suspending times but calling them into presence, when he quicksteps into, out of, between, and on the Two Worlds as he dances a butterfly effect. By opening a chiasm, he temporarily becomes the strange attractor, the butterfly effect, allowing habits and potentials to be visualized—even if evanescently. His actions force his Apachean audience out of complacency and into contemplation of the abstract made visible, for *Libayé* is a moving template onto which are etched the problems and possibilities facing contemporary Mescalero Apache society.

Although technically speechless, the *Libayé* figure often has English words painted on his torso, front and back. This strangeness of the intrusion of English into a thoroughly Apachean ritual both contrasts with and complements the strangeness of the figure himself, with the combination of human and animal elements. A spectator first notices the clank of the cowbell and the ludicrous costume, when *Libayé* dances into the ceremonial arena; the contrasts are greater for the elegance of the men dancing the Mountain Gods.

The Mountain God dancers appear in sets of four, each set with one or more *Libayé* clowns.[7] The Mountain Gods are beautifully and richly garbed: ocher colored buckskin kilts encrusted with jingling tin cones; tricolor waist sashes decorated with powerful symbols; red arm streamers to which are attached powerful eagle feathers; elegant head-dresses extending up to four feet above their heads and piercing the night darkness; finely wrought and decorated moccasins often with family or tribal designs; waists encircled by thick belts and sashes to which large, sonorous bells are attached so that cones and bells produce a lovely rhythmic sound in accompaniment to the singing and drumming providing their dancing music. Their upper bodies are painted nightly with symbols evoking Creation, a different symbol for each of the four nights they dance.

And then there is *Libayé*, dressed in shreds of Levi's cut off thigh high or perhaps merely diapered with old flannel. There are no soft moc-casins for his feet; rather, he wears worn-out tennis shoes or clumsy, heavy, high-topped work shoes. His headdress is a paper sack or a mask with the long ears of a donkey. The Mountain Gods' dancing produces music—his dancing makes only cacophony. His body has no beautiful painting; either he looks as if he were rolled in ashes and dust or he has English words painted on his torso.

"Think of him as contrary, *ʔichʔayuatʔé*" [oppositeness or con-trariness], Bernard told me. But it is difficult to think of him at all, for the mind wanders far from clowns and humor to the very edges of the organized and ordered world. Ashes, for ghosts, are conjured by his name and coloring. The orders of existence are challenged by his dancing pres-ence. While the Mountain Gods dance in difficult, exaggerated poses, he stumbles along, more often than not out of step and out of line. Where they are order and properness, he is un-order and inappropriateness. Yet his inversions are the reverse giving meaning and depth to the obverse—he is essential to the full understanding of the Mountain Gods themselves.

Perceptions of him are as contrary as is he. A maker (one who paints the dancers and controls the alienable songs and design sets used on them) is said to "own" a set of dancers, meaning that he has use rights to the actions that transform ordinary people into dancing personifications of Holy Beings. He also owns the words, music, and actions that transfer power from Power in The Real World to This World for a time. Makers are also called painters or owners (of sets of Mountain God dancers and the associated ritual) or even medicine men, the latter in recognition of their healing functions. One of the makers of dancers at Mescalero said, when commenting on Libayé in response to my musings, "He has more flexibility . . . He's a *boy*. He does all the . . . things. Whatever those [Mountain Gods] do, he kinda relates all the power back into him but so a lot of people won't notice it; that's one reason why they call him a clown."[8]

Libayé is said to be the most powerful, although appearing as the least impressive. When a portion of a costume has been danced off by one of the Mountain God dancers, there is an elaborate ritual that is performed before the Mountain God dancer picks it up again—unless the clown picks it up immediately. The power of dancing and blessing is power that must be respected by Mountain God dancers and spectators alike but is power that does not challenge Libayé. Since he is pure Power personified, Libayé can touch other powerful objects, such as dropped costume items containing a portion of the medicine power of the maker, without having to invoke ritual to de-fuse the power in the objects before he touches them. He attends to the most basic of human needs, as he carries water to the thirsty Mountain God dancers. Water is at once the basis for life and an important symbol of creation, for Father Sky, it will be remembered, impregnated Mother Earth with water and light to produce the Twin Warrior Gods, Child of Water and Killer of Enemies. As both water carrier and personified Power, Libayé is messenger of the Gods and messenger to the Gods; similarly, he carries verbal messages to and from the Mountain Gods. Libayé's very being calls into memory the order of the other, separate and parallel, world; he, as chiasm, both opens access to The Real World and stands guard at the access to the spacetime of that reality. Only Power can contain such power. And again the strangeness of a mere boy doing more than a man's work brings contrariness to the foreground.

By being a boy in the midst of men and by having more power than all the men combined, *Libayé* presents a situation that is the reverse of normal. When he dances, he is not a boy dancing; rather, he is the personification of Clown, the original godly figure who was so powerful that he called himself into existence. A portion of his backwardness, his contrariness, lies in his being simultaneously a human boy and a Powerful Being from The Real World. He is dressed with disregard for the usual canons of beauty, modesty, and good taste; simultaneously he is dressed properly—for a clown. He is a discordant, noisy figure and he is the sound of Power. He is both funny-strange and somewhat scary with his unholy combination of human and animal characteristics; and he is also awesome. First on the land and last in line, he becomes metaphorically first and last in everything, an ambiguity that only Power can comprehend. While the most powerful, he is also "very humble . . . All that noise is a decoy," in the words of Sidney Baca, one of the makers. *Libayé* is metaphorical creativity and dancing paradox.[9]

In those instances when the *Libayé* figure is painted with English words, both the creativity and the paradox become more acutely foregrounded and become fodder for community commentary. Even the words are contrary: first, because English is intruded into the midst of Mescalero Apache sacred ritual; second, because the Mountain Gods, who speak not at all—but communicate through body language, hoots, and eye contact—are accompanied by a moving screen painted with English, a foreign language; third, because the painting on the others is symbolic while *Libayé's* words are literal; and, finally, because literacy itself is a new phenomenon grafted onto a traditional figure that itself was grafted onto an ancient ceremony.

On one occasion the words "WAY TO GO LYN" were painted on a clown's body. I read these as "Way to go, Lyn!" in reference to a young Apache woman who had recently done well in a beauty contest; I assumed she was being publicly congratulated. However, Apaches, in the crowd close to me during the clown's dancing, read the same words as "Way to go, Lyn?" Their discussions, in Apache and English, centered around the advisability of an Apache girl competing in an Anglo event. What did this say about the way in which the Apache raised their children? About their values? Was it good to stand out of the crowd so much as to do well in a beauty contest? Did it perhaps show the New Mexican non-Indian communities the care with which Apaches treated their children? Did her demeanor illustrate the proper Apachean way of behaving? Was it good that she is beautiful in both the Anglo and Apache ways? Did it demonstrate that Indian women are beautiful and worthy of respect? Was she being showcased as a commodity; was she depersonalized? Were beauty contests good things? Did Apaches belong in them? The four words had opened a chiasm through which the Apache people could confront and contemplate their present behavior. Other ways of behaving were certainly possible. Did they wish to change and, if so, how?

On another occasion a *Libayé* clown had blatantly contradictory messages painted on his body. His chest read, "LTD FOR SALE," while his back stated, "LTD NOT FOR SALE." Here the conflict was more pointedly represented and the talk concerning the messages more straightforward. What does it mean to enter the Anglo world of economic transactions rather than remain in the Apachean one of reciprocity? If one has an LTD (or any car or pickup truck) that runs, why sell it? If it is running, why not sell it before it quits? If one has last year's LTD, is a new one this year appropriate? How can you haul many relatives and feed for livestock in an LTD? What good is a LTD? Information and opinion flowed quickly among the grandstand spectators. While I would not say that permanent or firm consensus was reached, people generally agreed, before that *Libayé* representation danced out of the ceremonial arena, that too much Anglo consumerism could spell the death knell for the Apaches yet there was also agreement that contemporary Apaches live in a consumer oriented world that threatens to take them over and homogenize them if they are not careful. That instance of a chiasm was one when people seemed to decide to reinforce their traditional way of life rather than modify themselves to the onslaught of larger mainstream American culture with its plethora of television commercials touting consumerism as the way of American life.

Yet another clown was emblazoned with "LOVER BOY" on his back and "OH BABY" on his chest. While the ceremonial time is one of relative freedom from sexual restraints, not everyone approves of this license. Parents used this set of English words to remind their children that everyone, Anglo tourists and tribal members, was watching and maybe they wanted to think about how they looked when they walked around the ceremonial grounds clinging to each other. Older people spoke, aloud, of the differences today in comparison with the time when they were young and exercised, they maintained, both more restraint and more discretion. Young people, especially teenagers, seemed embarrassed by the words, for sexual matters are not discussed in public at Mescalero; yet they giggled about the words and the actions they suggested while commenting on them in both English and Apache. The chiasm brought into being by this Łibayé's dancing and body painting was not one that resulted in change, profound or simple; it was instead a foregrounding of what is not usually the subject of conversation, allowing people to address themselves to some of the underlying values and proper modes of behavior Apaches are supposed to espouse and enact. The co-existing worlds brought into focus were those of real behavior and ideal behavior, suspended for a few moments and laid bare for public scrutiny and commentary.

Łibayé, when so painted, means whatever relationships he calls into play. He means that beauty contests are good and not good. He means that cars should and should not be, let alone whether or not they should or should not be for sale on a regular basis. He means that sexuality is and is not public. Look at him from one side and one set of relationships obtains; turn him around and another set comes into view. It is almost as though he were a computer graphics screen: you can see what you create and create what you wish to see. And that is the function of a chiasm: it opens the potential for new ways of thinking, behaving, perceiving, evaluating. It is non-judgmental and non-demanding. Chiasm simply, and profoundly, allows an expansion of potential, brings into being the thought of new possibilities or the possibilities of reinforcing and reaffirming what is already in place. And, by being controlled by powerful ones—whether animate or inanimate—there is also an implicit validation of both the rightness and flexibility of the base metaphor; for, while change may occur or a new tracing may be made, nonetheless the overall contour will remain the same. One, or one's culture, can change yet still maintain the essence of what it means to be Apache. By objectifying the intangible, processes and habits can be made manifest and therefore dealt with, whether that means initiating change or endorsing the status quo. It is all there, unordered and ready to be assembled, ready to be considered, ready to be brought into being just in the way Łibayé brought himself into being: by calling and naming, it can be.

The chiasm, as with the Clown, does not sit in judgment but

rather allows people to make judgments about those things that are usually not available for comment, those things that we just "know" but about which we have difficulty speaking. Hall (1983 : 211–12) has provided an analytic way of discussing the layers of any cultural complex by dividing it into three levels; he notes that

> primary level culture . . . is that variety of culture in which the rules are: known to all, obeyed by all, but seldom if ever stated. Its rules are implicit, taken for granted, almost impossible for the average person to state as a system, and generally out of awareness. *Secondary level culture,* though in full awareness, is normally hidden from outsiders. Secondary level culture is as regular and binding as any other level of culture, possibly even more so. It is that level of culture which the Pueblo Indians of New Mexico keep from white people. But it can also be the special culture of virtually any group of society. *Tertiary* or *explicit, manifest culture* is what we all see and share in each other. It is the façade presented to the world at large. Because it is so easily manipulated, it is the least stable and least dependable for purposes of decision making.

Chiasm operates at the primary level by making the usually hidden aspects of what it is to be Mescalero Apache visible and thus available for discussion. The base metaphor operates on the secondary level. The visual analogue of the base metaphor, the quartered circle, is on the tertiary level. But, while it is everpresent—as in salting food or on clothing designs—most Mescaleros also realize it represents the ordering of life as given primacy in the creation narratives so seldom shared with outsiders and rarely spoken of, in either Apache or English, in the presence of Anglos. So, while the quartered circle is tertiary level culture, it also reinforces secondary level decorum and values. Few indeed think about how cultural items enter the secondary or tertiary levels, even though they often participate in decisions made through chiastic openings. It is even rarer for an anthropologist to find a person who not only thinks of chiasms but also manipulates them; such people are far more important than key consultants, if they are willing to serve at all in the culture broker's role. Rarest of all is one who is culturally defined as a chiasm, such as a see-er or a singer, who is aware of traversing the space between The Two Worlds, can talk (in English and the native language) about such movement and what it potentially engenders, and is also willing to be, and capable of being, a mentor to an anthropologist.

The English words painted on *Łibayé's* body call into play the contrast and conflict between the English-speaking Anglo culture of the larger society and the Apachean culture embedded within it. The writing foregrounds matters of vital concern to the community but matters that are difficult to think about in the abstract. Apaches find it highly ironic that those matters, so very difficult to discuss, are displayed in public for all to see but that Anglos see only their perception of a clown, a foolish being, while Apaches realize the profundities being danced. These are primary level matters that are being showcased without the outsider audience being any the wiser. Matters considered are those such as what degree of accommodation are Apaches willing to make with the larger culture and what forms should such accommodation take? How can Apachean culture be preserved and enhanced in the midst of the Anglo way of life? What precisely constitutes Apachean culture? This is the usually buried and inaccessible primary level culture brought to the foreground where it can be considered seriously and perhaps modified, scrapped, or sustained.

Łibayé refocuses normal perceptions for a period of time and then retires while community members ponder his messages. He makes no definitive statements. Rather he opens the way for community consideration of alternatives. He questions. He allows community members to stand beside themselves for brief periods of time and he allows them to examine the things they do, or believe, and how they feel about those things. While he treads both on and through the mirror reflecting life in The Two Worlds, he neither is the boundary nor maintains it; he, as chiasm, provides clarified vision of the limits of boundaries as well as boundless possibilities and potentialities.

Not all makers use English words on the clowns they paint to accompany the Mountain God dancers. Sidney Baca, as a result of his own personal vision received when he was on a retreat to rededicate his group and his commitment to it, has a very different and active role for his Łibayé. Baca's Łibayé is also a boy, rather than a man, and he, too, is dressed in motley, dances ineptly, and exhibits other, usual clownly behavior. However, during the blessing sequences performed by Baca's Mountain God dancers, Łibayé dances to the front of the line, reaches into a pollen bag, and makes a miniature pollen painting of life's circle, ⊕, on the ground. He, and all the Mountain Gods, pray during this time while holy songs are sung by the maker and those men whose voices and drums provide accompaniment to Baca's lead voice and drum. This Łi-

bayé is arguing for an increased role of religion in the everyday life of the people. He argues, as well, for an integration of Apache and Anglo life as he wears a crucifix given each member of the group by the Bishop of El Paso when the group performed at a Catholic religious event in that city. Baca, like most makers, is known for his goodness and for his seriousness in pursuing a religious life in both the Apache and Anglo molds. Unlike some of the other makers, however, Baca paints his Mountain Gods only to bless or to cure, never for entertainment; this fact predisposes people to consider his *Libayé* to be more religious than some of the others. His *Libayé*, therefore, causes spectators to examine their own religious and moral lives, their own tolerance—or lack of it—for religions and religious behavior not their own. This *Libayé* is both conscience and potential. But whether through painted words or through actions, *Libayé* engenders a chiasm.

The meaning of any chiasm is an aggregate of the relationships within and between The Two Worlds. Neither *Libayés* in particular nor chiasms in general forge the meaning through boundary dissolution, as Handelman (1981), who considers ritual clowns from several societies, avers. In his masterful study of Puebloan clowns, Handelman found that ritual clowns have in common several characteristics: boundary dissolution, reflexivity, processuality, and transformation as well as having important functions in orchestrating the ritual events in which they appear. While his article is a masterpiece of comparison across cultures, I believe it a mistake to try to equate Puebloan clowns with Mescalero ones, despite their being present in the same general physical area and despite the fact that Puebloan people observe Mescalero ceremonials just as Mescaleros observe Puebloan ones and despite the Mescalero clown perhaps having been modeled on Puebloan ones. While I may be accused of being too Boasian in this regard, I will feel more comfortable with the comparisons of Apachean and Puebloan clowns after both are considered as chiasms, for my intuitive notion, from watching several Puebloan clown performances, is that they are very different with differing functions in their respective societies. The situation is different again at Mescalero, for, rather than dissolution or maintenance of a boundary, there is an opening, as with a doorway; The Shadow World is still here and The Real World is still there, parallel to the world we know, but—for a time—The Two Worlds are accessible to each other. The Two Worlds glimpse each other across the chiasm while each spins on its own axis.

The accessibility engendered by the vision of the other World brings potential change onto the stage and allows the current conditions to be named and to take center stage for a time.

Chiasms, and *Libayé* in particular, are at once symbolic of the ordering, and potential un-ordering, of the universe. This is not disorder, for disorder implies a lack of order; rather it is more accurate to say *Libayé* is both order and un-order: arrangement and segmentation, categories and elements, or paradigm and syntax. Babcock (1978a:29) has addressed this issue.

> Clown or trickster or transvestite never demands that we reject totally the orders of our sociocultural worlds; but neither do these figures simply provide us with a cautionary note as to what would happen should the "real" world turn into a perpetual circus or festival . . . Rather, they remind us of the arbitrary condition of imposing an order on our environment and experience, even while they enable us to see certain features of that order more clearly simply because they have turned insight out.

The "arbitrary condition of" ordering is poignantly ever present for third and fourth world people who live with the daily reminder that much of their lives is controlled by the sociocultural norms of another group. Yet, and I suspect this also contributes to ethnicity, there is freedom to choose modes of action and interaction even within the confines of a larger, controlling culture. It is to these concerns that the Mescalero Apache clown is addressed. "The code which is being broken is always implicitly there, for the very act of deconstructing reconstructs and reaffirms the structure," notes Babcock (1978b:99). The code of the Mescalero Apache life way, being primary level culture, is indeed taken for granted on most occasions; it is this code, and its relationship to the larger mainstream American code, that *Libayé*'s chiasm opens for manipulation, whether it is through English words rudely painted on his body or through his solemn dance and pollen painting in the midst of his usual contrariness.

Libayé's playing with the orders of being for Mescalero Apaches potentiates destruction as well as construction. His very appearance is a challenge to life as it is known for he alone of all the dancers is *not* dressed or painted in accordance with the base metaphor. Taken as a group, the Mountain God dancers are globally stable, but *Libayé* is locally unpredictable—and hence a very real, chaotic threat. In his behavior (as chiasm), he represents both paradox (his contrariness) and duality. Miller (1974:49–50) finds that

> this duality is embodied in traditions of sacred clowns and fools . . . [who] commit one unspeakable violation after another, and yet this capacity also enables [them] to see otherwise than through the spectacles of a culture—to incorporate noise into culture and thus be its creator . . . Inevitability and surprise are necessary correctives to each other. If everything is inevitable we are turned to stone, rigid and inflexible. If everything is surprising we live in a world of chaos, mad. We have to keep a foot in each world.

It is the foot-in-each-world function that *Libayé* performs so eloquently for the Mescalero Apaches, although committing unspeakable violations is not a part of his persona. He provides a way for the Mescalero world to avoid chaos, despite changes in ordering that accompany acculturation.

Clowns, particularly Puebloan ones, have been of continuing interest to scholars of the Southwest (see, for example, Bunzel [1932], Handelman and Kapferer [1980], Honigmann [1942], Laski [1959], Makarius [1970], Parsons and Beals [1934], Ray [1945], and Steward [1930]). Hieb (1972:186) says that "the clowns are a point of articulation with everything Zuni and everything foreign to the traditional Zuni world view." Or again, when writing of the Hopi, he declares, "[clowns portray] life as it should not be" (1979:184). Life as it should be and life as it should not be; life as it is and life as it might be: all this and more is vested in the ritual clowns. By dancing potentiality, they call possibilities into creation and in so doing are comparable across Athabaskan and Puebloan lines. Yet their roles are very different, too.

As an example of the differing roles of clowns within the Southwest, consider this incident. During a 1978 ceremonial event at San Juan Pueblo, I was trying to take still photographs for Dr. Sue-Ellen Jacobs, who was then engaged in fieldwork at the Pueblo while living there. She had the required camera permit attached to the camera I was using, as well as a permit on the camera she was using. A minor secular official, who also had ceremonial status, threatened me with bodily harm and destruction of film and camera, unless I stopped taking pictures, permit notwithstanding. He is of a family not friendly to the family with whom Jacobs was making her home; this, Jacobs and I decided later, was the cause of his inappropriate behavior toward me. Regardless of his motivation, he insisted camera permits were not transferable from one person to another and did not adhere to the camera to which they were attached. With eye signals and head nods, since we were not close enough to speak during the altercation, Jacobs and I agreed it was not worth the fuss and I returned the camera to her, thus making it impossible for her to have simultaneous shots of front and back views of dancers, as she had hoped to obtain with my help and as the Pueblo authorities had understood when granting both camera permits. Just a few months prior to this incident, I had photographed a similar dance event for the Pueblo involving school age children under the direction of the very same secular official who was denying my photographing this day. All photos from that previous session had been turned over to the Pueblo; they were subsequently returned to me to make any copies I wished before becoming the permanent property of the Pueblo. Thus, my bona fides with the Pueblo had already been established, providing the reason Jacobs assumed it would be acceptable for me to assist her in her work by operating the second camera.

Immediately after the public confrontation over the second camera, the clowns, who had been cavorting as Puebloan clowns do while also maintaining control of the dancers' lines, began unmercifully teasing the minor secular official—in English so as to increase his discomfort before the many tourists and anthropologists present. The clowns challenged his masculinity, pretended to take pictures of him, called him names, and mimicked his officious behavior with me, while suggesting he was so unsure of his manhood that he had to attack a woman, and a defenseless white woman at that. The teasing and verbal castigation continued throughout the day until the dancing was over. The hapless official had no choice but to take the rebukes in silence or leave the dance plaza.

None are so powerful—officials or not—that they dare challenge the Kossa, the San Juan Pueblo clowns. But about the only thing that the San Juan clowns share with the Mescalero one is power, for the Mescalero clown does not coordinate the dancers with whom he appears, does not speak, does not tease, does not act as community censor, and does not single out miscreants for public correction. If the Kossa are also chiasms, or if they open them as I suspect they do, it will have to be demonstrated by someone much more familiar with San Juan Pueblo culture than am I. For the moment, it seems premature to assign chiasm status to all clowns simply because they perform a clownly function.

At the same time, I believe Mescalero Apache clowns do share some things in common with other ritual clowns around the world. Peacock (1978:218) writes that

> Though the Javanese enjoy the clown and transvestite partly because they break taboos, release tensions, and permit the disorderly mixing of normally segregated categories, they also appreciate these figures . . . because they *demonstrate the underlying unity of the cosmology* . . . [emphasis added].

The underlying unity of the cosmology, as present in the base metaphor and its visual analogue, is not, however, restricted to the domain of religion for the Apachean clown, as can be seen when the clown sports words such as "Lover Boy" on his body. Rather, for the Mescalero, the unity is both of This World and of The Real World, for the two are constantly impinging on each other.

For example, a person who intends to become involved in serious betting on the horse races in Ruidoso, immediately to the east of the Mescalero Apache Reservation, might well seek a blessing from a ritual specialist who has "horse medicine." Horse medicine is a gift from Power, but a gift that must be shared and ritually attended in order for it to sustain its validity. Power resides in The Real World; it is shared with a person in This Shadow World upon the proper payment to Power and a commitment on the part of the person in This World to share the knowledge. A horse medicine person can, among other services, bestow good luck in racetrack gambling on one who seeks such a boon; the horse medicine person, however, does not respond to such requests unless they are made with the proper four requests. And, just as Power demands payment of gifts and ritual recognition, so the horse medicine person demands payment and ritual recognition as well, usually in the form of four voluntary gifts when the request is made. But there is an additional ritual payment demanded of the gambler; a likely payment would be a tenth of all winnings given, with appropriate ritual statements, to the first Apache person seen after collecting such winnings. To do otherwise is to risk offending Power by the selfishness of the winning gambler; dire consequences can be expected as a result.[10] It is difficult in the extreme to separate out the cosmology from the everyday here. The requests and payments in fours are, of course, a reference to the base metaphor; once again, cosmology is a part of the everyday. In like manner, *Libayé* connects the everyday and the cosmological in a ritual context; when so doing, he both shares in, and differs from, characteristics of other clowns throughout the world.

Chiasms in general, and *Libayé* in particular, then are conduits, similar to an earth navel, but often portable. Ortiz (1969:23–24) defines earth navels as the points at which the above, middle, and below intersect and to which all things must return. According to him, earth navels are fixed for the Tewa speaking Puebloan people. For the Apaches, I would argue, there is no fixed place where the intersection occurs, save some caves and mountains; earth navels, or the points of intersection between The Real World and This Shadow World, are chiasms and are as easily people and events as they are places. Nor are chiasms just linear; rather, chiasms have fronts, backs, sides, spaces, times, thoughts, and actions as portions of their dimensionality. For the Mescalero Apache, sacredness is not necessarily a permanent endowment. Nor is the boy who impersonates Clown permanently a chiasm; he becomes one only when painted and performing in a manner such that his presence opens a chiasm. Places may be chiasms at one time and lose that function at another, just as the Mescalero ceremonial arena is moved every generation or so in order for the ground to recover from the excess of power to which it has been exposed. Since the Apache were, until very recently, a highly mobile people, it makes sense that their equivalents of earth navels, chiasms, would also be portable.

But while portable, these chiasms are not ephemeral. They are the stable and tangible, if evanescent. People move about; sacred spaces come and go and are redefined; times trace their patterns and people cycle through both times and spaces. What is constant is Clown, or Singer, or Cave, or Mountain: these are constant chiasms. As a chiasm *Libayé* is both agent and agency for movement: between This Shadow World and The Real World of gods, ghosts, spirits, times, and especially Power. Most people do not themselves make journeys through chiasms; instead, others open chiasms for them to peek into potentiality and consider possibility. For most people, the chiasm has a surfeit of Power they are ill equipped to handle, so the crossings are trusted to the powerfully strong. At Mescalero they tend to be singers or healers or clowns or, some say, witches. Where these powerful people are, there are chiasms. The Two Worlds meet through them and they become what Turner (1975:80) termed switchpoints for social action. They are also switchpoints for thoughts about social, ritual, or symbolic actions. As chiasms, they allow penetration and flow between This World and The Real World.

Probably *Libayé* is the least threatening chiasm for the Mescalero, since he is, after all, only a boy enacting the role of Clown, even if it is a ritual clown. Bouissac, as quoted in MacCannell (1980:93), maintains that clowns function to remind us of the arbitrariness of conventions:

> The semiotic operation of the clown act enunciates negatively the fragile balance of culture always threatened on the one end by its own excesses. Something can be overdone to the extent that the most basic cultural categories are overturned.

Mescalero Apache clowns, however, do not over-do nor under-do; they simply do, but in a clownly way. *Libayé* lampoons, calls into serious question, reminds, deconstructs, and sometimes even suggests possible construction—all this to provide the avenue for possible new structuring, innovative order, or perhaps, a return to previous patterns or simply to query the present. By so doing, he allows communication with the ineffable. He offers a way to think about and discuss the unarticulated. Rather than overturning "the most basic cultural categories," *Libayé* focuses attention on what is not seen and allows others to see through his iconography and movement. Any potential overturning resulting from *Libayé*—or any other chiasm—will be cast in terms of the base metaphor; as long as there are Mescalero Apaches, the people will be able to say their new order, or category, is really just the same thing as that which it replaced. *Libayé* and chiasms quite literally open the conduit to potential and its inherent power. No wonder he is said to be the most powerful figure of the Mountain God dancer set, even if he is a motley boy. The chiasm he represents is a lens through which the community may see itself as well as a doorway through which significata can be exchanged. As such, he is a never ending stream of information, giving form to ideas and values.

One does not treat a chiasm lightly, for the power that emanates from such an opening or switchpoint can easily be perverted. One is literally playing with the building blocks of cultural life. Moving a block has an effect on each of the others. A rapid disruption of one block can cause the entire edifice of the cultural artifice to crumble. No wonder clowns are treated with such respect.

As a heuristic device, think of Łibayé and chiasm in the way in which physicists had to confront the properties of light early in this century. Rigorous experiments were conducted that conclusively demonstrated that light is composed of waves. But equally rigorous experiments were conducted that conclusively demonstrated that light is composed of particles. When such a paradox exists, the premises underlying the hypotheses and experiments must be carefully examined. How can it be that a discrete phenomenon, light, can be two contradictory phenomena? The questions and answers, as well as the experimental results, were puzzling until it was realized that the way in which the question is asked, or the way in which the experiment is constructed, in large measure determines the results. If one looks for waves, thereby filtering out particles, then indeed waves can be seen. Similarly, if one looks for particles and filters out waves, then indeed particles appear. However, by asking the question differently and by designing experiments such that both aspects of the phenomenon of light can be manifest, albeit at somewhat separate times, then the beautiful complexity of light, in its no longer contradictory forms, can be observed.

From one vantage point and from many times, Łibayé is a clown. He burlesques or engages in the most sacred of acts, although he is but a boy. Simultaneously or removed in times, he is also Clown, Power personified, a moving chiasm. It all depends upon one's own sophistication and the way in which he is approached, as well as, of course, the way in which he is conceived and painted by the maker. Łibayé is both nothing and everything—and there is no contradiction or paradox here. Neither aspect is right or wrong; both simply are. While no paradox or contradiction exist, nonetheless premises must be reconstructed. Each aspect is a portion of the other. Whichever is being foregrounded at the moment, that is what he is and represents. No one representation negates any other. It all depends upon the way in which the questions are posed, the ways in which perceptions are adjusted.

Similarly, his work or function is whatever is being accomplished at the moment. Now he is a little boy dancing ineptly behind a beautiful array of exquisite men dancers. The next moment, as his painted words capture audience attention or his actions stun minds into new thoughts, he is the Power of the ill-understood and the unknown from The Real World. Neither aspect is more important or relevant than the other. Both are required to understand the work of the ritual clown at Mescalero. By being all and nothing, boy and god, Power and profanity, last and first, rags and elegance, Libayé is chiasm personified.

Entropy can be averted by opening a chiasm, allowing tomorrow to be visualized as well as allowing now to be performed. Thus, chiasm is an opportunity for interactive and reflexive process which may involve reversal, inversion, transformation, innovation, or thought as well as action. Each time a chiasm is activated, choice occurs. To decide not to change is still choice, although we usually recognize choice in its more active character. Invoking a chiasm is not in itself determinative, but rather is only potential.

Anthropologists, and social scientists in general, usually discuss position, or the synchronic, because momentum and movement, or the diachronic, is so difficult to apprehend and communicate. Thus we speak in terms of synchronic *or* diachronic, field *or* ground, stasis *or* disorder, serious *or* comic. These terms are complementary descriptions of the same set, the same "reality"; each member of a pair is only partly accurate, while neither is inaccurate. In cultural terms, both aspects of sets must be present for a society to be vital, for a culture to be on-going; a culture cannot remain static and never-changing and still be vital in a changing world. Culture is continually emerging, continually changing, and continually being reaffirmed. Libayé and chiasm, then, are both necessary to understand the homogeneity and change that characterize the contemporary Mescalero Apache cultural scene. We can never see the whole of a culture nor all of its evolutionary processes at any one time; but we can see images of it as it is at one point in time (or times) and from one perspective. We can also see images of what it might be. Thus, a chiasm does not cause creativity or change. It does facilitate them, makes them possible; it allows action to occur by the community or those in charge. Chiasm is potentiation, not an ultimatum. The Mescalero Apache use Libayé as a chiasm; other cultures use other symbols, characters, events, actions, statements. If I read Toelken and Scott (1981:80) correctly, Coyote is a chiasm for the Navajo, as this dialogue between Toelken and his primary consultant, Yellowman, illustrates:

> Toelken: "Why does Coyote do all those things . . . ?"
> Yellowman: "If he did not do all those things, then those things would not be possible in the world."

CHAPTER 6

Singing for Life

The possibilities for organizing life, whether ceremonial or everyday, are beyond the bounds of imagination; human ingenuity is truly awesome to contemplate. Yet there are underlying needs to which we all must attend: needs for food and water, shelter, warmth, sex, companionship. Recognition of these needs and the various ways of fulfilling them formed the basis of anthropological functionalism early in this century. We humans also seem to need some connection with the larger world, whether or not we grace it with religious terms. To my knowledge, there is no society without a system of either religious or metaphysical philosophical thought and rationale. Further, people seem to use their religion or metaphysics to justify their particular way of structuring their lives from among the almost infinite possibilities. And, while there may well be—indeed, usually are—individual rites and rituals within the bounds of the system, religion seems more satisfying when shared with others. Even metaphysicians seem to require each other's presence, in person or through the medium of writing, for conversation and contemplation. Mescalero Apaches, like people throughout the world, ground their everyday behavior in a system of religion and philosophy that today has its widest currency in the girls' puberty ceremonial.[1]

It is not surprising to find a mass influx of people centering on the ceremonial mesa during the first week of July for the girls' puberty ceremonial, given the attitude that the reservation is the proper place to learn to be an Apache and given the belief that one must consciously strive to remember those aspects of life that are truly important. This ceremony encapsulates all that is important and proper to contemporary Mescalero Apaches. It is a four-day, four-night refresher course to some and, for others, a time of serious indoctrination. It is the epitome of the traditional—as the many enactments, recapitulations, and transformations of the base metaphor demonstrate—and yet it provides opportunity for change through the chiasms represented by the singers, the clowns, and the ceremony itself.

Regardless of whether the ceremony is a refresher course, new indoctrination, validation of tradition, or birth mother of the newest behavior, it is an event that is important enough for working people to schedule their vacations in early July, if at all possible. It is important enough to drive hundreds, or sometimes even thousands, of miles to attend. Houses on the reservation overflow with relatives and friends. Camp-out homes of tipis, arbors, tents, campers, and recreational vehicles surround reservation houses and soon move up to the ceremonial mesa to surround it as well. It is a time to renew both religious precepts and friendships; and, perhaps most importantly for the majority of the people, it is a time to be with extended family and friends, to be again with the tribe as a whole, and to bask in what it means to be Mescalero Apache.

Those Apaches who live off the reservation often express the feeling that they should go "home" to the reservation in order once again to make contact with the things that *really* matter. Even those who live on the reservation are beginning to say that remembering the things of importance is sometimes difficult. They blame television and say they are becoming more like Anglos in that they are now busy with concerns of making a living and getting ahead in life. People of all ages make a conscious effort, therefore, to be Indian at this time. Jobs, even if primary during most of the year, are secondary to homecoming and the ceremonial.

Oftentimes, those people whose jobs or careers take them away from the reservation for long periods of time (as for military service) will send their children home to the reservation to live with grandparents or other relatives in order to have the children "learn what's right." For these families, the homecoming is particularly important as a time of reunion. Even those whose primary homes are no longer on the reservation make a concerted effort to be at Mescalero in July during the annual public girls' puberty ceremonial.

Everywhere signs of Indianness are present. Girls who usually wear barrettes in their hair can be seen with feathered hair ties; boys who usually have the latest electronic beeping toy appear with miniature bows and arrows. The ceremonial time is important for making statements about ethnicity and, for many, redefining life and what it means to be a contemporary Apache.

During the last week of June, the tempo of life gradually increases on the reservation until the excitement is almost tangible. People begin reconstructing their camp-out homes on the ceremonial mesa, gravitating back to their own family's traditional camping area year after year. Pickup trucks, looking like moving forests, glide along the lower mesa roads and, upon reaching the unpaved, dirt portions of the upper mesa road, lumber like top-heavy behemoths, swaying now this way then that with a groaning of lower gears. Clouds of dust rise from the unpaved roads, clouds formed mostly by the trucks but also by the activity of the boys and young men who, under the direction of their fathers, uncles, and grandfathers, unload the freshly cut oak boughs into piles close to canvas, plastic, and the straight, long, slender, peeled evergreen poles that will form the frame of a tipi. The unloading accomplished, they hop back into the now empty trucks and await an elder relative's slipping behind the wheel and bumping back down to the paved road where they quickly disappear, only to return a short while later—again crowned with greenery. The heavy, difficult work of moving all that green wood is accomplished in a spirit akin to celebration.

Meanwhile, other family members begin to work with the unloaded boughs. Poles are set upright in a tripod as the beginning of a tipi; other, thinner, younger, green poles are bent in dome shapes for shady arbors, while yet others anchor squares or rectangles that will soon support tents. Discussions are held about the relative merits of using plastic to cover the tops of the arbors: sure to keep out any rain that may fall in this summer rainy season but drippingly hot if the days are cloudless. Most families compromise by using a light colored plastic, if possible, thereby lessening the heat buildup from the darker colors while retaining the waterproofing. Others eschew plastic entirely and rely on the time-proven methods of tightly intertwining the boughs so they are virtually waterproof; if they do begin to leak during the summer's thundershowers, there is always the tipi or tent for shelter, while silent prayers of thanksgiving are offered for the much-needed moisture. Yet rain at ceremonial time causes ambivalence: it is welcomed, for it is always needed in this desert/mountain region, but it must not rain too hard or at the improper time or the ceremonial will have to be suspended temporarily. That could well mean that people would have to strike camp and leave the ceremonial mesa to return to more mundane concerns before the ceremonial is completed. Those inside tipis and tents or under the arbors make the enforced rest of a rain into a session of family news and general information, while toddlers experiencing their first ceremonial learn to keep hands off the walls of tipis and tents so that the walls's surface tension is not broken and they will remain waterproof.

Even while busy erecting camp-out houses, people take time to greet returning relatives and friends. New friends are welcomed, too; more likely than not, they will be instructed to pitch in with the work of erecting the structures. A newcomer is apt to become the butt of jokes referring to that person's inability to master immediately the complex tasks of simultaneously bending and securing poles for the arbors, or of tipi frame erection, or of the subtleties of tying down the bottom of the tipi cover, or of securing it taut over the skeleton of the frame. As with all joking, this joking occurs only if the person appears to be able to take a joke and to tease back in return; otherwise, of course, the joker would lose status by embarrassing a guest.

With some families, setting up the camp-out area is accomplished with copious quantities of beer—preferably Coors—or *tiswin,* an Indian corn beer, when it is available. Other families bring out refreshments only when the work is finished. Still others merely place food and drink in a prominent place with the implicit invitation to help oneself. Although all three meals for each day of the ceremonial will be supplied by the families of the ceremonial girls, snacks are always available in family camp-out homes.

Women, and sometimes their men, whether associated by blood or by marriage, begin emptying out vans, pickup trucks, and cars of bedsteads, mattresses, linens, blankets, quilts, sleeping bags, cookware, tables, chairs, ice chests, towels, clothing, and all the other paraphernalia the family will use for the next week. "Closets" are made from boxes or suitcases placed under beds. Rope tied onto the inner surface of the tipi poles above adult head height forms a rod for hanging and draping items.

Things are placed not only on top of tables, benches, and chairs but also underneath them. A dipper is always in plain sight, ready to be taken to the nearby tap to slake thirst; it is also used to ladle out iced tea and Kool-Aid and as a serving spoon for traditional foods that will be available. Ice fills chests to be topped by soft drinks for the children and beer for the adults. Everything has a place; most camp-out homes are models of clever stowage.

Similar activity bustles all around the ceremonial mesa and on the mesas immediately above and below it. But inside the cyclone fence enclosed ceremonial mesa itself, a slightly different scene unfolds. While the larger encampment spills into minuscule valleys and climbs the north ridge in seeming abandon, all is rigid order inside the cyclone fencing, for it is here that the girls who will be having their puberty ceremony have their camps. Each girl's family is allotted an area just large enough for a tipi, tent, and arbor—all contiguous to each other, rather than with breathing space between as is the rule in the general camp-out area. Even as the surrounding camp-out homes are being built, the girls' area is already well ordered. The neat row of tipi-tent-arbor sets, one set for each girl having a ceremony, forms a south line facing the long cooking arbor, itself fronting the ceremonial dance arena.

Further to the south, behind the girls' encampment, lie the camps of some of the singers of the ceremony and their families, for it is the singers, the *gutąął,* who orchestrate the ceremony. The Head Singer always camps here; other singers may choose to do so or may instead camp in their family's traditional area. The Head Singer, however, is usually closest to the center of the camp area inside the fence. It is a positional metaphor that is expressed with this placement, for the Head Singer's orchestration of the ceremonial is akin to the ceremonial's orchestration of life.

Most people credit the ceremony with being responsible for the impressive increase in tribal numbers within the last century. Each time the ceremonial is held, the Mescalero Apache people recall their own history and difficulty in simply being able to gather together in sufficient numbers to hold this important event celebrating the initial menses of a girl, a girl now capable of becoming a mother of the tribe.

The Mescalero Apache Tribe increased from fewer than five hundred people, by the Army's 1873 census figures, to more than twenty-five hundred people, by the tribe's 1988 figures. Within a few generations they have moved from being a beaten, hunted, decimated people to being a people with an enviable, and envied, position of prestige and relative wealth. While contemporary Mescaleros acknowledge the vital role played by excellent tribal leadership, especially that of Wendell Chino in his more than quarter century of tribal presidency, the increase in numbers of enrolled Apaches is attributed primarily to the resuscitation of the ceremony after the period of enforced quiescence. Indeed, the tribal population did not begin its more spectacular increase until after 1912, when two significant events happened: the Mescalero Apaches were joined by their "cousins," the Chiricahua—who had been imprisoned with Geronimo in Florida, Alabama, and Oklahoma—and the United States government lifted the ban on public gatherings that had effectively prohibited the ceremony.

The Mescalero people have been on their reservation only since 1873. For several years immediately prior to that date they were supposedly prisoners of war, although the Apaches disappeared and reappeared with frustrating frequency, as Army records attest, calling into question their prisoner status. They had been held either at Fort Stanton or at the Bosque Redondo of Fort Sumner. At the latter they were joined by the Navajos who had survived the Long Walk. When the Mescalero were finally placed on their own reservation, the federal government, through the resident Indian agent, forbade gatherings of Apaches. There was a saying common at that time that more than six Apaches in any one place constituted an uprising, so public gatherings were banned. From the people's perspective, the ban was devastating: one must have guests for a ceremony, to say nothing of needing, at minimum, a singer, godmother, dancers, cooks, servers, and, not insignificantly, an audience. If there could be no gatherings, there could be no ceremony. Additionally, a ceremonial event is an expensive affair and the people were impoverished.

There are some who say that the period between 1873 and 1913 was not a quiet one, at least in regard to girls' ceremonies. They say that people would disappear into the mountains periodically, where they would hold small ceremonies of one day or two day's duration for their daughters who had come of age. Others maintain that the ceremony was not sung, but rather was kept in memory against the time when they could once again hold it publicly.

In 1912 the federal government rescinded its order—perhaps because the Territory of New Mexico became a state that year and the

Apache problem was no longer of primary concern to the federal authorities; perhaps there were other reasons. The Mescalero people were told they could gather together as a tribe once a year to have a celebration: on the fourth of July! After considering the offer, the Mescalero elders told the Agent they would prefer to wait until the Chiricahua joined them to begin celebrating again. They did this for several reasons: out of respect for the Chiricahua, who had also been prohibited from their ceremonial practices; out of the need for extra people for a full complement of helpers, religious practitioners, dancers, and audience; and also from the need for sufficient time to stockpile the goods necessary for a proper ceremonial. In 1913 the ceremonial was again held publicly; it has been held each year since that time with the exception of a year when the population was severely hit with the Spanish influenza.

Today people say they adhere to the July 4th date in order to make it easier for those who have jobs off the reservation to return home, since July 4th is a national holiday. So the first week in July, always including the fourth as one of the days, has become the time for the annual ceremonial.

There are some who are not so charitable in their attribution of the reason for having the ceremonial in the summer. They state that they continue to hold the ceremonial at a time that will overlap with July 4th as a way of thumbing their collective nose at the United States government. It is considered a good joke that the United States government's day of national celebration is completely enmeshed in a traditional Indian event, even though in recent years an Anglo-American style Fourth of July parade has been added to the general festivities surrounding the ceremonial, making the entire occasion one of festivity with parts that are very Anglo as well as parts that are totally Indian. While Mescalero Apaches are patriotic citizens of the United States, there are still unpleasant memories of times of incarceration and virtual enslavement that make the July 4th date one of delicious irony for some.

Not every girl who has begun to menstruate since the last July ceremonial will participate. Some girls choose not to have a ceremonial; one can be, indeed *is,* a woman upon menstruation—with or without a ceremony. The only defining characteristic of a woman is that of an adult female person, who, in turn, is one who menstruates; therefore, one is a woman upon menstruation. A ceremony is not necessary.

Some parents and guardians choose to hold a private ceremonial of one, two, or four days, rather than have their daughters participate in the public one. A ceremonial can be held at any time of the year and at any place, providing a singer agrees to sing there; summer remains the favored time, however.

Bernard believed that the truly proper time to hold the ceremonial was at the summer solstice, *shaʔ sizi*—or sun standing still, in the sense of straight up and down. This is when the aboriginal year began and when it still begins for those whose business is the religion and religious life of the people. Singers do not enter into discussions of whether or not the government is being mocked by the July 4th date. Instead, they note that it is a practical time, given people's work schedules, and it is close to the solstice, which occurs the third week of June. Singers must be practical as well as philosophical. As Bernard said when he was first Head Singer for his people, "When our religion goes, we go as a people." He was practical enough to realize that sometimes accommodations must be made. He would not compromise with the content of the ceremonial nor with its unfolding,[2] but he was willing to compromise on the date by saying that while it was best to hold the ceremonial at the solstice, it could, of course, be held at any time of the year. For the singers, the girls and their families, as well as for many of the other participants and audience members, the ceremonial itself is predominant, with the date being ascribed lesser importance.

During the course of the ceremonial, the singers recount tribal history from the beginnings to the present. *Níaguchiláádaʔ*, in the beginningtime when the world was being made, they sing: when the people were formed into a group, in the beginningtime; in a Land of Ever Winter, by the shores of a lake across which one could not see, in the beginningtime; when the people began their migrations, in the beginningtime; when the Grandfathers walked Mother Earth, in the beginningtime. They sing of all this and more, much more, as they re-create the world and, in so doing, assure its continuity, harmony, and balance.

Singers must memorize long stories of the people, their travels, and accounts of tribal interactions from the beginningtime to the present. They must have prodigious memories, not just for songs and recitations, but also for sequences of ritual activities that take place over the course of the four days and the four nights of the standard ceremonial. The task is complicated by the fact that the songs are not in colloquial, contemporary Apache, but rather are sung in what the singers refer to as "the classical language." And, indeed, it is to them much like Latin or Greek, or even Chaucerian English, is to a contemporary speaker of English.

The Apache classical language contains the roots of the present day speech; it is a language rich with allusion and metaphor. And it is a language that must be interpreted to the girls who are having their ceremony. It is not taught to women, although some women have learned it from having heard it for so many years. There are two ways for women to learn the ritual language: either for singers to instruct the godmothers, *naaikish*, in the meaning of particular words and phrases with the appropriate actions that those words or phrases are supposed to engender, or for a *naaikish*, who has learned through listening or being instructed, to teach a younger woman. Mescalero Apaches prefer to teach through example, allowing one to learn from observation rather than direct instruction. Nonetheless, each *naaikish* translates appropriate actions and meanings for the girl she is shepherding through the intricacies of the ceremonial.

Since the ceremony's songs are a recitation of ethnohistory and a re-enactment of events from the beginning of cosmological and historical time, there must be a way of including recent events for those who will come after. The ceremonial is kept current by a provision allowing each of the Head Singers to add a song, if he so chooses; this song is supposed to encapsulate tribal history during his tenure as Head Singer. As with all the ceremonial songs, it is rich with poetry, allusions, and metaphors. The manifest content may be about a horse, for example, but the latent content is tied to each of the words used and to allusions and metaphors built on them and on the relationships between them, as well as to where the song is placed within the structure of the ceremony.

The singers—who sing to celebrate the achievement of an adult role for the girls, who sing tribal history, who sing of the present in the past and the past in the present, who sing their people into existence—truly are singing for the life of the tribe. As they do so, they recapitulate the base metaphor constantly and also open and close chiasms. Just as time and space are shown to be linked through star timing in synchrony with song singing, so, too, are other glimpses of The Real World offered during the ceremonial.

While camp-out enclaves are being made ready, the singers and godmothers are also preparing for the ceremonial and checking to be sure all has been secured that must be ready at each proper moment. Tules, for carpeting in front of the Holy Lodge, must be gathered. There must be a sufficient quantity of cattail (*teł, Typha latifolia*) pollen and the proper mineral-laden earths for painting. A ceremonial basket must be secured, woven sunwise if possible and, if not, then blessed. The deer hoof rattles must be checked to be sure their handles are still fully beaded and the hide thongs holding them together are still in good repair. Ceremonial clothing must be made ready for the girls, their singers, and godmothers. Yucca stalks must be gathered; sticks must be carved for the singers to lean upon and other, smaller ones, for placement around the fire pit as a song count. And the poles must be secured for the ceremonial tipi, the Holy Lodge, an activity replete with rituals of its own.

It is customary for men only to go into the mountains to cut and bring out the twelve poles that will form the Holy Lodge. While each of the twelve is gathered with care, special rituals surround securing the Four Grandfathers, the first of which is marking chosen trees with a pollen circle and cross: " . . . to us a cross is . . . the four directions of the universe coming together, converging . . . the circle . . . means the Powers of the universe encircled [that] makes God, for His Powers are spread out but you put them all together again and there's one God. So that's why they bless it like that." (This quote and the ones following concerning the Grandfathers are from Bernard and are recorded in my unpublished field notes for June 28, 1975.)

After harvesting the Four Grandfathers, the primary structural poles of the Holy Lodge, are brought to the ceremonial mesa by means of a four-stop circuit that self-consciously replicates creative acts and invokes the base metaphor. At the first stop, prayers are addressed to the East Grandfather, the one representing the first day of Creation: "From the East, hence . . . a Power to see a new day . . . to see wisdom in this day and light on Earth. For you, we have stopped; have pity on us." The Head Singer and his assistants might well sing the entire time the Grandfathers and other eight poles are being brought into the ceremonial arena.

On the second stop, a singer may intone words such as, " . . . the Power to grow; the Power from which . . . Summer and Rain come from, the South; we pray to you that a people might live, [that] they may share of your generosity."

The third stop is for the Third Grandfather, the one for the west and the third day of Creation: "The third stop is for the West . . . from which the power of *Power* come from . . . We stop for you that a people might always have Power to endure. We have stopped for you."

The final stop is on the north side of the ceremonial grounds and is for the Fourth Grandfather and the fourth day of Creation. " . . . from the North, the Power to harden our faces . . . We stop for you that we will endure life and all its hardships . . . And then that is complete; they have done four stops and they have paid respects to all the universe."

The Four Grandfathers and the eight other poles are now ready to be raised to form the Holy Lodge, an activity that should take place before sunup on the morning of the first day: that is, before the full disk of the sun clears East Mountain to shine fully on the ceremonial mesa. To this point, all has been male; but, when the poles are to be raised, mothers of the girls having their ceremony and godmothers who will shepherd them through it join the singers and assistants in the ceremonial arena. The mother or godmother of the girl for whom the Head Singer is singing places her hand on each of the Grandfathers in turn as they are raised into their upright positions, thus signifying that there must be both female and male for a home to be constructed properly and for it to be complete.

Everyone is busy and, as is characteristic for the entire event, there are always multiple activities occurring at the same time. It is almost like being at a three-ring circus: it is difficult to know where to focus attention, for it is impossible to see it all at one time or in any one year. Women and men coming together in the ceremonial are also symbolic of their needing to come together, to work out whatever differences there may be, so that the tribe may continue and increase. For it is the ceremonial and its attendant rituals that are seen by the Mescaleros as the crucial factor in their ethnicity and their success in coping with the rigors of survival as a people in a pluralistic society not of their making. As Bernard noted (tape recording, August 27, 1975),

> Our ceremony, the puberty rites, is the most important religious rites that we adhere to today . . . The female————the woman of the tribe, when she reaches womanhood, this elaborate ceremony is held over her. Not, not because she has reached puberty, but because she is a *woman*. And, then, everything is done————for her that a people might live. That a people will *always* live. Every year we have this to regenerate ourselves as a people.————————That . . . we will make her strong, and gener-

ous, and kind, and proud so that she will bring forth *strong* warrior child that . . . will protect the people. ――――――This is the way a people perpetuate themselves . . . this is [done so] a people might live.

Benard's words are to be taken both metaphorically and literally. The characteristics the ceremony imbues in a woman—strength, pride, generosity, kindness—are the characteristics Apaches strive to achieve in their own lives. Men are expected to be brave, above being kind; kindness is a virtue ascribed to women, although there are many stories of brave women and kind men. Bernard describes the importance of generosity in a tape recording on August 17, 1975:

> . . . the four laws of our people are honesty, generosity, pride, and brav-ery . . . a people, they cannot be great if they have no sense of generosity about them. For it is out of generosity that a man sees the world and what a man is worth in this world. He cannot be proud, if he is not generous, because he has nothing to be proud for and brave for. And he cannot be honest, for all honesty has no basis if it is without generosity. So――generosity, at the end, is the most important law that we have. It is the value that we have cherished from the day we became a people to today.

Men are brave in their role as warriors; women are kind in their role as nurturers. Both men and women, however, are expected to be kind and brave in appropriate circumstances. But no person can be a proud adult, with straight carriage and head held high, unless that person is also generous; generosity is the primary quality. It is this quality of character that has caused some difficulty in contemporary times when people are torn between adhering to the traditional value of generosity and the opposite, newer movement toward accumulating goods and money for their own individual households. Such contrary pushes and pulls make contemporary reservation life difficult at times.

It is especially important to be generous with one's own family, those in the matrilineage. But it does not do to forget the kin of one's father. They, too, are relatives, but believed to be more distantly related; usually emotional affect is stronger for those in the matrilineage. Yet all relatives deserve generosity and respect. Nor is any person in the tribe to be ignored; if at all possible, generosity must be spread to all Apaches. Of all possible personality characteristics, the one least understood among Apaches is that of selfishness. The ideal person is also generous to all outsiders, excluding only those whose actions have earned them enemy status.

In the above quotations, when Benard was instructing me, he was very precise. The messages delivered to Apaches in attendance at a ceremonial are more subtle and less overtly didactic. No one, for example, would presume to tell another adult to be more generous, unless, perhaps, one were senior in the lineage or held a particular position of responsibility in the family; then, the only ones to be so addressed are likely to be other family members rather than people in general. However, the message of the importance of generosity is made abundantly clear throughout the course of the ceremony, even when not overtly stated as it was when Bernard was instructing me. Generosity is particularly apparent in respect to food. Food is given away: three times a day the relatives of girls having their ceremony provide food for all in attendance, Indian and non-Indian alike. Entire matrilineages, extended in every possible direction, contribute to these massive give-aways of food.

The food that is given away at mealtimes is usually prepared and served by matrilineage members, extended through the generations and sometimes laterally (e.g., wives of men in the matrilineage) when extra people are needed. Thus, not only do mother's sisters and maternal grandmother's sisters and their daughters, and daughters's daughters, help but also help comes from the male siblings of each of these and sometimes from women associated with those men. Oftentimes assistance is also received from the sisters, mothers, grandmothers, and nieces from the father's side, too. It is becoming more common to see women from other tribes or non-Indians assisting, too, as marriage ties are becoming more common outside the Mescalero Apache Tribe. Decisions about who will help and when are made on a practical basis: who needs how much help and who is available to provide it. It is expected, however, that the matrilineal relatives will help with all necessary chores and will also assist with the monetary expenditures that must be made. Friends, too, may offer assistance and be pressed into service. There is a virtual obligation on matrilineage members to assist, if, that is, they expect to maintain their good name in the family. Help from the others is a bonus when it occurs. But some families choose to have only the relatives of the ceremonial girl's mother assist.

On the first and last days of the ceremony, there is a surfeit of food generosity; food is conspicuously abundant as it is thrown, literally, from the beds of pickup trucks to waiting crowds who joyously dodge oranges, apples, soft drink cans, candy, and tobacco while also trying to catch the goodies as they fly by. Generosity is very clearly seen in this conspicuous abundance of food. And, since food is necessary to sustain life, to be generous with food is truly to be generous with the very stuff allowing life. It is easier to hold one's head high when one is known for her/his generosity. Pride legitimately flows from generosity.

Generosity is also represented on the person of the girl having her ceremony. Over her elaborate buckskin two-piece dress, she wears layers of jewelry. Much of the jewelry is provided by her female relatives and those males to whom she is related through her mother. Her father's family also usually provides jewelry as well. Sometimes the jewelry a girl wears has been given to her, and sometimes it is loaned for the duration of the ceremonial.

Relatives of a girl will have also demonstrated their generosity in the months leading up to a ceremonial, as they assist her natal family in securing and storing goods for the coming event. These may be bolts of cloth, coffee, lard, flour, sugar, salt, tobacco, and such; or the relatives may instead have contributed skins or beads, as well as time and effort to help make the girl's dress and moccasins and the hundreds of "tin" cone jingles, fashioned from food cans, that festoon the dress. Or they may have given their time and energy to gather the reeds, pollen, minerals, and grasses needed. Oftentimes, male relatives offer to provide the skins out of which a girl's costume will be made. These skins must be as blemish free as possible and tanned with special care, or so most people believe. Increasingly, however, people are succumbing to the temptation to buy skins that have been commercially tanned and bleached, thereby saving themselves a long, time-intensive, and smelly process, since brains and urine are part of standard tanning and curing equipment.

The tribe as a whole contributes to those who choose to have their daughters' ceremonials during the July holiday, for beeves from the co-operatively run herd are given for slaughter to provide the basis for stews that will be fed to participants and audience alike. There are also contributions of water, electricity, toilet facilities, a public address system, police services, and cash. Those who choose to have a private ceremonial for their daughter will still be offered water tanks, portable toilets, police, and beef. No matter where an Apache person looks during a ceremonial, there is a display of generosity—not just to tribal members but to all who come to witness the event. Even those considered with less than charity on most occasions are treated kindly and generously during a ceremonial.

Kindness is not a characteristic generally associated with Apaches in the Anglo popular view. Anglo literature is replete with tales of Geronimo or other raiders who swept down from the mountains, driving off horses and cattle before the settlers knew what hit them. There are also a myriad of stories of the cavalry successfully following an Apache trail, only to be ambushed by those same Apaches from behind or the sides; and there are still other stories of pillaging or of slave raiding and trading. Then, too, there are the stories of Apachean atrocities against all non-Indians, usually without concomitant stories of the events that led to the interactions that are remembered as being so bloody. Yet within the bounds of tribe, or within the bounds of friendship, kindness is a highly developed art. Further, it is accomplished in such a fashion that neither giver nor receiver need be embarrassed; in the Apachean value and decorum system, no one should be diminished by a kindness given or received. If a person perceives a need on the part of another, the person should fulfill the need, assuming it is within the person's abilities to do so. Thanks are neither expected nor given; to say "thank you" in such a situation sets up a hierarchical situation where there should be equality. On rare occasions, one might hear *"daabaaʔiłhénsi"* [roughly, I am grateful for it]; but this would be used only when the receiver was surprised that the giver perceived an unspoken or hidden need and then fulfilled it precisely properly. Thanks are given in other ways.[3]

Those who are portrayed as vicious warriors are the same people who will not make a joke in public unless all those present are well known to each other. Joking is all too easily misinterpreted. Misinterpretations can cause embarrassment and a loss of face—not for the person who is the butt of the joke, but for the joker who displayed such insensitivity as to embarrass another in public. Thus, kindness to another and kindness for the feelings of another are intimately tied into kindness toward self. This is not to say that joking is unpopular. On the contrary, as Basso (1979) has shown for the Mescalero's Western Apache "cousins," joking is an exquisitely developed form of verbal art. But kindness and consideration take precedence over the transitory joy of joking.

Apachean kindness cannot be equated with the Anglo interpretation of the word, however; sometimes Anglos perceive neglect where Apaches see kindness. It is a kindness to allow another the autonomy to find her/his own way, even if the way chosen is a destructive one that is known to be so to the other. Anglos see neglect of duty in failing to minister to the one who is lost; Apaches observe decorum by noninterference, even while they may grieve internally for the self-destruction evident.

Through the exercise of generosity and kindness, a person develops pride and strength of character. This pride is inherent in being Apache. Even their name for themselves, ^{n}dé, is thought of in capital letters, THE PEOPLE, very much in the sense of the chosen and proper humans. Creator gave the Mescalero Apache people serious responsibilities for the maintenance of balance and harmony in the universe. Despite incursions of every imaginable sort by the larger mainstream Anglo culture, Apaches have persisted and have maintained their responsibilities. They have every reason to be a proud people, a pride that is on public display during the July ceremonial time.

Strength of character—developed through generosity, kindness, and pride—is only half of the measure of strength the people possess. There is also high positive value placed upon physical and emotional strength. The strength to best enemies, whether on the battlefield or more recently in the courts, the strength to withstand incarceration on a minuscule portion of the land they once roamed and controlled, the strength to fight back from poverty and disease, the strength to maintain their language and customs despite enormous pressures to acculturate: these, too, are important components of the strength Apaches seek and display.

Strength is reinforced through the dignity lent by having a long history, one that predates by centuries the coming of the conquerors, a history kept alive in the ritual language as well as in stories told to children or related around campfires on cold or rainy days and nights.

A proper person does not emphasize one of these four qualities—generosity, kindness, pride, and strength—to the detriment of the others. Balance is necessary in the behavioral values and characteristics, as in all other aspects of life.

These characteristics are to be understood also as a transformation of the base metaphor. Just as the East, with all its associations, is the beginning point of the celestial and cosmological base metaphor, so generosity is the cornerstone of its transformation into the qualities of an ideal Apache person.

The qualities are also detailed in song and verbal instruction to the girls having their ceremony. Most of the instruction can be heard by any who choose to crowd around the Ceremonial Tipi, or Holy Lodge. The importance of bringing these characteristics to fruition in oneself for the good of the whole people is stressed overtly. But also the characteristics are demonstrated quietly and reinforced for each adult. Many instances of the base metaphor are visible but not stated. As the tribe as a whole contributes to the enormous expense of holding a ceremony, so each individual contributes to the tribe. All food is shared until there is no more to share; similarly, adults recommit to sharing their best with their people until there is no more of them to share. The people perpetuate themselves through a community and individual commitment to all that is deemed necessary to make a proper Apache.[4]

Girls are assisted in becoming proper Apaches through the puberty ceremonial. The ceremony is a celebration of the achievement of womanhood for girls, a time of homecoming and sociability, as well as a reunion with the primary life force, Creator, who is made manifest through natural phenomena, especially through the sky, sun, and Mother Earth. Mother Earth, in turn, has as one of her proper and holy manifestations White Painted Woman, ʔisdzanatłʔeesh, who is also ever changing. At various times in the ceremony, the girls are said to be White Painted Woman; it is her life that theirs will emulate. It will be recalled that when White Painted Woman first appeared in the East, she was a young, beautiful woman. During the course of a day/year/lifetime/eternity, she gave birth both to living beings and to proper ways of behavior as she walked over the Earth to the West. By the time she arrived in the West, she was changed and appeared as an ancient woman. Nonetheless, she reappeared the next day/year/lifetime/eternity in the East, again young and beautiful. Just as White Painted Woman traversed the Earth, so will the girls being honored traverse the Earth in their lifetimes, changing in the process from infants to children to adults to old women. And, just as White Painted Woman brought the items and knowledge of Apache civilization and the exquisite gift of children, so will the girls having their ceremony renew the civilization of the Apache through their lives and works and give the tribe new life through the children each will bear. While each girl is honored as now being a woman, she is also honored for the mother she will become.

The girls' puberty ceremony, then, is a ritual drama, a re-enactment of Creation, with contemporary pubescent girls/women enacting

the role of the culture heroine, White Painted Woman. It is also an event
that foregrounds the base metaphor and chiasms. The ceremonial is, of
course, readily understandable to Apachean people. Non-Indians find
that the interpretive task is facilitated by following the base metaphor
through the event, paying attention to those times when balance, circularity, the number four, and the interplay between sound and silence occur. The patterns of these components of the base metaphor allow insight
into how the singers sing for life—both that of the girls and that of the
tribe. In the following composite description of a girls' puberty ceremonial, I have joined together events from several individual and July ceremonials.

THE FIRST DAY

In the predawn darkness there are only wisps of smoke coming from the
cooking arbor and some of the camp-out homes, as the singers and their
assistants begin to assemble at the west end of the ceremonial arena. Even
the active children are still asleep, as is attested by the reluctant whines
heard when parents begin waking their children so they will not be late
for the starting of the ceremony.

The few off-reservation and non-Indian spectators who have
braved the early morning chill sit on the north side of the ceremonial area
directly opposite the large cooking arbor, watching as several singers and
makers [ʾanaaguʾłiin, One Who Makes Them (the Mountain God dancers); an owner of a set of dancers] emerge from behind the cooking arbor.
They have been singing and praying near the girls' quarters while each
godmother dresses her charge from the left, the side of the heart and
therefore the side closest to Creator. First comes the left moccasin, then
the right. Next comes the soft buckskin skirt made heavy with its fringe,
each strand of which ends in a handmade tin cone. The buckskin over-
blouse, with its elaborate beading and more tin cones, follows. Finally
the scarf is added, attached at the shoulders so it can cascade down the
back. Finishing touches are provided by jewelry, beaded work, porcu-
pine-quill work, turquoise, and silver. Shy girls, usually between eleven
and fifteen years of age, disappear under the layers of clothing and decoration to emerge as the living representations of White Painted Woman.
As the final items of the costumes are put in place—the scratching stick

(for the girls are not to touch their bodies during these days) the pollen pouch, and the drinking tube (for the girls' lips will not touch water for these four days)—the singers come to the northwest side of the ceremonial grounds and stand near the spectators in the north grandstands. The makers, when they are present, and usually the fathers and/or uncles of the girls, array themselves behind the singers. At this time of dawn, the sky lightens quickly. The Head Singer moves to the west end of the ceremonial arena and, facing east, begins to sing a prayer to the Powers of the universe while also addressing them with cattail pollen blessings. The others, supporting him and his actions, pray silently.

Strong young men check the placement of the heavy, evergreen poles for the Holy Lodge, *ʔisʔaʔanebikughʔą, Old Age Home*, inside which the most significant aspects of the ritual will take place during the ensuing four nights. Beginning with the Head Singer, the singers bless the poles with pollen in the crossed circle pattern. These poles, usually between twenty-five and forty feet long with the longer poles the more desired ones, are blessed at both butt and tip ends. The twelve evergreen poles that will form the skeletal structure of the Holy Lodge are arrayed in a circle, bases toward the center, behind (to the west of) the singers. Grasses (to prevent lightning striking the Holy Lodge) are tied to the tops of the four primary poles, the Four Grandfathers. The circle formed by the poles opens to the east and has a basket at its center. The singers continue their prayers as they sprinkle pollen from the base to the tip of each Grandfather pole.

Prayers continue as the mothers, grandmothers, and godmothers of the girls join the singers. As the singers sing to each Grandfather in turn, beginning with the East Grandfather and moving sunwise, the gathered women "send forth a voice," a high-pitched ululation of reverent praise and pride that is arresting in its intensity and pitch.

Meanwhile, the young men who are raising the poles pause four times, once for each cardinal direction, before bringing the poles to their full upright position. Soon all Four Grandfathers are standing upright, supported by the combined strength of the men who strain against the weight of the green poles. Gradually, the Grandfathers are tilted in toward each other, with the East Grandfather bearing the weight of the other three.

Each Grandfather is a multivocalic symbol. The First One, East Grandfather, represents the first day of Creation and all that was created on that day in the heavenly firmament. He is called *ʔeɫtsesizi*, First Standing, or East; this Grandfather is sometimes termed *Bikʔéguʔiyaa*, According to Whom There Are Sky Elements and Beings (that is, Heavens, Sun, Moon, Earth, Wind, Lightning, Thunder, Rainbow, Rain, Cloud, and Those Who Depend Upon Them [Plants]). The Second, South Grandfather, represents the second day of Creation and nonmammalian animals. He is called *Naakisizi*, Second Standing; this Grandfather is also termed *Bikʔégunaagishnaatʔa*, According to Whom There Are Flying and Crawling Beings (birds, reptiles, insects, fish, and snakes). The Third Grandfather, West Grandfather, represents the third day of Creation and the rest of the animals. He is called *Taasizi*, Third Standing; he is also termed *Bikʔégubijedidii*, According to Whom There Are the Four-Legged. This Grandfather has another name as well, *Hanyaadighaʔsizi*, or Going Down Standing to indicate the sun setting in the west. Finally, the Fourth, North Grandfather, represents the fourth day of Creation and people. He is called *Diisizi*, Fourth Standing. He, also, has two additional names: *Bikʔégudiⁿdé*, Creator, or According to Whom There Are The People [Apaches] and *Shaʔibiyaiyusi*, or Standing Winter, which refers to the northern sun standstill, or the winter solstice. It is said that the Fourth Grandfather represents the weakest of all Creator's efforts, for it is only people who require all of the others for their survival. The Four Grandfathers stand as reminders of Creation, as reminders of the people's dependence upon the natural world, as visible reminders of the balance and harmony created by Creator, and as reminders of the interdependence of all Creation. Their collective term, *Shi Tsuye Tɫendiɫ*, My Grandfathers Together, carries with it the connotation of being intertwined in a human sense or, in an inanimate sense, spiraled together, each supporting the others.

After each of the Four Grandfathers is standing upright, the spiraling begins. The East Grandfather is the primary support; South Grandfather begins a controlled slide until it rests upon the primary pole. A young man, who has been holding the rope attached to East Grandfather, begins to run around the poles, holding the rope taut, as he lashes them together with deft wrist action, while the proper songs are sung to the Grandfathers being raised and leaning on each other. When the Four Grandfathers are in place, each of the other eight poles are lashed to them. A young man then climbs up the frame to fasten the white cover immediately under the tufts of evergreen that have been left on the topmost portion of the poles. Meanwhile, other men cover the bottom two-thirds with freshly cut oak branches. Soon the Holy Lodge is completed on the outside. At the very top are tufts of fir; the middle portion is covered by white canvas or other cloth, while the bottom is covered with closely intertwined oak boughs.

This description of the significance of the Holy Lodge and the explanations in the following pages of other aspects of the ceremony were given by Bernard in a tape recording of September 21, 1976, unless noted otherwise.

> The main Ceremonial Lodge is made of twelve evergreen fir trees. These poles represent eternal life for us. And the twelve represent the twelve moons of the year[5] . . . The four main structure poles . . . correspond to the four directions of the universe, the four seasons, the four stages of life––for in the natural world everything is based on four . . . These twelve poles that form the tipi, to us represents the balance of Power, goodness, generosity; all that is good in this world comes from this tipi, this Holy Lodge . . . It says to us, "Come forth, my children, enter me. I am the home of generosity, pride, dignity, and hope." . . . The Four Grandfathers hold up the universe for us . . . These poles are heavy; it takes many men to lift them . . . When these poles are being raised, the mothers of the daughters put their hands on the poles. And that signifies that the home is not a home without the woman; and even though this ceremonial structure is going up, it also has to have the help of the woman even though she is physically not able to put it up.

The ceremonial tipi recapitulates the visual aspect of the base metaphor. It is, of course, a circular structure; the cross is formed by imaginary lines drawn from east to west and south to north along the cardinal directions. These directions are indicated by four rocks, one in each of the cardinals, that lie on the periphery of the fire pit in the center of the Holy Lodge.

The basket that had been in the center of the circle formed by the butts of the poles is now brought out in front of the Holy Lodge. It is a handmade basket containing grama grass, pollen, eagle feathers, and tobacco.

> . . . . basket represents the . . . heart of a people; it has all the important things. It has grass in there: food for all that we live on, the animals. The feathers represent Eagle . . . We get our authority to live as a people

from Eagle. He is God's earth authority. That's why we wear the [eagle] feathers . . . feathers are our authority and pride . . . Tobacco is man's hope and his prayers . . . the basket is industriousness.

Although the Grandfathers are named for the cardinal directions and represent them, they are actually displaced so that the *ch'enetł'u* [literally corral, but usually termed "runway" in English] can be open at all times to allow unobstructed passage of the morning sun's rays into the center of the ceremonial tipi. While some men construct the runway, others begin to lay a carpet of tules (*Scirpus lacustris*) where runway and Holy Lodge join: "cattail to us means cleanliness and freshness" (Bernard, June 28, 1975). At the same time, men inside the Holy Lodge put finishing touches on the central fire pit, flanked by the cardinal stones.

> The fire pit . . . signifies the woman and the poles represent the man. Men are the shield; they protect. The woman is the center, being protected . . . Everything revolves around the tipi . . . it's a people. The cover is men. The fire is woman, warmth, love, and perpetual labor for a family to live. If there's no woman in here, there's no rhyme or reason to it . . . Everything is male in that lodge except the women and the fire.

Later on, in the late afternoon, one of the godmothers will take a coal from a cooking fire in the communal cooking arbor and kindle the fire in the center of the Ceremonial Tipi.

Outside the Holy Lodge, while the runway is being finished and the last touches put on the fire pit, the singers face east and pray. The Head Singer slowly raises his left hand as he sings and prays. His palm faces outward; painted on it, in red, is a round symbol of the sun with rays emanating outward to the four directions.

The godmothers lead the girls to their places on buckskin mats placed on the quilts and blankets on the top of the tules, just as the Head Singer completes his last song prayer and his left arm is fully extended. When the timing is proper, the full disk of the sun completely tops the mountains east of the ceremonial mesa and strikes the upraised palm, thus presaging the more foregrounded sun pulling of the last morning.

> When men offer red paint to the sun—red signifies male and men. That's the background of the sun. The two basic colors of the universe is yellow and red, yellow for women . . . And the sun is the physical representation of God . . . [As the sun rises] goodness washes over you.

This miniature of the last day's sun pulling is spectacular, although few see it, for attention is focused on the girls and the ministrations of the godmothers to them.

Goodness washes over the girls, too, who kneel, either upright or, if they are tired, resting on their heels while a line forms to the southeast of them. The girls' mothers stand behind them holding burden baskets filled with food, candy, tobacco, and money; the girls' fathers and uncles stand to either side, inside the runway and directly in front of the Holy Lodge.

First through the line are the singers, with the Head Singer leading and the others following in order of the length of time they have sung. Each singer kneels in front of the girl occupying the southernmost position; this is the girl for whom the Head Singer sings. He reaches into her pollen bag with thumb and forefinger to begin the cascade of golden pollen for the blessing sequence. First he sprinkles it behind his head to the east, then to the south, and west, and north, calling down the blessing of Creator as represented in the pollen. Next he blesses the girl by sprinkling pollen just beyond her body between shoulder and chin height: a rivulet to the east, south, west, and north, then from the west to the east by marking the crown of her head to her forehead, moving to the south on her right shoulder, to the north on her left shoulder, and from south to north across the bridge of her nose. The movements form a cross inside a circle with the girl as the pivot. She is encased in a blessing. He moves to each of the girls, from south to north, blessing each in turn and being blessed himself.

> Pollen is applied to them. They are blessed with pollen. Pollen is the color of yellow. The yellow color represents God's generosity. It also represents the south, from which the warm winds bring rain that a thirsty land might drink and bring forth its bounty of fruit and meat.[6] And they are . . . blessed that they will be fruitful and bring forth strong sons that they will be mighty warriors . . . that they will bring forth strong daughters that will become the mothers of a warrior race; that they will perpetuate themselves in a good way, a holy way, with the Powers of the Four Directions.

The girls reciprocate the blessing sequence for each of the singers. Each singer will bless each of the girls and, in turn, be blessed by them. As the last singer is kneeling in front of the first girl, the Head Singer moves to the front of the spectator line to assist them in moving to positions before the girls to give and receive blessings. Anyone who wishes to be blessed may go through the line. Infants and children too small to perform the blessing sequence for themselves have their hands and arms moved by their caretakers. Those who have specific complaints linger to rub some of the pollen on the afflicted part(s) of their bodies, or they may whisper a request for a blessing to an afflicted or weak area. Anyone who is sick or troubled will go through the line, as will those who seek to remain well and partake of the blessings of Creator and White Painted Woman as mediated through the girls. The girls are known to be especially holy during this time of their ceremonial.

Singers and godmothers keep a careful watch for signs of fatigue on the part of the girls, for there is still more strenuous activity to come. At times the line is so long that not all waiting to be blessed will be blessed in public. Those remaining in the line, if it is halted to proceed with the next segment of the ritual, will go to the camps of the girls behind the cooking arbor after the morning's public events, there to be blessed and to bless in private.

The Head Singer motions away those still in line; the godmothers assist the girls in going from their knees to their abdomens. Each girl lies face downward with her head to the east and her chin resting on the accumulated blankets as her godmother presses and molds her into a fine, strong woman. The hair is smoothed over the girl's shoulders and back; then the molding begins: first the left shoulder, then the right; next the left and right sides of the back; then the left hip and the right hip; the left then right thigh and calf; the left and right foot. As she is pressed, so will she become.

As the godmothers near the feet, the basket with the grass, feathers, tobacco, and other ritual items is taken out to the east where it is placed on the ground in a direct line with the entry to the Holy Lodge but at the very edge of the ceremonial arena. While the singers sing and the godmothers ululate, the girls run along the north side of the dance arena, around the basket, and back along the south side of the arena. The basket is moved three times, each time closer to the Holy Lodge, and the running girls encircle it three more times. Bringing the basket in closer to the Holy Lodge each time makes a statement of the sorrow of the parents—their girls are now women and soon will be leaving their natal homes to establish their own homes with their own children. The basket being brought in closer to their religious home symbolizes the parents' natural desire to cling to their daughters a little longer, to delay their moving into full adult roles and lives.

The four runs around the basket also symbolize the four stages of life: infancy, childhood, adulthood, and, as the basket again nears the Holy Lodge on the west side of the ceremonial arena, old age. As the primary characters in the ritual drama, the girls reenact the legendary journey of White Painted Woman who walked to the west as an old woman and returned from the east again a young woman. At the conclusion of the fourth run, there are again simultaneous actions. In front of the Holy Lodge the girls' parents and other relatives shower them with tobacco, candy, piñons, fruit, and money spilled out of the burden baskets they have been holding. The spilling from the baskets signals the end of the public rites for the morning and triggers massive give-aways by matrilineal members of the girls' families; sometimes matrilateral relatives participate in these give-aways as well. The relatives throw candy, oranges, apples, soft drinks, cigarettes, loose tobacco, and small household items (such as ladles, spatulas, and bowls) from the beds of pickup trucks parked in front of the cooking arbor. People of all ages dash to pick up the gifts (while dodging the barrage of continued throwing), for these are special items that have been blessed. The give-away is also a display of public generosity, and it is a way of expressing thanksgiving for having a daughter who has become a woman. At Mescalero, when one celebrates, it is appropriate to do so with food given to all and gifts distributed in keeping with one's means.

While those in the assembled crowd, many of whom arrived before or with the sunrise, scamper for the gifts, the girls return to their camps. There each girl's godmother talks to her of sex and her responsibility for motherhood. The singer gives his "daughter," as he will refer to the girl for the rest of her life, Indian bananas (*huskane, Yucca baccata*) and says, "Be fruitful all the days of your life; obtain food and not be lazy." He repeats this, and the feeding, twice more. The fourth time, the godmother feeds the girl; as she does so, she tells her, "May you bring forth in this world strong male children so they will protect your people." If at all possible, the feeding and instruction are done in Apache; however, some of the girls now do not understand the language sufficiently well to be instructed in Apache so they must be spoken to in English.

Even before the singer and godmother finish feeding the girl and instructing her, those who have not yet been blessed form a line outside the camp-out home of the girl by whom they wish to be blessed. At the conclusion of the feeding, they are admitted one, or a few, at a time. Each kneels in front of the girl, who is sitting on a bed or a chair, and pollen blessings are exchanged.

During these blessings the Head Singer goes to the camps of each of the girls in turn to bless the traditional foods that will be eaten as a part of the breakfast. Mescal (*Agave parry* or *A. neomexicana*), Indian bananas, piñons roasted and in stews, mesquite beans (*Prosopis glandulosa*), various wild berries and seeds, nuts, dried meat, Spanish bayonet flowers (*Yucca elata*), venison: all are favored for this meal. The Head Singer also blesses the breakfast food to be distributed from the cooking arbor, usually meat stews, fry bread, and coffee.

Each girl's family has a fire in the cooking arbor, where food is cooked for all who come to the ceremonial. A breakfast of fry bread and coffee is available each day, with some families also providing a meat stew with potatoes and perhaps a chili stew as well. In the camps the relatives and very close friends eat traditional foods, as well as the usual breakfast fare distributed to all comers. Some families choose to share the traditional foods as well. If they do so, or if the Head Singer demands that they do so, the traditional foods are spread in a line in the ceremonial arena close by the cooking arbor. A dipper festival ensues, for, without a dipper, there is no proper way to bring the food from the communal containers to plate or pan to take back to share with immediate family members.

Meals at first seem to be almost an intermission in the ritual drama. Yet they are also a logical extension of it, since mothers—including White Painted Woman, whom the girls represent—not only give life but sustain it as well.

After breakfast, participants and spectators alike rest—some at their camps, some at their year-round homes, and some at local motels or the homes of friends and relatives. But for the mothers and female relatives of the girls, finishing breakfast is not a signal for rest time; it merely means it is time to check tipi stores to begin preparing for lunch and dinner.

The tipis in the girls' camps are used primarily for food storage and preparation prior to cooking, while the tents and arbors are the living areas. Some of the final food preparation does take place in the family arbors, particularly for things such as salads, while the large cooking arbor is the preferred place to prepare foods that must be cooked, such as coffee and stews. Stews are cooked in new twenty, thirty, or forty gallon aluminum cans that are placed in fires, next to them, or on grates over them. Male family members butcher cattle daily to provide the meat. Some family members may have slaughtered deer or elk or antelope that has been kept in family freezers for this occasion or has been preserved through the more traditional means of jerking—cutting into thin, narrow strips and drying. Fry bread browns in bubbling lard inside cast iron pots on the fires, while the women tending to the shaping and cooking of the fry bread laugh and talk together. It is the making and cooking of fry bread, with its attendant sociability, that forms my own most delightful "women's work" memories of Mescalero. Coffee is cooked "cowboy style"—that is, coffee and water are placed in large cauldrons and boiled together. While some women tend to the cooking fires, others prepare salads in the tipis and family arbors.

Lunch and dinner menus are the same: meat, potato, and chili stews, some with red (dried) and some with green (fresh) chilis; meat and piñon stew; vegetable stews with chili; salad (usually potato or macaroni—occasionally tossed); fry bread; pinto or mesquite beans; coffee; Kool-Aid; fruit, either fresh (watermelon, apples, oranges, cantaloupe) or canned (peaches or fruit cocktail). People are served as many times as they choose until all that has been cooked has been distributed. But, since there is sufficient variety and portions are generous, seconds are seldom sought other than for fry bread (a favorite of both Indians and Anglos), coffee, or Kool-Aid. Some Indian families prefer to cook their meat themselves; in this case, raw meat is given them to take to their own camps for preparation. For those who prefer Anglo style fast food, there are concession stands serving hamburgers, hot dogs, chili, coffee, and soft drinks. Food is in abundance.

Singers and godmothers are always fed from the fires and larders of those for whom they are working. The food is in such generous proportions that usually they have sufficient quantities to feed their immediate families as well. So, while audience members eat their meals in the grandstands or at makeshift picnic tables or in their family camp-out areas, the ritual specialists' immediate family members eat in their own tipis or tents behind the girls' camp area.

While ceremonial participants rest in the afternoon, the spectators are entertained. If it is July 4th, there will be a parade. On the other days the entertainment is from the rodeo or dance contests and powwow dancing. Some who are members of the ritual drama audience become performers in these events. An all-Indian rodeo, with competitors from many states, takes place on a mesa to the northeast of the ceremonial grounds. The animal activity of a rodeo does not mix with the holy activity of the ceremonial; they are separated, therefore, in space and time. The rodeo attracts good contestants, since prizes are generous and points can be earned for the annual all-around Indian-cowboy championship. Increasingly, some Anglos come for the rodeo event only and ignore the ceremonial. As long as there is an audience for the ceremonial to validate the experience by seeing it and accepting gifts of food within its context, it does not matter to the Apaches that some ignore the most important activity and concentrate on the ludic. As Bernard said, "[We had] horse racing and gambling [hand game and bets on the races] in the old days –––government outlawed it. Now, rodeo takes its place."

Dance contests in the pan-Indian powwow style take place in the ceremonial arena and partially overlap in time with the rodeo. And in the 1980s a Fourth of July parade was added, with Mescalero celebrities, children, elderlies, and floats from various on- and off-reservation groups.

Dinner is served between 5:30 and 6:30 P.M., depending upon when individual families have their food prepared. Long lines form on the arena side of the cooking arbor. While waiting, people often see friends and relatives in their own or other lines. There is much hugging, greeting, admiring of new babies or commenting upon the growth of children, and much switching of places. It is not considered impolite for one member of a family to hold a place in line for the entire family—much to the annoyance of visiting Anglos who do not understand the local canons of politeness where one member of a family may well represent the entire extended family, whether standing in line or speaking in a meeting. Anglos feel angry when one person suddenly becomes ten or fifteen or twenty as they approach the serving tables.

After dinner the mounting tension is almost tangible as darkness begins to descend and the huge bonfire is prepared and lit in the center of the dance arena. At this time, if it has not already occurred in the late afternoon, an owner of a set of Mountain God dancers sends one of his clowns through the girl's camp area as announcement for the girl(s) for whom his group is performing to assemble further up the mesa, out of sight of tourists. There, the girls(s) will be seated in lawn chairs and be blessed by the Mountain God dancers who encircle them in an invisible, healing protective curtain. Women associated with the owner of the group and the dancers, as well as the relevant godmother(s) are present during this special blessing. They quietly stand on the north side, forming a protective wall for the girl(s) and then dance in place during the singing and drumming that accompanies the blessing dance.

When the sun no longer colors the mountains and deserts to the west and when the bonfire in the center of the ceremonial arena is roaring, jingling noises can be heard from the east as the Mountain God dancers prepare to enter the dance arena. Their maker and his assistants have been busy for the past few hours praying, drumming, and singing while the entire group of Mountain God dancers has been painted and costumed and the private blessings have been danced for the girl(s) far up the side of the mountain above the ceremonial mesa—out of sight of spectators.

Each group of Mountain God dancers is associated with particular designs on headdresses and sashes, as well as with a set of designs to be painted on the bodies. These designs, along with the songs, are passed from one maker to another at the time that the rights to the group are transferred. However, that does not mean that the designs remain the same through time nor that each maker uses the same set of designs as those who preceded him did. Designs can be, and are, changed through a dream or through the seeking of a vision at a sacred place. In a similar fashion, songs can be changed, although they seem to remain more constant through time than do the designs.

To Anglo eyes the designs seem to change each night. The dance steps are strenuous and the men must dance close to the fire; therefore, they sweat even on cold nights, and the designs painted on for one night's dancing seldom are in condition for dancing on the second night. This is not a problem, however, since each of the designs in a set is normally used only one of the four nights; the men have to be repainted each day for each night's performance. Any part of the design remaining on a body from a previous night's dancing is simply painted over for the next and subsequent nights. While the same precise design is not repeated, the elements are combined in a different manner for each of the four nights. Each representation is said to be a transformation, or reinterpretation, of the designs that preceded it and that will follow it. The transformations within a set of designs for any one group of dancers are often said to be

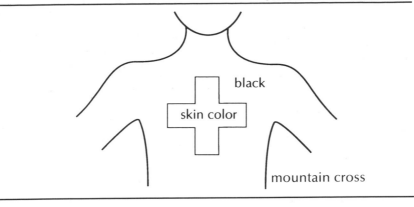

Fig. 6.1 *Sidney Baca's first night design. (Drawings 6.1 through 6.4 by Laura Kline.)*

"the same thing" from one night to the next, and all of them are generated from the base metaphor, unless the particular maker [also called owner/painter] has had a vision or dream instructing him to use a different design. Reduplication, so long as it is done evenly, does not disturb what is perceived as sameness; neither does color reversal affect sameness in this regard.

As an example, Sidney Baca, whose group of Mountain God dancers has recently used new designs that came to Baca during a rededication experience, uses a set of designs that, while fixed, also allow for some variation. On the first of the four nights, Baca uses *dził ʔluzi*, [mountain cross], that appears through making the field black and leaving the mountain cross design in skin color, as is illustrated in figure 6.1. On the second night, he paints just *dził*, [mountains], in white on a black field (fig. 6.2.).

Night three allows for wide variation, but variation still generated from the base metaphor, as he will paint a white design on a black field. The design will be either *sųųs* [star] in one of two variations, or *tse nų ʔbił* [spinning rock], as in figure 6.3., a-c.

On the final night he paints either *shaʔ*, [sun], in yellow on a black field, or a different *sųųs* in yellow on a black field, as figure 6.4., a and b show. Each of the designs can be generated from ⊕ (see figs. 4.17–4.22).

The general costuming of the Mountain God dancers is the same among the groups—buckskin kilt, paint, head covering, headdress, sash, moccasins, and on each arm a red streamer with four eagle feathers attached. Each dance group is identifiable by its distinctive body painting

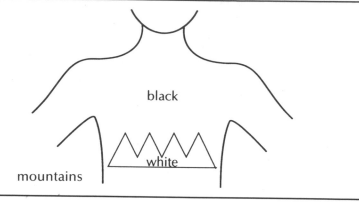

Fig. 6.2   Sidney's second night design.

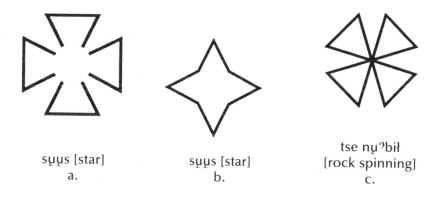

sụụs [star]
a.

sụụs [star]
b.

tse nụʔbił
[rock spinning]
c.

Fig. 6.3   Sidney's third night design choices.

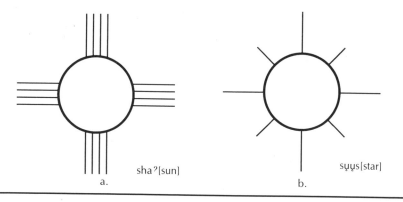

shaʔ[sun]
a.

sụụs[star]
b.

Fig. 6.4   Sidney's fourth night design choices.

design sets, sashes, and headdresses. There is no mistaking a Mountain God dancer or the group to which he belongs.

The dancers' A-line wraparound buckskin kilts are fringed and fitted with beaded or skin decorations, as well as with jingles cut and shaped from food tins, that make a jingling noise each time movement is made. Kilts are held up by worked leather belts (often with bells attached) and red sashes wrapped over parts of the heavy belts, or tied on just below them. The mid-calf length buckskin moccasins are often decorated with bells either at the top or at the ankle. A glance at the toe of the moccasin tells the ethnic identity of the dancer: plain toes mark a Mescalero man, while a turned-up toe, or toe guard, is chosen by a Chiricahua man. If there are no bells on the moccasins themselves, a dancer will often add a leather strap with bells around each leg. The dancers are moving music, and they move whenever they are in the ceremonial arena.

A head covering of black fabric—canvas, heavy cotton, suede, dyed buckskin, or heavy doubleknit—with small round openings cut for each eye and the mouth is topped by a bilaterally symmetrical headdress made of yucca and woods with decorations of feathers and paint. These elaborate headdresses with their "horns," as the upright projections are sometimes called, give rise to the English colloquial term for the Mountain Gods: Horn (var. Horned) or Crown Dancers.[7] A scarf around the neck completes the head wear. The headdress of each group member is the same and is painted with designs matching or repeating an element of the design set painted on the dancers' bodies. Thus, with the exception of the palms of the hands, a dancer is completely covered with paint or costuming from the soles of his feet to two or more feet over his head. He becomes the anonymous personification of a Mountain God. And even when one knows which man portrays which Mountain Spirit, no one calls their names while they are costumed, for to do so would call the God himself—few mortals have the power to deal with such a Presence. Neither do the men speak while costumed with their headdresses in place. It is said that a man will suffocate, if he puts on the mask of the headdress without believing in what he is doing and in the traditional religion.

Usually there is a dance set (four Mountain God dancers and one or more clowns) for each girl, although at times two girls will share a set of dancers. Sharing is most apt to occur when the girls are sisters or first cousins through their mothers' side of the family, or when there are more girls having a ceremony than there are sets of Mountain God dancers. In this latter instance, the closer the kinship relationship between the two girls, the more likely it is that they will share a set of dancers. In contemporary times, some of the sets of dancers who used to be painted are in "retirement," sometimes because there was no one to assume the responsibilities of being an owner/painter/maker and sometimes because there is a guardian relationship in operation whereby a nonsinging, nonpainting, nondrumming adult holds in trust the rights to a set of dancers for a minor child. And there is one instance where a group was retired recently when all the stored costumes were burned in a freak fire; this was taken as a sign that the group was not to be painted—at least for the present. Thus, there is now a shortage of Mountain God dancer groups.

As night falls, the air chills everyone except those close to a fire. Blankets are wrapped around sweaters, jackets, and shawls as people settle into grandstand seats or into the lawn chairs they set up on the very edge of the ceremonial arena—on all sides save the east. The spectacle is awesome when the fully costumed Mountain God dancers converge on the dance arena, jingling rhythmically as they move, their headdresses piercing the darkness above them. The dancers pause in their trotting step just outside the east entrance to the dance arena; they stop close to the spot where the basket was placed earlier in the day for the girls' runs. There the lead dancer gets the others in step by striking his thighs with the sticks he carries in each hand. *Libayé*, the clown, mimics each movement of the lead dancer, but usually a bit late. When all are in step and when all noises—from the bells and the tin cones to the strident note from the cowbell slapping against the clown's buttocks—are in synchrony, the lead dancer moves his group into the dance arena. They raise their arms and sticks as they approach the fire and emit a hooting sound resembling that of an owl in timbre but that of a turkey in repetition and speed. They are said to be praying as they make this noise. Their movements and vocalizations are said to be "blessing the fire."

When the lead dancer is within a few feet of the fire, he lowers his arms and sticks and bows his head; then the line steps backward, still facing the fire. The sequence of approaching, hooting, lowering, and retreating is repeated three times; on the fourth approach the dancers dip their bodies first to the left, then to the right as they approach the fire. They move so quickly in their four dips to each side that their arms seem like windmills. This time as they retreat the lead dancer again slaps the sticks on his thighs as he guides the group once around the fire, making a complete circuit, before stopping on the south side of the dance arena. The blessing sequence is repeated from here, then from the west and north—each time with one complete circuit of the fire between stops for the cardinal directions. After the fire has been blessed, the group moves to the Holy Lodge, where the sequence of blessing is repeated from each of the cardinal directions in order (east, south, west, north).

In recent years another pattern has emerged, practiced by the members of Sidney Baca's group. After Baca formally received his charge through inheritance, he took a pilgrimage to a sacred mountain, where he sought and received a vision. He had originally intended his pilgrimage to be a rededication of his group and a commitment of his own time and effort. But the vision he received led him to modify his group and once again to have the clown assume a central role, as it is said he did in the "old days." The clown for Baca's group performs blessings with pollen before the group addresses the fire and after it has finished a blessing from each of the cardinal directions. He also performs pollen blessings around the Holy Lodge. These blessings are in the familiar circle-with-cross pattern, but sprinkled on the ground where the Mountain Gods and *Libayé* will soon be dancing.

Additionally, Baca's group includes women who dance in support of the men who sing, drum, and dance. Usually women are admitted only to the outermost circle of dancing while in the arena. But with this group, the women are an intimate part of the blessing sequences and the fire sequences, albeit in subsidiary roles as they stand behind the men singing and drumming for the dancers.

When the blessings are completed, the women retire to the sidelines, where they remain unless they choose to dance in the women's line that moves around the fire and between the dancing Mountain Gods and the general audience. They do not again actively participate with the men until the last song of the night that Baca and his assistants sing, the "Going Home Song." Even writing the name allows a peace to descend around me, for it is, to me, the most moving of all the songs sung and the time when the most group cohesion is felt—it is almost tangible. With the women, dancing slowly, this time intermingled with the men who are singing and drumming, the group begins to move from the western edge of the ceremonial arena, immediately in front of the Holy Lodge, to the eastern entrance/exit. As they slowly move along the north side of the ceremonial arena, they are joined and encircled by the dancing Mountain Gods. When the last note of the song is sung, all are at the eastern edge of the ceremonial arena, where the Mountain Gods take their leave and the women return to pick up their chairs and retire to their camp-out homes, at least for a time. But all this is hours away.

In the early part of the night, Baca, with his assistants who drum and sing after his lead, move to a position in front of the Holy Lodge where benches have been placed. The Mountain God dancers and their Clown(s) now dance with dramatic posturing, stamping, and gesturing around and around the bonfire, always moving in a clockwise, or, as they aver, a sunwise direction. Even when there is no singing or drumming, the dancers keep moving; they are never still the entire time they are in the dance arena. It is particularly impressive when there are several groups of dancers in the arena at one time; in this case, they all dance to the music of one maker, while the other leaders and their assistants await their turn on the bench. The Mountain God dancer sets dance to the music provided by any of those who drum and sing.

As the first maker begins his drumming, a large cardboard is placed on the ground in front of the benches where he and the chanting men sit. Young boys congregate around the cardboard carrying evergreen sticks they have gathered from near the Holy Lodge. They join the adult drummers and chanters by beating in rhythm with their sticks, and occasionally they also join in singing the choruses of a song; those who had been part of the audience become performers.

The dancing of the Mountain Gods signals the women to join in the dancing as well. Their dance path is several feet away from the bonfire and the path of the Mountain Gods. Some of the first women to dance are the girls for whom the ceremony is being held; they are accompanied by their godmothers, who dance in front of them. Their mothers and close matrilineal female relatives, and perhaps their matrilateral female relatives as well, dance behind them: " . . . while the men are dancing, the women dance around them. There again, we can't separate the male from the female in our religion," Bernard stated in an August 1975 tape recording while explaining the ceremonial to members of a BBC film crew.[8]

The girls wear their ceremonial attire, of course, since they do not remove it until the last morning of the ceremonial—and then only for a bath before donning it again for another four days. Others wear everyday dress without jewelry that might make noise. Only the Mountain God dancers, the Clowns, and the ceremonial girls make noise in the dance arena; the sounds produced by the bells and jingles and jewelry on their costumes are perceived as music. All other sounds are avoided.

A shawl is added to the everyday dress of the women. The shawl is a piece of fabric approximately two yards long that is folded in half lengthwise and draped over the shoulders in such a fashion that the hands are covered and the twelve- to fourteen-inch fringe hangs down on the sides and in back. Only the women's legs move in performing the dance steps. However, the execution of the steps moves the body toward, then away from, the fire—and that movement produces a swinging motion of the fringing on the shawls that is mesmerizing and is considered beautiful. Proper women dancers move silently with a straight carriage and squared shoulders, propelled only by the motion of their knees and legs and the apparent motion of their shawls. The dance style seems effortless, although it is very difficult to sustain. The effect is almost ethereal.

The girls make only a few circuits of the fire before retiring to their camps to rest before their strenuous dancing begins. As they retire, other women begin to dance "in support" of the Mountain Gods. Mothers encourage their very young (four- and five-year-old) daughters to dance, too. The women most often dance in groups of matrilineally related kin. Sometimes women who are matrilaterally linked to them will join in, but usually a woman dances with her own sisters and first cousins through her mother. The groups of women that cause the most appreciative comment are those that contain three or more generations of a matrilineage. A few Anglos or non-Mescalero Indians may also join in the dancing, if they are particularly close to a family of women and are specifically asked to dance and if they have, or can borrow, a shawl. No woman dances without a shawl. Although women of all ages dance, those who dance longest are between about fifteen and fifty. The steps that appear so graceful and fluid are very taxing.

As the dancing of the Mountain Gods and the women dancing in support of them holds the attention of the spectators, the girls are led from their camps into the Holy Lodge by their singers and godmothers. Often the Head Singer announces that it is time to enter the Holy Lodge by leading a procession of himself, the girl for whom he is singing, and the godmother through the cooking arbor. The girl for whom the Head Singer sings is assigned the easternmost campsite, so the three must traverse the entire length of the cooking arbor on their way to the Holy

Lodge. The jingling tin cones on the girl's dress announce her presence as she moves through the cooking arbor. The time of night also cues the others to fall in line or to come immediately to the Holy Lodge so that the night's activities of the ritual drama can begin.

When the singers, girls, and godmothers are assembled in front of the Holy Lodge, the girls are led-in through the mediation of an eagle feather. Each singer stands with his back to the opening of the Holy Lodge, holding the tip of the feather while the girl for whom he is singing holds the quill end. Four songs are sung during the leading-in, and with each song a symbolic step is taken into the Holy Lodge. During this leading-in portion of the ceremony, the girls are said to be inviting in life and magnanimity for their people and themselves.

Cowhide dance mats await the girls around the inside periphery of the Holy Lodge. In the old days, it is said, the girls danced on buffalo hides, but today the hides are from cattle. The godmothers spread blankets for themselves and the girls to sit on while resting; it is here that they await the arrival of any of the singers, girls, and godmothers who were not ready in time to participate in the leading-in by the Head Singer.

While the girls and their godmothers arrange themselves inside the Holy Lodge, the singers arrange their folding chairs at the entryway to the Holy Lodge. The Head Singer details either the most junior singer, or one of the boys present in hopes of becoming a singer himself one day, to place wood on the fire. While they wait, they pray and smoke. Smoke is itself a form of prayer; at the same time, it is a channel through which prayers can travel to Power and Creator. All smoking inside the Holy Lodge is replete with ritual, recalling the crossed circle pattern, from the lighting of the cigarette to its snuffing out.

After everyone is inside and ready to begin, the Head Singer ritually smokes by lighting a cigarette from a bundle of thin sticks that have been placed on a pole of the Holy Lodge. As the taper is lit to become the lighter, it is offered to the Powers of the Four Directions, in a sunwise circuit a few inches above the fire pit, before being placed at the end of the cigarette. After the cigarette is lit, the taper is again offered to the Four Directions in a circuit over the fire pit before being extinguished on the ground. The Head Singer offers smoke and prayers to the Powers and blesses those present. As he extinguishes his cigarette, after making a sunwise circle with it, he begins shaking his deer hoof rattle and is immediately joined in the rhythm by the other singers. The girls rise to dance as the singing begins.

There are two dance steps that the girls use. The more common one, *naabik'aash—n*, involves keeping the body rigid while moving only the feet. By pivoting alternately on the balls and heels of their feet, the girls take four "steps" to the left, then four to the right, four to the left, four to the right, and so on in rapid succession, in time to the deer hoof rattle beat. The cowhide on which they dance is just wide enough to allow four lateral movements before they must reverse direction. They hold their arms in front of them by bending their elbows, raising their forearms, and making their hands form relaxed fists with the palms outward while the knuckles rest lightly on their shoulders. The position and step cause their clothing to move and the tin cones to strike one another, adding another sound to that produced by the percussion of the rattles and the men's voices singing in the ancient ritual language. The other dance step, *yeijish*, is designed as a rest step, although it, too, is strenuous to perform. Again the body is held still while the feet move. While standing in place with their hands on their hips, the girls kick one foot and then the other straight out in front. A part of the ritual for the girls is to make a physical sacrifice for the good of themselves and the ultimate benefit of their people; this they do through their modest behavior and demeanor for the entirety of the ceremonial as well as through their runs to the east and their nightly dancing. While singers and godmothers are careful to see their charges do not become too tired, they must often struggle against the commitment of many of the girls to dance each song and sit only when the singing stops. Some girls, of course, are less determined and must be prodded to dance. Blessings accrue to those who dance voluntarily.

Some of the girls report experiencing the opening of individual chiasms as they see into, and hear from, The Real World while they dance in their ceremonial in This Shadow World. Of those who report such experiences, there seems to be general agreement that they "see" the proper way to behave and that they feel a general euphoria. Some say that they recognize past inappropriate behavior while feeling no desire to continue with it; others maintain that, rather than seeing past behavior, they instead see the proper path for them to follow in the future. Still others report no such experiences.

Between the songs sets, the godmothers massage the girls' shoulders, backs, or legs if they are showing signs of fatigue. The Head Singer, too, keeps a close eye on the girls for signs of fatigue. When he feels they are becoming tired, he will change tempo so they can dance more slowly or he will take a longer break—perhaps smoking a cigarette between song sets—all the while watching the star clock and mentally timing the songs that still must be sung against the movement in the sky. Alternating the two dance steps with short rest periods, the girls dance for several hours each night while the singers sing of tribal history, of Creation, of the coming of the tribe to the present place, and of what is to be. Bernard described the dancing and the language of the singing in the tape recording of September 21, 1976.

> They're dancing . . . it used to be buffalo hides but now it's beef hides. They are dancing on it, gliding. They glide back and forth on these hides, shuffling. The men . . . sing to them and tell them, "These sounds that you make on this hide are sounds of a people walking and living. Dance on this hide——for it is your home. It is your food." The sound that it makes as a girl dances back and forth on it, it says, "This is the sound that a people will make on this earth. It is a pleasant sound, a good sound. Abide by it."

As the singers sing, the godmothers interpret for their charges and, at certain words, send forth their voices in the high-pitched ululation. The interpretation is particularly important for the girls to gain full understanding of the songs and the meanings attached to them, for as Bernard stated,

> The real stories are told in classical language and you have to stop and explain the language. The classical language is full of allusion so that each word stands for a series of related concepts and it needs strict interpretation. The classical language is the root words of my language. Even a girl who speaks good Apache . . . has to have it interpreted; that's what that woman [the godmother] is there for; my job is to sing—she interprets and tells them what I'm singing.

The girls dance from about 10 P.M. until midnight, then return to the dance arena to dance briefly with the Mountain Gods before going to their camps on this first night of the ceremonial. Social dancers replace the Mountain God dancers usually between 11 P.M. and midnight, or shortly thereafter. Sometime between 2 A.M. and dawn, the social dancers leave the dance arena. Those who retire earlier are lulled to sleep by the beating of the drums and the distant voices of the makers and their cohorts, who sing for the social dancers as well as for the Mountain Gods. Even she who is too excited to sleep, or too busy writing field notes by firelight or flashlight inside a tipi, finds that when she does lie down she is soon mesmerized by the passage of the stars viewed through the crossed poles of the tipi at its smokehole apex, while the drumming seems to reverberate through the very ground, becoming the metronome for her own heartbeat. The first day ends.

THE SECOND AND THIRD DAYS

There is no morning ritual on the second and third days. Afternoons are filled with powwow style dance competitions, the rodeo, and, on the Fourth of July, a tribal parade. In just the past few years, Bernard reintroduced a former practice—that of kindling fire with sticks and dried grasses.[9] He made both the base stick and twirling sticks from yucca; they were then given to the godmother tending the girl for whom he was singing. The godmother, in turn, assembled the other godmothers and the girls in the early afternoon. Each of the girls took a turn twirling the stick in the wood, creating the necessary friction, until fire was achieved. The fire is then shared with each of the girls' camps and, if desired, coals can be saved to ignite both the fire in the Holy Lodge and the bonfire around which the Mountain Gods dance later in the evening.

After supper but before the bonfire is lit for the Mountain God dancers, the war dancers appear in the ceremonial arena. They carry rifles loaded with blanks, bows and arrows, or lances. Their hair is usually long (even if it must be a wig) and is held in place with a plain headband. They wear loose shirts or are bare-chested. Each wears moccasins and a long G-string, often over Levi's or cotton pants. Now they are adolescent boys; in the old days, I am told, they were men who wore only buckskin and carried real weapons of war. They used to dance in front of the Holy Lodge to protect, symbolically and actually, both what occurred inside it as well as the people in general. Now they dance in an entertaining sort of way; yet there is an undercurrent of tension as they seemingly take delight in frightening the audience by aiming at particular people with their arrows and lances or shooting them with blanks, thus forcing the audience members to take a performer role. But, in general, theirs is now a benign dance, empty of its former threat. It is also removed in time from the events in the Holy Lodge, as the war dancers appear in the afternoon while activities in the Holy Lodge are only at night.

The bonfire, several feet in diameter, is lit at dusk from a coal carried either from the Holy Lodge fire pit or from one of the fires in the cooking arbor or the girls' camp-out area. The fire is fed until it is a roaring blaze, in preparation for the nightly dancing of the Mountain God dancers and the social dancing that will follow their performance. Beginning around 10 P.M., the girls will again dance for two hours or so in the Holy Lodge as the singers continue their sung narrative of tribal history and perform rituals that will protect the girls from the vagaries of the mundane world, rituals that include, on the second night, the "smoking" of the girls with tobacco. There are fewer songs sung on the third night so that the girls may have a longer time dancing on the edge of the ceremonial arena while the Mountain God dancers circle the fire. Again during this conjoint dancing, some people report experiences of exceptional clarity or understanding through the chiasm that is opened by ceremonial behavior, as they seem to enter almost trance-like states usually while dancing themselves but, for some, even while being spectators. And, of course, there are the discussions surrounding the possibilities brought into focus as *Łibayé* dances his role as chiasm.

THE FOURTH DAY

Again there are no morning rituals and again the afternoon program of powwow style dancing, rodeo, and war dancing occurs. But this night, inside the Holy Lodge, the songs and dancing will continue throughout the night, as was described in chapter 3. On this night, social dancing, which commences when the Mountain Gods retire from the ceremonial arena, will continue throughout the night, ending only as the predawn light appears, usually finding the dancers close by the dying fire for warmth.

Since time is reckoned at Mescalero from sunrise to sunrise, the pulling of the sun to wash over the girls in their Holy Lodge occurs at the end of the fourth day. By Anglo time reckoning, it is the morning of the fifth day. With events "counted" differently, such as these on the fourth/fifth day, the arbitrary nature of time segmentation becomes readily apparent: Anglos begin their new days at midnight, while the Apaches begin theirs at full sunrise. The fifth sunrise of the ceremonial occurs during the pulling of the sun on the last public day. This fifth sunrise is simultaneously the end of the fourth day and the beginning of the second set of four days, when the girls will remain on the ceremonial grounds with only their close female relatives and their godmothers —when the public aspect of the ritual is over, when the singers go home, when the Mountain God dancers return to their everyday lives, and when the private mother-daughter and godmother-daughter aspects of the ceremonial begin. (These latter aspects of the ceremonial will not be considered here.)

These days are ones of ritual time. And, since time and space are collapsed in ritual drama, time is simultaneously the here/now and also the here/now/ago, while the space in which the drama occurs is both of This Shadow World and The Real World of Power, spirits, truth, and Creator. Thus, days can be, and often are, canceled in This Shadow World, for our pitiful human segmentation of time has no meaning in The Real World.[10] Canceling a day in This Shadow World does not affect The Real World. The ceremony consists of four full days of ritual events regardless of the number of times the earth spins around. And since days are reckoned by sunrises, there obviously can be no new day, unless the full disk of the sun visibly rises over East Mountain; at least, there is no ritual day.

On the last day, as on the first day, people assemble before dawn for the final ritual activities. Some of those present have remained up all night, dancing or simply lending their presence in support of the girls who must also remain awake all night. Some have stood all night long watching the events transpire in the Holy Lodge, stamping their feet against the cold and huddling into blankets or ski jackets. Some have set mental or metal alarm clocks in order to arise two hours before dawn. There are many people present, for the singers maintain that this is the most important day since the universe is re-set on this day and people once again resume their responsibilities in keeping the proper order, balance, harmony, and rightness of the world.[11]

Just as in the old days, the girls' families distribute presents of cloth, dippers, knives, tobacco, scarves, and other items to those who have danced in support of the girls throughout the night. The presents are a tangible reminder of the endurance of the dancers and their dedication to tradition as they dance all night to lend their strength to the girls who must also dance all night with only short breaks. In the old days, they say, the men would also pay the women for the honor of dancing with them all night. Money was proper payment as was a shawl, a blanket, or even sometimes a horse. As one old man said, "It was the gentlemanly thing to do."

Mingled with the laughter and pleasure of those who social danced all night is the jingling of the girls' dresses and the percussion from the deer hoof rattles of the singers, for the girls have been dancing—with only two short breaks—the godmothers have been counseling, and the singers have been singing throughout this, the last, night of the ceremonial. Everyone recognizes that it is a strenuous night for the girls, but it is considered to be a part of their sacrifice both for their own strength and, through them, for the strength of the tribe. Bernard's comments here and on the following pages are from the tape recording of September 21, 1976.

> These girls have been dancing for four nights. On the fourth night they dance from when it gets dark to daylight with a break around midnight.[12] It is a physical ordeal for them. But they must go through it . . . It is a sacrifice they make . . . their physical contribution that they make that a people can be strong and healthy.

Throughout this night's singing, the singers have placed sticks around the Holy Lodge's fire pit: one stick for each set of four songs and another stick for each "tobacco song." These sticks, provided by the Head Godmother, model the shape of the Holy Lodge when they are all in place. About two hours before sunrise, there is an increased tension, as there is much to be done before the sun tops East Mountain. As the last song is sung and the last counting stick placed around the periphery of the fire pit the singers rise, signaling the godmothers to take the girls back to their living quarters. There the girls' hair and bodies will be washed in yucca root suds, repeating the actions of the first day when the girls were cleansed and dressed. This ritual also foreshadows duplicate cleaning and undressing activity that will take place at the end of the eighth day, long after all the visitors have departed.

Other things are occurring while the girls are being readied. The singers change from their everyday clothing to their best Indian attire;

when next seen in public, they will be wearing their best buckskin shirts, their brightest shawls draped around their waists, their symbolic jewelry, and their best moccasins.

Meanwhile, all tules are taken out of the Holy Lodge and replaced with fresh ones. The folding chairs for the singers are placed so they face east and are behind the girls, whereas previously they had faced west and toward the girls, and had been between the girls and the spectators.

The girls have their faces painted with white clay by the singers. Their arms, from fingertips to elbows, and their legs, from thighs to feet, are also painted. They thus assume tangible aspects of White Painted Woman.

> The girls' faces are painted white signifying that they have achieved; they have done their ordeal. They have lived four good days and they will be running. Running signifying a physical effort that they must do in order to prove themselves that they are worthy mothers . . . That white paint is the sign of purity and of the Mother Earth . . . They are called White Painted Woman, because white is the color of purity, these four days.

But before the girls' final ordeal, the singers must pull the sun, and that which was given form by the men, the Holy Lodge, must be destroyed by them.

The singers sit on the tules spread on the ground at the entryway to the Holy Lodge again with the Head Singer in the southernmost position and the others following to the north in rank order. Even though light increases quickly, they seem to be unhurried as each carefully paints a rayed circle on his left palm (fig. 6.5). The Head Singer again picks up his deer hoof rattle and begins singing with his left palm facing his left thigh and at thigh level. The singers sing a song. In unison they move their left arms so that their left elbows are at about waist level with their palms turned toward their own faces while they sing their second morning song. Once again they lift their left arms, this time to about mid-chest height, and again turn their left hands so their palms are at shoulder level and facing the south as they sing the third morning song. For the fourth, and final morning song, their left arms are raised slightly above shoulder level; their left palms now are at a right angle to their left arms with the palms facing due east. Just as the last note of the last song is sung, if the timing has been carefully attended to, the sun's complete disk fully tops

Fig. 6.5   Bernard painting the sun symbol on his palm prior to pulling the sun July 7, 1983. (Photo by the author.)

East Mountain to illuminate the sun symbol painted on each palm! It is awesome and truly spectacular (fig. 6.6).

Unless he has been persuaded to allow another the honor, the young man who had placed the white covering on the Holy Lodge on the first day once again shinnies up the poles, this time to disengage the lashings and lower the covering. Whoever is holding the rope attached to the covering, when it is removed from the Holy Lodge, is entitled to keep the covering. While the young man is working to disengage the cover, other men on the ground take away the oak boughs that had covered the bottom of the Lodge.

Meanwhile, inside, the girls are being blessed and sung to. People crowd in, even though the eight subsidiary poles are beginning to fall. As the last pole falls, leaving only the Grandfathers, the girls are revealed sitting on the ground, each with her singer and godmother kneeling in front of her. Again, as on the first day, people form lines in front of one

Fig. 6.6 *Singers Bernard Second, Medicine Bird Runningwater, and Paul Ortega (background) singing a sun-pulling song on July 7, 1983. (Photo by the author.)*

or another of the girls; each singer takes a seat to the left of the girl for whom he sang while each godmother stands to the right of her charge. The girls sit with their eyes downcast as the singers bless them. Each singer paints his daughter with red ocher or white clay, using his own unique design both on her and on each of those whom he blesses with paint.

Again, as on the first day, lines of people move in front of the girls, but this time it is the singers who perform the blessings, painting the face (or, with some singers, both sides of the face or the forehead) with the same symbol he has painted on the girl and on her godmother as well. Most people believe that this paint is meant to be left on until it disappears of its own accord, although nowadays some people wash or rub it off upon leaving the ceremonial mesa rather than appear, especially off-reservation, like "painted savages." Such concerns are alien to the few Anglos who line up to be painted, for they wear their paint as tangible marks of acceptance. This time there is no hurry—all who so desire will be blessed, men on the left sides of their faces and women on the right. Those with particular afflictions whisper of their need to the singer, who, with the palms of his hands outstretched, rubs the afflicted area while he prays. Rather than with pollen, these blessings are accomplished with white clay and red ocher. After the face painting blessings, each girl grasps the base of an eagle feather while her singer holds the tip; they are led out of the Holy Lodge.

> Now they have been brought out of the tipi after the four
> days of religious functions.————They have been brought out.
> They have been brought by an eagle feather. They, tell them,

> Four days you have walked your land and done good.
> Now hold this eagle feather, the symbol of authority,
> And walk out of your home.
> Go forth into the world.

The girls are escorted to a white buckskin that has been placed on the ground in front and to the south of the runway that is now lined by the girls' fathers and close male relatives. Four crescent moons, painted on the buckskin either with cattail pollen or with colors evoking the directions and said also to represent life's stages, form the stepping-stones each girl walks upon, left foot first, before her final run. As the girl under the tutelage of the Head Singer steps on the first crescent, the first song is sung; one additional song is sung for each of the other three crescent moons as she steps on each one in turn.

And she will be told,

> Now you are entering the world.
> You become an adult with responsibilities.
> Now you are entering the world.
> Behold yourself.
> Walk in this world with honor and dignity.
> Let no man speak of you in shame.
> For you will become——
> The mother of a nation.

At the end of the fourth step and the fourth and final song, the first girl is pushed off the buckskin by her singer, the Head Singer and by her godmother. The other girls follow the first one by quickly stepping on each of the four crescent moons and, like her, run to the east around the same basket that was used on the first day's run.

They are singing to them as [they are] running and they are telling them,

> You will be running to the four corners of the universe:
> To where the land meets the big water;
> To where the sky meets the land;
> To where the home of winter is;
> To the home of rain.
> Run this! Run!
> Be strong!
> For you are the mother of a people.

Three times the girls run around the basket and return to their singers and godmothers, with their fathers standing in attendance in front of the Holy Lodge. At the end of each of the first three runs, the basket is placed further and further from the frame of the Holy Lodge where the girls' fathers and close male relatives still stand. Each time their daughters run, they run a little further from them; no matter how much a parent wishes to hold onto his child, there is a time when that child must leave both parent and home. On the last run, the girls encircle the basket four times before each girl takes from the basket the eagle feather with which she was led into and out of the Holy Lodge. But instead of returning to singer, godmother, Holy Lodge, and male relatives, as she had done on the first three runs, this time she is met by her mother and close female relatives who lead her, still running but now also rubbing the white paint off her face, to her camp behind the cooking arbor. While a girl may eventually be separated from her father, her matrilineage will be with her for the rest of her life, as it has been with her from the time of her birth. At this very moment the Four Grandfathers come crashing to the ground simultaneously; their clamor forces the audience's attention to the western end of the ceremonial arena. By the time the spectators have turned around again to watch the east and the basket, the girls and the basket have disappeared.

> During their last run they are running to their destiny; they are running into the hard world of adulthood . . . the hard world of a hunting world, a war world . . . When the last run is completed, food will be thrown out that a people might be fruitful and multiply to many.

What began five mornings ago with the erection of the Holy Lodge and the distribution of food ends with the destruction of the Holy Lodge and the distribution of food (again from the beds of pickup trucks) as well as the two breakfasts that are served after the giveaways. One breakfast is of traditional foods, blessed with pollen, in the center of the dance arena; the other is of Anglo-influenced foods in the cooking arbor. In between has been goodness, holiness, the affirmation of the essential rightness of the world, and the place of humans in it. The importance of honor, pride, generosity, bravery, dignity, strength, family, and tribe has been celebrated and reinforced for all. As the last of the dance songs sung to the girls in the Holy Lodge states,

> In your country,
> In your plains and green mountains,
> You have lived four days
> In holiness and goodness.
>
> In your country,
> In your plains and green mountains,
> You have existed four days
> In holiness and goodness.
>
> *Naaisha.*
> I have done this.
> Here
> It ends.

The four public days of the ceremonial are at an end, and, while almost everyone is busy catching food from the pickup truck give-away or eating breakfast, there is a final, private ritual that takes place in the tipi of the girl's camp. The singer, who has controlled her life from the moment her parents or guardians approached him to sing over her, now kneels before the girl for whom he has sung (fig. 6.7). Softly he speaks to her, telling her she has lived for four days in holiness and blessing; telling her she is a good woman who will never do anything that would cause others to speak ill of her; telling her that she is from a fine family which is justifiably proud of her; and telling her she now has more power than does he—for she can now become the mother of The People. It is a moment that invariably brings tears to the eyes of her parents or guardians and the few spectators privileged to be present. The fourth ceremonial day ends.

Quickly people move off the mesa, some to return to relatives' homes on the reservation and others to return to their own homes on or off the reservation. This is the saddest time for me: packing up and leaving the tipi that has been home for the past four days; leaving the camp area where I have lived with family and friends and have greeted and become reacquainted with others; hugging babies that will be taller next year; lingering over a last cup of coffee with the women and men to whom I am closest—it is always poignant. All who have been there report being changed by the experience. Of course, the girls for whom the ceremony was held are now publicly acknowledged as women; this is a major change from being a child. In traditional times, many would marry soon after having their ceremony. Now, however, there is junior high school and high school to finish and, for some, college before marrying and raising a family. Yet, oftentimes and to the surprise of nonparticipants, the girls are not the only ones who have been changed.

Anglos who have stayed for the four days and four nights experience an exhilaration they describe as "moving" or "strange" or "incredible" or "unexplainable." Usually they report later being encouraged that a traditional ceremony is still important to a people they had thought almost fully assimilated. A few go home and imitate parts of the ceremony for their own daughters. None say they have experienced a chiasm, but all outsiders who have spoken to me about the ceremonial describe thinking of things in new ways or seeing puberty in a new light.

While the Apaches present are fully aware of the many demonstra-

Fig. 6.7 At the conclusion of the 1983 rituals, Bernard kneels before his "daughter," Sonya Geronimo, while parents Helen and Snyder Geronimo (backs to the camera), and godmother, Delfina Yaanaakai, look on.

tions of the base metaphor—in the ceremonial tipi, in the four runs around the basket, in the singing of songs and their very structure, by the dancing, in the salting of food, in the number of days of the ceremonial, in the number of Mountain God dancers and in their designs—the Anglos have no such points of reference. The messages and forms of the base metaphor are repeated endlessly; they serve as a lived mnemonic for the Mescalero Apaches.

Similarly, the importance and inevitability of circularity, with its attendant directionality, is reinforced repeatedly during the ceremonial. All dances are circular; the runs of the girls describe circular paths; the Holy Lodge is a circle; the ceremonial arena is a circle; the blessing sequence forms a circle; and on and on. Nor are reminders of balance and sound/silence lacking, as with the dancing of the women in the ceremonial arena in contrast to, but in support of, the dancing of the Mountain Gods.

Watching the ceremony of a niece or a daughter brings memories of one's own ceremony, or that of a sister or aunt, or planted memories of their mothers before them. Just as White Painted Woman circles endlessly through life, so life circles endlessly through The People and so an individual life will end but that of the tribe will endure. It will endure, that is, so long as the people maintain their proper direction, their proper way, their inherent balance and harmony. So long, perhaps, as they do not buy and sell LTDs with Anglo regularity. References to the base metaphor are constant for Apaches throughout the ceremony. Some Anglos do note the repetition of acts four times or the importance of circular movement, but most are oblivious to the vitally important statements being made through the verbal, graphic, plastic, and enacted transformations of the base metaphor, just as most Apaches, while acknowledging that something important has occurred, are unable to cite chiasms being opened; rather, talk is of the actions of the *Libayé* figures or the changes in the ceremony.

During his tenure, each Head Singer has the opportunity to add one song to the part of the ceremony that is sung in the Holy Lodge—the part of the singing recounting the people's history. Such additions are to incorporate important tribal events in the time of the Head Singer, and, thus add to the history of the tribe as a whole which, in turn, will be recounted again and again throughout the time that the ceremony is sung. Even those who do not stand behind the entryway to the Holy

Lodge and do not hear the songs being sung are nonetheless fully aware of what is being sung. They are reminded that they have been a people for a time longer than any person can count. They have together and individually faced and conquered many enemies and threats to their existence. They have survived. They have the tools and knowledge to survive in the Indian as well as in the Anglo world. Which will they choose? And what will happen when a singer sings out of turn or changes things that people thought were inviolable?

Such an event occurred in 1985 when Willeto Antonio, the Head Singer before Bernard Second, came out of his semiretirement to sing a private four-day ceremonial. Willeto will not sing on the ceremonial mesa anymore, believing the ground to have been over used and also objecting to the plethora of tourists and to the carnivalesque atmosphere. He will occasionally sing private ceremonials, even though they take a tremendous toll on his energy, since his stroke and virtual confinement to a wheelchair. In 1985, beginning on the very first day of the private ceremonial, Willeto's songs were very different from the ones usually sung. To cite only one example, he had songs for, and names for, each of the twelve poles of the Holy Lodge, as well as having names for each of the runway poles. People were certainly attentive to these new and potentially dangerous moves.

Head Singers, by their very existence and through their songs and power, function as chiasms, allowing the society to examine itself and to contemplate change. They also have, as a part of their responsibility, the ability to change directly the ways in which people behave; this they demand in response to a vision that comes to them from The Real World or because of an injunction delivered in a variety of ways. But while Head Singers may demand change, they cannot necessarily expect a positive response.

After hearing Willeto's songs naming the previously unnamed poles, recounting the genesis of palm trees, and the like, several people struck camp and left the ceremonial grounds. One man said that he "just don't like people changing those things; maybe it is not so good." He decided he'd rather go to El Paso and Juarez, Mexico than remain on the ceremonial grounds and listen to what he believed to be heresy. And a woman, the mother of three children, was truly terrified; she said that she feared that the ground would open up, "like in California earthquakes," as a result of what she perceived to be blasphemy. She dismantled her camp and took her children home, fearing that disaster was imminent.

Others were more charitable and suspended judgment on the song changes of the first and, as it developed, subsequent days. Their feelings were that singers were powerful de facto and, if a singer changed something as sacred as the ceremonial songs, then there must be good reason for it—even if the reason had not been shared. Further, most people believed that if the singer was acting contrary to Power, it would redound to the detriment of the singer rather than the people: Power seeks power.

Bernard, who was in attendance as a helper to Willeto for that ceremonial, found that their visions of the proper ceremony diverged during 1985, despite the fact that both had learned to sing from the same men. Yet Bernard would not contradict Willeto nor allow anyone to talk against Willeto's vision or practices in his (Bernard's) presence. Nonetheless, Bernard did not approve, even if he was loath to criticize but rather sought to understand the underlying motivation, as his June 17, 1985 statements indicate:

> Willeto keeps saying "Sun Clan," but there are no clans [13] . . . He wants things to fit like they do in Pueblo . . . Western Apaches say *deshchín* for clan. We say *deishehí* when a woman is giving birth. At that time we can say, "Ha dideishchei?" Which one are you born into? Which *woman's* line? Like what's your family? . . . Willeto's married to a Pueblo and he's half Navajo—so that's where it comes from . . . It's *all* important; we need it all . . . Willeto named these [Holy Lodge poles] but they don't really have names.

Similarly, a few years previously, while I was sitting and talking with Willeto when Bernard was Head Singer at a ceremony, Willeto noted that, "Even if he [Head Singer] makes a mistake, I tell those others [other singers] to follow him." Singers do not correct each other nor each other's visions; and it is quite acceptable, to most people, to have different versions of any ritual or ceremony in existence at the same time. While I did not hear, nor speak to anyone else who heard, why Willeto made the changes to the 1985 ceremonial, Sidney Baca provided the explanation that seemed best to fit the situation: "Now that we know about all those things, like palm trees, it is good to have them sung, too."

Those who chose to remain for the full private ceremonial early in the summer of 1985 were rewarded by seeing an eagle fly in from the east on the last morning as the girl was completing the last of her ritual runs.

The eagle flew from the east to the west of the encampment area, pausing at the western edge where it began a series of wide upward spirals that finally took it out of sight. Eagles, the birds of authority, are good omens, especially when they fly in from the east. Regardless of whether or not a particular person approved or felt comfortable with the changes that Willeto Antonio inaugurated, all agreed that the ceremony had been finished in goodness and holiness, or the eagle would not have appeared.

Chiasms are openings to potentials, rather than specific mandates. Willeto's changes in the ceremonial may or may not become canon, although they are now more likely to be adopted by the other singers since Bernard's death. Only those who are pure channels, such as *Libayés,* or those with power can risk such changes, however. Change occurs through time, whether or not the change is as dramatic as were Willeto's 1985 songs.

The choices implicit when changes are contemplated are not ones that can be picked up at ceremonial time and put aside until the next ceremonial. They are instead choices that permeate daily life, not just in the precepts of sharing and kindness or bravery and dignity, but also in the choices manifest in simple, everyday activities. An acceptance of palm trees in the songs of the girls' puberty ceremonial brings with it subtle pressures to accept more of the larger, non-Apachean world. Apaches pride themselves on being able to take the best from those whom they encounter while retaining their own core of Apachean ethnicity; they do this through chiasms that open the tribe as a whole to the new, even while casting the new items in terms of the base metaphor. As long as the tribal memory of the base metaphor is intact, there is room for many changes, changes that will allow the continuance of the tribe in the face of great pressures to accommodate and assimilate, pressures to compete economically and in consumerism.

It is not only tribal memory that is recounted and reinforced through the ceremony, but also the memories of individuals within the tribe. Where there is conflict, as with the 1985 ceremonial changes, there is also a conflict in individual memories. Yet, through the enactment of the base metaphor, even within the changes like those in 1985, there is a binding tie made manifest through the fact of the ceremonial itself and its many replications of the base metaphor that place each person who participates, in whatever capacity, in the midst of an ongoing entity and way of life.

It takes very little to participate in a Mescalero Apache girls' puberty ceremony—only belief and proper living. Participation can be gained even without belief and proper living simply by being an audience member. But, when one does believe, then the singers can sing one into and through life, no matter how life changes through time. Singers, whatever their particular songs or visions, sing for all Apaches. They also sing for all people, for, as they sing, the essential harmony and balance of the universe is re-created and reinforced; *hⁿzhúne*—beauty, harmony, balance, grace—is reestablished. The exquisite rightness of the base metaphor, with its genesis in the very sky, is demonstrated yet again as the singers sing the girls in and through womanhood and the tribe into continued existence. Truly, the singers are singing for life.

CHAPTER 7

Crying for Death

This is the chapter I did not ever want to write. I do not deal well with death and had, at one time, promised myself never to address the topic in Mescalero Apache life and culture. Yet I am forced to attend to death, for it is a vital part both of life's living circle and of living life's circle.[1]

The following material, from my field notes of the far too many funerals I have attended at Mescalero, is used here with permission of the mother, Lorraine Second Evans, of the infant whose death and funeral are described. The afterwords are added because they are an integral part of the process of living and dying. I am pleased that the critical polylogues begun recently by Ruby (1982), Clifford and Marcus (1986), as well as Marcus and Fischer (1986) make such statements anthropologically permissible.

In standard mainstream American culture, we have many ways of ignoring the inevitability of death. We compartmentalize it in an effort, I suspect, to remove it from our thoughts and emotions. In our junior and senior high school family health and reproductive physiology classes, we teach our children about care of self, minimal public health, and about the physiology of sexual reproduction. But, curiously, we exclude the mechanics of these topics; even more curiously, we totally disregard death and dying. As a product of my own culture, I am uncomfortable with death and dying, although a recent catastrophic illness abruptly forced me to face the possibility of my own death and to become somewhat more content with the process. I like to think that I have come to positive terms with both the dying process and its conclusion, death. Yet, with Bernard Second's death and funeral in late 1988, it was obvious that I still have much to learn and assimilate. And, in typing the notes that follow, I was again moved to tears for remembered grief and for the head-turning arrested gait that I still experience when I see a child who resembles the one named Carrie, whom I so dearly loved and whose funeral and burial are described.

As will become apparent, the base metaphor and the construct of chiasm were both important in my own process of coping with Carrie's death. And, as I believe the field notes and subsequent discussion make clear, these same organizing principles also assist Apaches in their living process while confronting dying. The effects of alcohol at Mescalero render almost everyone an expert on the pain of living while confronting the death of loved ones.

The long quotation that follows is from my expanded field notes; bracketed comments are added for clarity and do not appear in the original notes. Parenthetical information appears in the original notes.

Saturday, February 25, 1978

Shortly before 7 A.M. (6:35?), I was awakened by a 'phone call. A man said, "Are you Ginger?" [It is my nickname.]

"Yes."

"You know Lorraine?" [The youngest in my fictive, adoptive, Mescalero family.]

"Yes."

"She wants you to know the baby died."

"Oh, no!" I just kept saying this several times. Then I don't remember what he said; I just was blank. I was in the dining room looking at the chair by the fagón [corner style fireplace common in houses in Santa Fe, where I lived at the time as a Weatherhead Resident Scholar at the School of American Research (SAR)] where Shag [Lorraine's childhood nickname] and Carrie sat just a few days ago.

"It was crib death," he continued.

"Oh no, no!" (Pause—I don't know for how long while I reached for kleenex to dry tears.) "When is the funeral?" My mind was racing: I had to get to Mescalero; the car probably won't make it; it's like I lost one of my own; I've gotta be with Shag; how could this happen?

"The baby was taken to Albuquerque, you know, for autopsy. I'll probably call you again."

"Who are you?"

"Raymond, Bernadette's brother." [And therefore fictive kin, since their mother and the mother of Bernard Second and his siblings, who had adopted me and my daughter, were sisters.]

"Thank you for calling me." Then it all went blank again. I went back to bed and cried myself to sleep. Then I had nightmares of sick babies who were dying.

[The following was written as a monologue as I made an effort to straighten out my thoughts; here my field notebook was functioning more as a personal journal.]

> My car won't get me there and back. I'll have to go on the bus for the funeral. And I'll take the [baby] food grinder I'd just bought for her to place in her grave. I cried again and Suzanne tried to comfort me. She doesn't want to go to the funeral . . . I tried calling both Bernadette's and Katherine's [oldest sister in the matrilineage to which Carrie belonged] but no one was home either place so I called Kathleen [nonrelated friend on the reservation] to take a message to them that I'll come down on the bus.

Another call at 8:30 A.M. The funeral is at 10 A.M. Monday. Then Raymond called again. He'll pick me up at the bus stop and Shag wants me to bring a baby Pendleton blanket. I'll rent a car, I think, because I have to also get ready . . . to go to Illinois for the job interview; I'll skip the Deer Dance tomorrow and go to Mescalero instead. I've got to get a new car; it's frustrating not to be able to use mine, for fear of losing another gear and being stranded, when I really need it.

Suzanne helped me stumble through the day and, although I thought I should stay by the 'phone, she insisted we go baby Pendleton looking. We didn't find one but she was quite correct: I needed to feel I was doing something. . . . I shudder to think of myself in Shag's position. And then I cry some more.

Sunday, February 26, 1978

Renting a car will cost about $150; that's too expensive for me right now. So instead I made arrangements to take SAR's Blazer.

After much searching all over town, I finally found a crib-sized Pendleton . . . This time I will drape the casket myself. I only wish I could have draped it over the baby instead. I called down to say I had the Pendleton and was borrowing a car to come down now.

Just as Shirley [administrative assistant at SAR] came in the door to give me the Blazer keys so I could leave, Bernadette called to say I shouldn't come down on the bus or borrow a car because she was going to drive to Albuquerque and would pick me up to take me to Mescalero early Monday morning . . . (She will have to drive most of the night, since it's about 4 hours to Albuquerque or here.) She said that it wasn't right for a mother (of the baby) to be alone at a time like this. Well, that did it and I started to cry again. (I really do feel like the baby was mine, too, especially since I'd been there to visit her shortly after she was born and Lorraine had brought her up here "to get to know her other mother" just last weekend.)

Monday, February 27, 1978

Got up at 3 A.M., expecting Bernadette at 4 but she arrived closer to 5 and we started out . . . I wondered why death makes you feel so alive as I watched the sun rise on the way down; but it soon disappeared behind clouds. It's going to be a cold, maybe snowy, day . . .

We got to Mescalero and Bernadette's just after 9. Shag saw me, came over, hugged me, and we both started crying. We three women had a cup of coffee—don't know where Bernadette's children are; with a relative, I suppose. (Before going to the Church, Shag said last night Bernard said he was going to have "to do something about" those working against his family. He said, "They are taking too many from one family. Adults are one thing, but when they start on innocent babies, it is something else." [This is a reference to suspected witchcraft or sorcery as the result of jealousy or fear.]) Then we went over to the Catholic Church [St. Joseph's Apache Mission]. On the way Lorraine said Carrie died in the hospital! They'd been running tests on her [she'd been quite ill the previous weekend when they'd been at my house] and she was to be released on Saturday; instead she suffocated Friday morning. All day and all night Friday Lorraine said they tried to reach me; that's why Raymond called so early Saturday—to be sure he got me. Lorraine said the mattress didn't fit the crib properly and it shifted over; Carrie's head became wedged between the crib rails and the mattress. Some said she was crying but her cries were ignored . . . She said the autopsy said . . . "sudden infant death" . . . Then she said the coffin was so tiny it looked like a shoe box.

She was right—it did look like a white shoe box except it had brass handles. At St. Joseph's, Lorraine opened the coffin and fussed with the covers before moving the coffin from the back to the north side by a heater because, "She'll be too cold." . . .

The white, soft antelope skin I'd given her in December had been made into a tiny shawl for the baby. And the gan [Western Apache Mountain God] print fabric was made into a two-faced blanket. I placed the baby Pendleton over the coffin as well. There was another baby Pendleton in green; ours was pink. There were also the yellow and white quilt she usually had over the baby, the nursery print blanket, and a little shawl of red doubleknit with white, blue, and black feathers appliqued in a fan and stars with ribbons, substituting for fringe, at all four corners. Carrie was wearing the ring and bracelet I'd given her. It was wrenching . . .

When the priest came in, the baby was moved from the side to the front of the church. The priest gave a resurrection/celebration mass. Bernadette held Lorraine upright as we sat through the mass. Shag kept wailing, "I want my baby," over and over. Someone sitting behind me kept handing me kleenex as I sobbed and cried, too. There wasn't any decent way to find out who it was, but I don't suppose it matters anyway.

After the mass, the tiny coffin was wheeled out to the hearse while we stayed behind to pick up the flowers [that had been at the funeral home and had been transferred to the front of the altar] to take them to Graveyard Canyon. Bernadette drove Shag and me into the Canyon, and I really didn't want to go—I'm not much good at funerals and I'm worse at graveside rites. As we drove into the Canyon, Lorraine said Carrie's grave is just in front of her "grandmother's" (Carrie's great aunt and Bernadette's mother) so that "her grandmother can take care of her." The family, once established, is forever.

The priest spoke about little souls going straight to heaven; then he left. Then the funeral parlor men started to lower the coffin, but the men of the family waved them off. They took their equipment and left. Bernard himself put the baby's coffin in the grave and placed her suitcase in, too. Now there were just Indians and me.

Bernard spoke, all in Indian, saying Carrie was a beautiful baby with beautiful thoughts who would remain beautiful for each tomorrow.

He himself placed her coffin in the grave and put in her large suitcase, too. [The redundancy about Bernard is in the original notes. The suitcase contained those things that were too intimately associated with her to be given to, or used by, others.] He then took a handful of dirt and tossed it into the grave. Lorraine repeated the action followed by Bernadette, then me, then the "real" (i.e., blood) sisters of Shag and Bernard. Next the men took turns shoveling in the dirt; I hate that part. Family men, ritual specialists, and friends shoveled.

It was alternately raining and snowing—big, wet flakes—and it was so very cold and muddy. I was cold, wet through, and had no more tears as Bernard put the rocks around the tiny mound: a large rock first to the north for her head, a little bit smaller rock next at her feet to the south, then a series of rocks to the east and another series to the west until the grave was surrounded and outlined by rocks.

John came over to speak, half in English and half in Indian, to Lorraine. Taking her hands in his, he spoke about his feelings on the death of a beautiful baby.

Then we women began to place the flowers from the church all over the rounded earth mound. Lorraine again began sobbing, "I want my baby back. Come back! I'm all alone again. I got no reason to get up in the morning anymore."

We picked some dried weeds (wild artichokes?) to brush ourselves off with as we walked back to Bernadette's VW, Bernadette, Melanie (who appeared from I don't know where), Shag, and I. We went to Bernadette's where extended family members had a dinner waiting.

. . . After dinner, Bernard sent Melanie to get my purse; she handed it to him. He gave it to me and said, "Here, there are some things you need to write down." He knows my steno notebook is always in my purse. It was as though I'd been hit in the solar plexus; I must be the anthropologist now, not the grieving other mother/auntie. It hurt. But he would not hurt me on purpose. Is it his way of getting me out of my grief, moving me beyond grief? Is he forcing me to re-recognize I am an outside insider? I think maybe he is saying each of us must find a way to go on and a good part of my way is through the distancing that must occur when I stop participating and again observe. Yet, this time, I am an integral part of that which I am to observe and, by demand, record. Sometimes I am very uncomfortable with this life I've chosen. Right now I hate being separated out. But I did begin my rough notes and it did help.

. . . (Bernard asked me the word for mud [*gushk'ish*, one of my favorite onomatopoetic words]) and everyone laughed at my accent. After a while I said, in regard to the accent, "Guess it must be from living so close to the reservation line." There were gales of laughter at that because of the jokes about the loose women who hang around the reservation line . . . But the joke also speaks to my own marginality as an Anglo intimately involved with at least some Apaches yet also an outsider—like a moth to a flame or like someone who haunts the periphery, the border.

. . . Irwin [fictive cousin/brother] kept calling me back to the dining room to come sit by him and eat some more. This, too, is pregnant with meaning. First of all, I'm too skinny to be really attractive, so a fictive, extended, male family member is performing a proper role by trying to fatten me up by feeding me so I'll be more attractive and reproduce for the family. Secondly, by wanting me to sit by him rather than with the women, he is denying my actual/adoptive family ties and making sexual innuendoes; this also has the effect of saying that although skinny, I am almost attractive so, by sitting next to me, he gets first shot in case I become attractive [and am redefined as nonfamily]. Also, there is a deeper meaning: Apaches are [outwardly] stoic, laugh in the face of death, meet and overcome death, and will prevail by strength of numbers; so, it was also acceptance of me as a kind of captive/adoptive [family member] . . . Maybe it was more, too. Jokes do a *lot* of work.

. . . There is altogether too much death. Sometimes it is very difficult to be an anthropologist because of the people you live with, work with, and learn to love. Your family is no less precious for being fictive or of a different color or speaking a different language. At some point the humanness transcends the differences and death is as striking as if it were in my first family.

Sunday, March 19, 1978

. . . Lorraine says she dreams of Carrie laughing and smiling so she thinks she made the passage OK and is happy. I said I still dreamed about her, too, and sometimes awoke crying. She says that Bernard told her not to touch Carrie in her dreams or "she'll take you with her." . . . Lorraine and I talked about my dreams and decided it would be prudent to tell Bernard of them and seek his advice. She also said she thinks her brother,

Warren, is playing with Carrie and teasing her. (Families are forever. Some members are here and some family members are there—but it's still all the family.)

Tuesday, March 21, 1978

Went to Bernard's early, with tape recorder and camera—as directed. He was treating my dreams of Carrie. He said my dreams of her were my wish that she was still alive.

We walked up the canyon, past the NIYC encampment place, to a tree where Carrie's cradle is along with [other ritual items]. "A baby's cradle is like a tipi: it is a home," he said. ". . . if a child, after he out-grows the cradle, dies, then it . . . is dismantled. But nothing is broken on it. It is dismantled and the frame on the bottom is left intact and the sun visor is not broken; it is just tied on to it. Everything is left intact. The only thing is it is disassembled and then put on a tree so that——it's put on a tree that will bear fruit . . . And the reason that's done is so that it says that, 'May you have a fruitful life in This World.' Now, if a child dies, then . . . the frame is broken; the sun visor is broken and there are holes put into the sides, you know, the buckskins that cover it. They are punctured or someway——put holes in there to signify that life has gone out of it. And they put it on a tree after it's all tied together, broken up; and that means that the child will have a home when he enters The Land of Ever Summer.[2] Right?"

He held the tape recorder while I photographed the cradle and other ritual items in the tree . . . He waited until I had finished photo-graphing before speaking again, "I hated to show you this, because, you know, I thought it might be disrespectful, then, then in a way I thought that, you know, like———in your writings——that would be good for you to have. And another thing is Baby Girl [Carrie's pet name in the family] loved you and you loved her . . . Sometimes it breaks my heart to think about her. You know, especially at night when I walk around and——how beautiful that she was and the happiness that she brought our family. And, I think, well, it is only me that I'm feeling sorry for because——she never suffered in This World.——There's no suffering for her. She's in The Land of Ever Summer with all her relatives. There's my mother, my brothers, sisters, grandparents: they're all there——give her love and re-spect. So I don't like to feel like that; it's bad for me . . . we walk a hard road in This Land . . . we have something to look forward to––in The Land of Ever Summer, then it makes sense out of life, because, as I said, . . . this life is only a reflection of The Land of Ever Summer . . . So don't worry . . . women––no matter how much they run around and scream about liberation 'n' all that, in the end it is still their maternal instincts are the strongest . . . And that's what you're feeling . . . It's alright, alright. She's with those who love her. . . . It's right to cry for my aunt, my sister, or my brother: those who I lost. But not *her*.––––I should be happy,––'cause, like I said, the roads of This Land are hard; it's difficult. And she's been spared that.––––And we envy her. And it seems like that the more we envy them and the more we want to follow them––the healthier and the better life gets for us. It's like a temptation: to keep on livin'."

[End of field notes and tape transcription.]

We walked back down the canyon, cut into the old encampment area, crossed the little wash, and walked back up the hill to his house, me hugging the camera and tape recorder, as if memories of her were not enough and what was fixed on tape and film now were the reality that once she was.

Living a good life, an impeccable life by the canons of Apachean conduct and decorum, means being enfolded in the embrace of family, whether in This World or in The Real World, The Land of Ever Summer. The family endures beyond the bounds of death; so, in a very real sense, family includes a potential chiasm. There are some who are here, in the now, and others who are there, in the before and the to be; family includes those who have been, those who are, and those who will be in the matrilineage. Matrilineages, and hence families, had their beginning when The People were formed into one group so very long ago by the lake in winter's land. They continue today and, as long as there are Apaches, they will continue far into the future, both in This Shadow World and in The Real World.

It is said that the very young and the very old must be listened to carefully for they are on the edges of the crossing between the Worlds, the area I call the chiasm; they have the ability to carry messages between the Worlds, regardless of whether or not they can speak. Their actions can speak, as well as can their voices. These beliefs help in understanding the equation of infancy and old age: both are a time of wisdom; both are a time when one is properly dependent upon others for sustenance and nurturance; both are within reach of the crossing point, the middle point, the fulcrum upon which This World and The Real World balance; and both must be respected for what they can provide to those of us in the other two realms of existence in This World—childhood and adulthood. We who are independent must assume the responsibilities not only of providing for the infants and the aged but also for the continued existence of This World in its physical and ritual senses. We must maintain the balance, and hence harmony, that comes into being when we in the middle positions attend properly to the infants and elderlies. We cannot shirk our duties or the universe may become unbalanced—literally unhinged—and cease to exist; or it may begin to exist in ways that are inimical to our own well being.

If the universe is *guzhuguja*, properly balanced and in order, then *juułgu*, being encircled, can be expected: children will be born and the old will die; the universe will continue as set into motion by Creator. Both the encirclement of the base metaphor and that of the family will endure. But when children die out of their time, the very fabric of the universe is rent. It is an indication of things being out of balance, of the order being upset, of it being a time to attend properly to one's own life and that of the tribe as a whole, perhaps even of an intrusion of The Real World into This Shadow World for purposes to be divined. A baby may die to take information back into The Real World; or there may be darker reasons.

Bernard Second suspected witchery was being practiced against his family because of his power. No person having senses intact would move against one of power; but it is easy to move against the weak, such as babies and some women or children. Regardless of the reason for the death, it occasions a chiasm in that the living are forced to confront their own lives and what they may be doing, or not doing, that perhaps makes it more likely that the inherent balance and order will be upset. The chiasm is also opened to allow the passage of the newly deceased from This Shadow World into The Real World of The Land of Ever Summer.

The belief at Mescalero that sometimes little ones are taken early because there is a need for communication between the Worlds must always be considered before precipitous action is taken, especially if witchery is suspected. Since the very young, like the very old, are closer to the point of articulation between the Worlds—the chiasm—they are excellent messengers. While the term "chiasm" is my analytic construct, it is built into the visual model of the base metaphor, as this discussion of March 19, 1978 between me and Bernard illustrates:

> CRF: . . . what's in the circle? [Bernard had just drawn ⊕ in my field notebook.]
>
> BS: Life, the universe; everything that is.
>
> CRF: All right. Now what are these two lines? . . . [indicating the lines of ⊕].
>
> BS: Four directions. There are, if you want to think of time, then think of time in all; *everything in this world is in four* . . . From the east to the west is the understanding of the world. And that means to show politeness, thanks for all the beings and plants of the world. From the north to south is a different power; that is the power of human endurance and all the consequences that hit humanity. And when I say humanity, I mean my people. *The middle is the point of understanding. . .*

Whether for good or ill, whether brought into being purposefully or as a consequence of other actions, the chiasm allowing passage between the Worlds—the middle point of understanding—is accessible at death and that means that there must be care, ritual care, taken to assure the stability of both places and times. Where Anglos postulate entropy, Apaches envision rampant chaos with no underlying order and with a dizzying increase in energy turned to no productive use, as with a fibrillating heart, when the universe is out of balance. Ritual allows humans again to assume the control necessary for the proper running of the universe. Not only is death brought into the realm of ritual, but also excessive mourning, such as I experienced at Carrie's death, is subjected to the stabilizing effects of ritual.

Death and funeral rituals at Mescalero conform to the base metaphor while also reinforcing it and reversing it. The base metaphor encapsulates all that is necessary to live a good and proper life while maintaining responsibilities for keeping the universe wound and running. But death is not living; and, even with a belief that the dead enter The Real World, The Land of Ever Summer, they do not enter it as living beings such as we are familiar with on the earth's surface. Crossing the chiasm separating life and death alters the kind and quality of living. Therefore, it is inappropriate to do as we, the living in This World, do; rather, it is appropriate to reverse what is normal while still conforming to the ordering principles of balance and harmony. The base metaphor is not disrupted by death; it merely is run backward, or differently, for a period of ritual time. Harmony and balance have been altered so the base metaphor's usual dictates are also altered.

In van Gennep's productive model of rites of passage, whether life crises (such as birth, death, marriage, etc.) or calendrical (seasonal festivals), there are three stages: "rites of separation from a previous world, *preliminal rites,* those executed during the transitional stage *liminal (or threshold) rites,* and the ceremonies of incorporation into the new world, *postliminal rites"* (van Gennep 1960:21). Turner (1967:93–110), working from van Gennep's model, brought anthropological attention to bear especially on the importance of the middle stage, the liminal, that he termed "betwixt and between."

In most cases at Mescalero, the dead are buried on the fourth day after death. These four days are liminal ones for the newly deceased, as well as for the relatives. The family has been ruptured and the newly deceased person has not yet joined the family on the other side of the chiasm in The Real World. This time is the most dangerous for those still living, as both the deceased wishes to have some of the still living make the journey, too, and the still living are tempted most to join their family in The Real World.

The newly deceased person is neither in This World nor yet incorporated into The Real World—the person is, and is in, the chiasm. It is this between-ness that characterizes liminality. As Turner (1967:93) put it, "if our basic model of society is that of a 'structure of positions,' we must regard the period of margin or 'liminality' as an interstructural situation." In this instance, the two structures are those of This Shadow World and The Real World; the newly deceased is at the middle point of understanding, the middle of the butterfly or Lorenz effect, poised at the articulation of here and there. Rather than being in a state of transition, Turner (1967:94) preferred "to regard transition as a process, a becoming, and in the case of *rites de passage* even a transformation." This latter view accords well with Apachean perceptions, for the newly deceased person is believed still to be present, although invisible, while gathering information to share with those in The Real World; the newly deceased is in process of moving from This Shadow World to The Land of Ever Summer.

It is also during this transition process that the newly deceased is most often seen, fleetingly or in signs, by the still alive. The newly deceased must "gather tracks," revisit those places and people of importance to her/him during the lifetime, no matter how brief or how long the person existed in This Shadow World. As one of the proverbs states, "Shik?ekehe nahush daał," [I will walk again in the tracks I have left.]

Without the proper ritual accompaniment, the newly deceased may be caught permanently in the transition process, forever entombed in and at the chiasm, unable to return to This Shadow World nor to be incorporated into The Real World. Therefore, the rituals for the dead are of particular importance.

In contemporary times, it is most usual for bodies to be taken to funeral homes for preparation according to state law. Clothing and jewelry will be taken to the funeral home by family members; sometimes the clothing is contemporary, but most people prefer to clothe bodies in their best Indian traditional clothing.

Some people maintain that the dead were buried immediately upon death, in traditional times, while others maintain that the four day period between death and burial has always been the norm. I tend to believe that the four day delay was preferred in more recent (i.e., within 400–500 years) times, because of the Shell River Prophecy, a prophecy given to the Mescalero by one of their holy men at a place they call Shell River [Yellowstone River?], usually located in present-day Montana near the Wyoming border and Yellowstone National Park. The event occurred during the time the people who became known as the Mescalero Apache were migrating into the Southwest. The holy man appeared to be dead, only to manifest life again on the fourth day. It developed that he had been on a spirit journey to The Real World where he learned, and shared, much that was of importance to the Apache people at that time; he also delivered a prophecy that provided information about what was to occur in the future and that assisted the Mescalero in finding and recognizing their new homelands as they were traveling south from their original home in the Northwestern part of Canada.

Ritual specialists in particular maintain that people should not be buried prior to the fourth day after death, just in case the person, whether holy man or ritual specialist or not, is really on a spirit journey as happened in past time. Waiting for four days is also in keeping with general cultural precepts. So, while people may say that the newly deceased should be buried as soon as possible, it often works out that what that means is that people are buried four days after death occurs.

Notification of death should be given first to family members by family members, but as is often the case, especially in alcohol related deaths from accidents, the news spreads quickly throughout the tribe. Extended family and close friends gather, either at the home of the deceased or at the home of the eldest member of the matrilineage, to offer assistance. This assistance takes many forms, from provision of food or money or goods to providing services necessary for the maintenance of daily life, such as child care, cooking, errand running, and so on. Bereaved people have a tendency to ignore their own needs, so cooked food is often brought to the home where the family gathers or, without being asked, people simply cook what is available. This home is also the location of planning and provisioning. When food is brought to the home or when one comes to grieve, negotiations also occur that result in being sure that the body is properly adorned with shawls and blankets, in paying for the casket and associated funeral expenses, in seeing to the ritual specialist to conduct the funeral and those needed for graveside rites, and especially in insuring that someone from the extended family will always be at the funeral home while it is open and the body may be viewed.

Apaches prefer to have family members present with the newly deceased at all times to keep the dead body company, to protect it from malevolence, to insure it is treated with dignity, and to greet those who come to mourn or who come out of respect for either the dead person or other members of the family.

To show respect for the dead, friends send flowers to the funeral home and bring shawls or blankets with them when they visit the body or when they visit the home where the extended family gathers. The shawls and blankets are draped on the coffin, with their depth signifying the numbers of people who held the dead person in high regard. They are also a visible statement of the closeness, or bond, between the newly dead and the giver.

Since babies have been in This World only a short time, it cannot be expected that there would be many blankets or shawls donated. Thus, Lorraine's request that I bring a baby Pendleton blanket was one that is understandable, given the conventions surrounding the proper way to treat the dead. Carrie was only four and a half months old when she died—much too young to be gifted with shawls and blankets. Had she been older, her own dance shawls would have been part of the funeral goods draping her coffin; instead, her mother made tiny shawls for her of soft antelope skin and double-knit fabric. It is not considered to be a proper funeral without gifts of shawls and blankets, so family members provided what is usually provided by the community at large. Had the funeral been for an adult, then some of the shawls and blankets would have been redistributed to those who assisted the family or who came a long distance to attend the funeral, for there is a strong, though not verbalized, belief in reciprocity: what goes around comes back around. As an example, when Bernard Second died, I brought my full-size Pendleton blanket, my shawl, and my daughter's shawl—all of which draped his body. However, Bernard had been adamant that he not be buried with "things," but rather that they be shared and distributed among his many friends and extended family. So the Pendleton was given to the president of the tribe, as recognition of his attendance at the funeral and as thanks for the eulogy he delivered. What had been my daughter's shawl was given to a Western Apache medicine lady who had traveled several hundred miles to attend the funeral. My own shawl was buried with him for several reasons: as a comfort to me, to insure that he had something that had been close to me close to him so he would be less likely to try to take me with him; as a public sign of the nature of our relationship, and to show the family in The Real World the esteem in which he was held in This Shadow World.

For adult funerals it is usual to have the flowers that flanked the body in the funeral home—and that were then placed in front of the altar in church, finally being carried to the grave site—given to participants and helpers, save for a few that are left at the grave site. The funeral described here, because it was for a baby, differs in minor details from those for adults; in large structure, however, it conforms to the expected norms.

After notification and provisioning (both very important aspects of Apachean generosity), there must be the viewing (at the funeral home) and the funeral service (at one of the churches on the reservation or, rarely, at the grave site.) Finally, there are the burial rites that take place at the grave site. In these events there is a constant interplay between Native and Anglo sites and customs. The body is removed to a funeral home (Anglo) where it is dressed and decorated (Native) so it may be viewed (Anglo) prior to the church funeral (Anglo) and actual burial (begins as Anglo and ends as Native.) The mix of Anglo and Native practices is characteristic of contemporary life on the Mescalero Apache Indian Reservation.

Almost everyone at Mescalero today professes to be Christian, at least nominally, while also maintaining a belief in some aspects of Native religion. In addition to the Catholic presence, there are mission churches maintained by the Assembly of God, Baptists, Church of Jesus Christ of Latter Day Saints, and Dutch Reformed as well as meetings of smaller groups without special buildings, such as Bahai. There is no shortage of Christian (or non-Indian) services from among which to choose. Many of the Christian sects also have burial rites that are performed at graveside. Even while Anglo customs are followed, they are given an Apachean character by actions that are appropriate to Mescalero decorum but are not a part of Anglo practice: actions such as the wailing (accepted as a proper way to express emotion at a funeral) or the redistribution of donated goods. At the conclusion of the Anglo grave site rites, the Anglos—whether from the churches or funeral home—leave the grave site. It is at this point that the Native funeral and burial rituals begin.

Either after or during the placing of personal belongings that were not distributed to others,[3] Apache men—most often religious or civic leaders—speak of the newly deceased. The speaker is recognized by his movement to a position to the immediate east of the grave. At times it is arranged in advance who will speak, and at other times one who wishes to speak will make that desire known at the grave site; I have never known anyone to be refused who wished to speak. In contrast to Anglo practice, if the newly dead person was not a good or pleasant person, this will be mentioned, along with whatever positive can be spoken about the deceased. For a child, of course, there is only good that can be mentioned. These speeches are always extemporaneous and are analogous to Quakers' "speaking in the Light," for it is believed that only truth can be spoken, or the words will choke the person trying to speak. Sometimes the speech is poetry and beauty; at other times it contains an admonition to those still alive to change their ways before it is too late. Often the speaker notes the void left with those in This World when one moves into The Real World; and often comfort is extended to the closest family members of the newly deceased. In contrast to the formal speeches made during tribal meetings, these speeches have only two parts: the substance and a closing. There is no formulaic opening validating the speaker's authority to speak and there is no recapitulation of the essential point. Yet, they are still considered to be in balance. By the division into only two segments, the speeches seem to have an implicit message that there is the here and the there and that the speech is designed to close the gap between the two.

While the speeches occur, there is often a continuation of burial rituals. Sometimes, as for highly esteemed people such as Bernard Second, all other burial rituals are suspended during the speeches and eulogies. Whether during or after the speeches the first dirt thrown in is by women and men in the family—that is, in the matrilineage. Sometimes the motions used to toss in the dirt recapitulate the blessing sequence with a small amount from each of the cardinal directions in turn. The rest of the dirt is then shoveled in the grave by family members and close male friends. Women do not participate in the shoveling of the dirt nor in the placement of the rocks that outline most graves.

In normal practice, any ritual action begins in the east; but for burials, the first rock is usually laid at the head which is to the north, if at all possible. Then a rock is placed at the foot, or south end. A bracket is opened by the east side placed rocks that fill the space between the north and south placed rocks; the only opening is therefore to the west, the direction that the dead take in their beginning passage to The Land of Ever Summer. Finally the bracket is closed with the filling in of the west side rocks from both the north and the south; the movements deny the usual ritual sequence of east, south, west, north and contradict the blessing sequence of the cardinals in east to north order followed by connecting lines from south to north and west to east. Or, alternatively, the first rock will be placed in the west with the next three marking, in turn, the south, east, and north; this, of course, reverses the normal blessing sequence with a resultant non-life bracket being formed. Regardless of which formula for rock placement is followed, the newly dead person is now irrevocably separated from the still living and has returned to the womb, the womb of the Earth Mother. The chiasm opened by death has been closed by burial and each realm now traces its own pathways, until once again they interconnect through a chiasm.

The life path tracings for the still living include several additional rituals, beyond those at the grave site. Upon leaving the graveside, the mourners pick plants—sometimes living, sometimes dormant—to use to begin the ritual cleansing, "to brush off death." As soon as possible, bodies will be bathed, hair washed, and clothes changed to separate further the things associated with death from living people.

Recently, people began sharing a meal after a burial; it is self-consciously seen as a time of incorporating the still living into a new whole that continues despite the loss of a loved and respected one. It is also a time when Apachean generosity is again on display. Nonresidents of the reservation who attend these meals are usually given food to take with them, for their own journey home. When the rites are for a child, it is customary for the meal to include only family members; for an adult, the meal is offered to all who attended the funeral and burial.

It has also become customary for any who so desire to reminisce about the deceased after the funeral and burial—during the meal, immediately after the meal, or at another, smaller gathering several hours after the meal. At this time, jokes about the deceased or those sitting the wake are rampant; people both laugh and cry during these times. Or perhaps some will sing songs particularly associated with the deceased or songs designed to speed the newly deceased on the journey to The Land of Ever Summer, if a ritual specialist is present and knows such songs. Each of these activities serves to bind together the survivors and, through grief shared, move all to a state of acceptance.

Attention is paid to natural phenomena as well. While Apaches almost always attend to natural phenomena, immediately after death and burial the phenomena are taken as signs of the passage of the deceased or as coded information from The Real World. Usually the interpretations can be made by the families, but at times ritual or religious specialists will be asked for their interpretations, which will then be discussed and compared with lay interpretations.

Although not a part of the notes for the baby's funeral, it is quite common to have a medicine lady or medicine man, that is, a ritual specialist whose expertise is in herbs and healing, perform a ghost medicine ceremony that rededicates a home to the living by exorcising remnants of the recently deceased. In traditional times such ceremonies were not as necessary, since it was common practice to burn both the tipi home and the belongings of the deceased. Now, however, with the move to a consumer economy and with much of a family's assets in expensive tangible goods, including houses, it is rare for personal belongings to be burned. To my knowledge, homes are never destroyed, although a family may well move to another one soon after the death of a person—particularly if the person had died in the house and sometimes even if the person who died simply had been living in the house.

At the conclusion of these rituals, including the ghost medicine ceremony and perhaps moving, it is expected that people will resume their normal lives. That is not to say that the recently deceased are forgotten; they are not. Rather, it means that the separate tracings of lifeways are expected to be following their proper paths so that the pathway of those from The Real World no longer intersects with or greatly influences the pathways of those in This World—until, that is, another chiasm is opened either through a ceremony or through another death or birth. It is believed that once proper funeral, burial, and postburial rituals are completed, the essential order of that segment of the universe is restored. If a person finds it difficult to continue normal life, then more stringent measures are taken that are designed to restore the person to proper order, so that she or he will not upset restored balance and harmony through excessive grieving.

As my notes quoted above indicate, Lorraine, even though she was Carrie's mother, made what Anglos would call a good adjustment while I made a poor one. She had certainly not forgotten her child, but she was at peace knowing, through her dreams, that her child was incorporated into the portion of her lineage made up of deceased family members in The Real World.

By contrast, I could not stop having nightmares. Whatever Anglo anxieties may have produced them, they were treated in an Apache fashion, as Bernard forced me once again into the anthropologist's role by directing me to take camera and tape recorder on our brief trek into the canyon. By showing me the purposefully destroyed cradle and by forcing me to confront the finality of death, while simultaneously "telling" me both that I had a job to do and that my feelings were legitimate, he was teaching me the Apache way of coping with death. One feels badly, talks about the feelings, grieves, understands the feelings, and then lets them go. I had not let them go and was allowing them to color my life and, by implication, the lives of my fictive family. But, rather than chastise me for my inappropriate behavior, Bernard told me that sometimes he, too, missed her and that he considered my excessive reaction to be a natural one brought about by my being a woman and a mother, even if a liberated one. He kept switching pronouns and, in so doing, equated me with his feelings and him with mine while also telling me that some sorrow is not appropriate. What he did not say, but what he intimated, was that a new order, one without Carrie, was in place and I could only cause upset and chaos by insisting on the primacy of an old order.

Carrie's cradle was broken, not disassembled; her cradle home had been freed to serve her in The Land of Ever Summer. The broken cradle was placed in a non-fruit-bearing tree—such an explicit metaphor that it required no explanation. Her home was in The Land of Ever Summer; mine is in This Shadow World, if I dared face it and decided "to keep on livin'." I could take my Anglo anthropologist things—notes, pictures, and recordings—and cling to them, if I needed to, rather than recognizing that the pathway I was to follow was one being trod by living family members while Carrie's was with the ones no longer living in This World. But, whether I accepted or rejected the temptation to keep on living, it was time to stop crying for death.

CHAPTER 8

Living Life's Circle

Until very recently Mescalero Apaches were nomadic, when considered over long periods of time, or transhumant, when viewed from a shorter time perspective. That is to say, when vision encompasses hundreds or thousands of years, there is a steady nomadic trail of south-southeastward movement for Apachean people; but when time is collapsed, nomadic movement is less apparent and the people can be seen as transhumant, moving in a pattern defined by the natural resources being utilized. In the short term, Apachean people established camps where they lived for seasons or years before again moving further southward. At these camps, women, children, and the elderly had a tendency to stay put seasonally while the young men warrior-hunters followed the animals upon which the people depended for their protein, bringing their kills back to the base camp as either fresh or dried meat. The living situation then was of a semi-permanent base camp utilized for several seasons or years and from which people moved to hunt or moved seasonally to exploit various vegetal resources before all returned to the base camp, usually for the winter season. Base camps were then moved as dictated by animal migrations or as vegetal resources were depleted, or in danger of becoming so. Some maintain that there was a steady movement southward, on the eastern side of the Rocky Mountains, in accordance with the Shell River Prophecy. Regardless of motivation, the patterns of short term transhumance and long term nomadism holds.

Regardless of the time depth under examination, Apachean people were mobile, not sedentary. Elderly people, when I first began dedicated work at Mescalero in 1974, used to tell me that it was very difficult for their parents and grandparents—those first on the reservation when it was established—to get used to living in the same house at the same site year after year, for they believed that the ground got "dirty" from too much human habitation and needed to "rest." Indeed, this attitude is still quite prevalent today and accounts for the vigorous scrubbings some houses receive periodically. A sedentary life style is one that has only recently been imposed on Apaches as a result of the reservation system, that, for them, has been a fact of life only since the 1870s.

There is much house changing even today. Deaths are one reason people change houses. Another reason is modernization, as when a family moves to a temporary home while their permanent one is brought to code or modernized by the addition of facilities or rooms. Housing has been a primary concern of Wendell Chino and the various tribal councils he has led, since, as late as the early 1970s, much reservation housing was substandard. With so many families needing better housing or just adequate housing, a lottery system was established whereby all those eligible for improved housing were placed in a pool from which were drawn the names of those who would get the next available new housing. Housing assigned by this system sometimes seemed almost like a game of musical chairs; people would live in their new house for a short period before "trading" with another family. In an informal study I did in the mid-1970s, with a smaller sample follow-up in the mid-1980s, it was apparent that trades were usually done to allow relatives through the matrilineage to live closer to each other. Mobility is still a fact of Apachean life, although it is mobility circumscribed by new, and sometimes bothersome, rules and regulations.

When a people are mobile, whether in the long or short term, they have a tendency not to acquire vast amounts of heavy goods. This, for Apachean people, was especially true before they acquired, or reacquired, the horse. Prior to the widespread use of horses in the seventeenth century, all movement was accomplished on foot, with dogs as pack animals and the motive power for travois. No sensible person, who must contemplate a move in a few seasons or years, is going to encumber him/herself voluntarily with heavy belongings. Nor are they going to be willing to cart around a heavy load of religious paraphernalia. Religion, and its accoutrements, must be as portable as household and personal goods, an idea foreign to those of us with the Western European model of life firmly entrenched and who have our own long tradition of huge, permanent edifices built to serve both spiritual needs and as large reminders of the transitory nature of life.

The presence or absence of large religious structures, such as the magnificent European cathedrals, make important cultural statements that are reinforced through other cultural means. In our American elementary school social studies classes, for example, we teach our children about the importance of the sky and natural phenomena to agricultural peoples; we tell them how the annual inundation of the land by the Nile undergirded the ancient Egyptian economy as well as their mythology, cosmology, and, of course, their calendar. Depending upon the texts we use in our schools, we often also teach similar arguments for other ancient peoples. The assumptions in such texts and, indeed, the scholarly assumptions until very recently, are that calendrics and astronomical phenomena were necessary to agriculturalists but not to hunters and gatherers, those presumed to have a lesser level of cultural complexity. The sky was vital to sedentary people and not to nomadic or transhumant people—that is the essential message. Many even believed that once people perceived the regularities of the sky, it was possible for them to cease being foragers and hunters and to become sedentary. But, as is apparent in the chapters of this book, an intimate knowledge of the sky was, and is, also the property of a people who chose, and still choose, to be nonagriculturalists. People can be skywatchers and skyknowers without being ground tillers.

The Mescalero Apache vision of the cosmos forms their perceptions of many other systems of proper behavior. Apaches conceptualize a vast circularity that encompasses the entirety of the universe, both that known and that unknowable to mere people. Their vision of life is a cosmic one, a cosmovision. In their sojourn here, they live life's circle.

Apachean people had no cathedrals, no elaborate medicine wheels, no bejeweled or encrusted symbols of religious fervor, and no permanent structures against which to measure or contemplate the workings of the celestial sphere. Instead they had $^n da\textipa{?}i$ $bijuuł$ $sia\textipa{?}$, ⊕, life's living circle. It is such a simple figure, only a quartered circle, yet it encapsulates so very much. It is not only the design for living but also it is the design for changing. As Apaches often say, "Nutł'eł shihintslé na-gutlé," (strength comes from change).

The quartered circle is everything—and it is just a little circle with a cross. It is a portable religious/philosophical system that is one of the more powerful mnemonics I have ever encountered. It "speaks" of the beginningtime and of Creator and Creation as well as of behavior in the contemporary world. It speaks of how things were, are, should be, and will be.

The most powerful symbols are those that speak multivocalically, with many voices appropriate for many occasions, and with polysemy, with many meanings, as Turner (1967:50) notes: "By these terms [poly-semy and multivocalic] I mean that a single symbol may stand for many things . . . For a few symbols have to represent a whole culture and its material environment." For the Mescalero Apache, the dominant or key symbol, $\oplus$, is an even more powerful evocation than what Turner had in mind working from his Ndembu (African) data. Not only does it repre-sent the culture and its material environment, but also it represents ob-servations of the natural world and the behavioral imperatives that are said to flow from those observations. In other words, it is the base meta-phor upon which all social, psychological, philosophical, and moral life is predicated. Perhaps best of all, it is easily portable and need not even be represented in permanent form; it can be almost instantly created as the need arises for its use. And in each re-creation of the base metaphor, the people are reminded of its almost infinite layers and nuances of meaning.

Turner (1967:50−51) also addressed the meaning of symbols:

When we talk about the "meaning" of a symbol, we must be careful to distinguish between at least three levels or fields of meaning. These I propose to call: (1) the level of indigenous interpretation (or, briefly, the exegetical meaning); (2) the operational meaning; and (3) the positional meaning. The exegetical meaning is obtained from questioning indige-nous informants about observed ritual behavior. Here again one must distinguish between information given by ritual specialists and infor-mation given by laymen, that is, between esoteric and exoteric interpre-tations . . .

On the other hand, much light may be shed on the role of the ritual symbol by equating its meaning with its use, by observing what the Ndembu do with it, and not only what they say about it. This is what I call the operational meaning, and this level has the most bearing on problems of social dynamics. For the observer must consider not only the symbol but the structure and composition of the group that handles it or performs mimetic acts with direct reference to it . . .

The positional meaning of a symbol derives from its relationship to other symbols in a totality, a *Gestalt,* whose elements acquire their significance from the system as a whole. This level of meaning is directly related to the important property of ritual symbols . . . , their polysemy.

Turner's system of symbolic meaning moves from that based with the people, the exegetical, to that primarily dependent upon the observer, the operational, to that of a different level of abstraction, the positional, where the focus switches from questioning and observation to analysis. When the meanings are used in combination, this system provides an important means of understanding the symbolic representations of another culture.

With regard to the Apachean base metaphor, the exegetical material has been provided in previous chapters through quotations, primarily from Bernard Second. His eloquence requires no further elaboration. On the operational level are my own comments and, often, misunderstandings, as well as the ways in which I was instructed in proper Apachean behavior. The positional level is that around which this book is organized. For the Mescalero Apache, the polysemy of their primary visual symbol, the quartered circle with its myriad of associated meanings, is collapsed into the dense, yet simple, drawing of the base metaphor. In order to access its multivocality and its polysemy, I postulated chiasm that corresponds to the center point of the visually represented symbol.

Turner's data were ideational and then represented in a variety of specific elements within the Ndembu natural and created environment. My data focus on one symbol which itself generates the others, rather than finding them, ready-made, in existence in the world about the people. Chapter 4 illustrated a few of the almost limitless forms that can be generated from splitting, reduplicating, and combining the elements in the visual depiction of the base metaphor. Such elasticity allows not only new ideational interpretations but also new geometric models of the ideational. It quite literally is all "the same thing," although it took me years to see how.

This same elasticity is what has allowed the Mescalero Apache culture to remain so vital and strong despite quite literally four hundred years of pressure to accommodate to Spanish, Mexican, or American perceptions of the proper ways to live, think, believe, and behave. And, I am willing to predict, it is the elasticity of the base metaphor and its visual analogue that will allow the continued persistence of Mescalero-ness into the future. That is not to say that there will not be change; there will indeed be change, some of it radical. But as long as the people manage to envision, through chiasms, modifications that are "the same thing" and to cast changes in living, thinking, believing, and behaving in terms of the base metaphor, they should endure as a separate, identifiable people, a people whose ethnicity provides the means of living life's circle.

My only concern is that alcoholism, with all its destructive ramifications, will become even more of a problem than it is currently. Unfortunately, the established behavioral pattern of taking responsibility for one's own life at a time when it is appropriate to do so applies to alcoholics as well. Alcoholic behavior is self-destructive and all too often has devastating consequences for others as well. But the noninterference principle operates very strongly at Mescalero. In abiding by this principle, many parents, for instance, do everything possible to get their children ready for school but believe deeply that, if the child does not wish to attend school, there is virtually nothing the parents can do—even forcing attendance will be unsuccessful—for the child, it is believed, will sit there but not pay attention and therefore will not learn when s/he is forced to do something against individual will. Being an alcoholic is a decision of individual will for which no one else feels responsibility—either in genesis or termination. Alcohol besotted brains do not see the beauty in the universe, cannot remember the songs that reconstitute life, do not recognize the transformations of the base metaphor in everyday life, and—while still loved—those with such brains are incapable of living up to the expectations for normal behavior with its generosity, sharing, pride, and dignity. This *can* destroy the people, despite the ubiquity and elasticity of $\oplus$ and the base metaphor it represents.

When contemplating the worst possible scenario, that of losing all that it means to be Mescalero Apache, Bernard Second used to shake his head, as if to clear the unpleasant internal visions, and state that it could never happen as long as the religion was intact and people still had eyes to see and the will to watch the natural universe as it apparently slowly spins around us. It is all there in the sky, in the four seasons, in the solstices and equinoxes, in the circularity of repetitive patterns, in the balance between plants and animals, rain and sunshine, thunder and lightning, night and day. All one has to do is attend to that surrounding life. As Bernard spoke into my tape recorder on March 19, 1978 saying,

> . . . all this together, God has given that to us. It says, "Here. This is what I have made you, made you a correct people, a good people, and I have given you *all* these things . . . because I want you to show Me what you are about . . . Therefore, I have given you *all* this that you might live on it. Bikʔéguda ʔ-i ʔinda ʔ, shi zha! Shi zha!" That's what He said to us and then He said, . . . (The Creator, but there again, who knows if He's masculine or feminine . . .), "Diiyan nashiyaakuguł," split Me into fours and I am the four directions of the universe again. And bring Me back together again; I am *one* again."

The Creator is all around and is also manifest in ⊕, as is all of life and living. All one has to do is look around and listen. "Listen to the Wind," Bernard would tell me, "it speaks to you." When we forget petty humanness and listen to the sound of the universe, it becomes clear both that life's circle is an on-going one and that people can live life's circle. It has been through the holy men, the singers, the religious specialists, that the Mescalero Apache people have maintained their sense of being a people. Those same specialists have consistently reiterated the importance of the base metaphor, the importance of paying attention to the natural world, of listening to the music of the spheres, and of seeing *guzhuguja* [everything in order] in *juułgu* [circularity], as well as recognizing both of them in *ⁿdaʔi bijuuł sią ʔ*.

"Can people draw the universe?" I asked Bernard during the March 1978 visit to Mescalero.

"Sure!" he replied, as he took my notebook and pen and carefully drew:

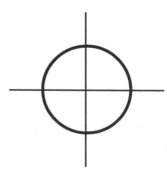

A Brief History of
Mescalero Apaches

THE PAST

Picture a vast open area stretching as far as the eye can see. In every direction the land is so flat that it appears to be like a plate. Covering the land is a variety of grasses, some so tall they reach to the chest of a full-grown man. Cutting through the grasses and deeply scarring the land are arroyos, some formed in times so long distant that they have cut thousands of feet below the surface of the land. Dotted over the land are moving black masses of buffalo (*Bison bison*), great shaggy beasts with massive heads. Far to the west, on clear days bereft of moist air and dust, the peaks of what we now call the Sacramento Mountains, the tail of the Rocky Mountains, can be seen.

East of the mountains on the vast plains the Spanish were soon to name the Llano Estacado, there are small bands of people, moving in synchrony with the buffalo. They almost disappear into the tall, thick grasses; their presence can be discerned only through smoke from their fires unless one is very close to them indeed.

Francisco Vázquez Coronado and his company of adventurers/explorers came into this land on their 1540–1542 expedition from Mexico. They sought gold and other metals to enrich both themselves and the Spanish crown; they sought new lands to conquer and control and, with the labor of the people on those lands they expected riches from the mines they expected to find. They were to extend the Spanish sphere of influence, if not control, to encompass the unknown lands north of the Valley of Mexico and into present-day New Mexico, Texas, and Arizona. The priests among them sought souls. For the glory of God and king they moved up the Rio Concho through central Mexico to, and beyond, the Rio Grande, through what is now Arizona, Texas, and New Mexico and finally onto the Llano Estacado.

Historians cite the Spaniards for their plethora of documents. They were inveterate letter writers, petitioners to king in Spain or to his viceregent in Mexico City. Whenever they traveled, they kept detailed lists of the contents of carts and trunks. The priests were no less busy than the citizen-soldiers in this regard, writing to their clerical superiors or to King or Viceroy. When they traveled, whether priest, citizen-soldier, or military, at least one among their number was detailed to keep the daily log containing information on how far they had traveled, what they had seen, places they had named, people they had encountered, relationships among themselves, and personal comments. These documents reside in archives in Spain, Mexico, and the United States and, for contemporary scholars, are more valuable than the gold the early explorers sought, for the documents are a window to the past.

Pedro Castañeda was one who provided a narrative of the Coronado expedition. In his narrative, there is the first mention of people believed to be ancestral to present day Apaches, encountered shortly after leaving Cicuye (later termed Pecos.) Now there is only a remnant of the massive church the Spaniards later built there in the midst of the pueblo whose ruins lie almost halfway between present day Santa Fe and Las Vegas, New Mexico. The low walls of the prehistoric Indian pueblo have been restored and stabilized to allow our minds' eyes to envision what the site must have been like in the eighteenth century. But all that was yet to come as Castañeda wrote almost two hundred years previously. He states,

> The army started from Cicuye, leaving the village at peace and, as it seemed, contented . . . Proceeding toward the plains, which are all on the other side of the mountains, after four days' journey they came to a river with a large deep current, which flowed down toward Cicuye, and they named this the Cicuye river [Pecos River] . . . After ten days more they came to some settlements of people who lived like Arabs and who are called Querechos in that region. They had seen the cows [buffalo] for two days. These folks live in tents made of the tanned skins of the

cows. They travel around near the cows, killing them for food. They did nothing unusual when they saw our army, except to come out of their tents to look at us, after which they came to talk with the advance guard, and asked who we were . . . That they were very intelligent is evident from the fact that although they conversed by means of signs they made themselves understood so well that there was no need of an interpreter . . . These folks started off from here the next day with a lot of dogs which dragged their possessions . . . they do not have any crockery in this region. They do not make gourds, nor sow corn, nor eat bread, but instead raw meat—or only half cooked—and fruit . . . people follow the cows, hunting them and tanning the skins to take to the settlements [the pueblos] in the winter to sell, since they go there to pass the winter, each company going to those which are nearest . . . there are a good many more of these people than there are of those at the settlements. They have better figures, are better warriors, and are more feared. They travel like the Arabs, with their tents and troops of dogs loaded with poles and having Moorish pack saddles with girths. When the load gets disarranged, the dogs howl, calling some one to fix them right. These people eat raw flesh and drink blood. They do not eat human flesh. They are a kind people and not cruel. They are faithful friends. They are able to make themselves very well understood by means of signs. They dry the flesh in the sun, cutting it thin like a leaf, and when dry they grind it like meal to keep it and make a sort of sea soup of it to eat. A handful thrown into a pot swells up so as to increase very much. They season it with fat, which they always try to secure when they kill a cow. They empty a large gut and fill it with blood, and carry this around the neck to drink when they are thirsty. (Castañeda in Winship 1964:232–36, 279–80)

Tall, well-built, kind, friendly, intelligent people: not at all the picture dime novelists and Hollywood would portray. Nor is it the picture received through the accounts of the United States Army or settlers some three hundred years later. The Spaniards met the Bedouins of the American plains and found them to be unafraid of a formidable mounted Spanish force. Coronado's expedition left the Valley of Mexico with 1,000 horses, 500 cows, 5,000 rams and ewes, and more than 1,500 Indians and servants, as well as the explorers and churchmen (Winship 1964: 302). While the group had shrunk somewhat before reaching the plains, they were, nonetheless, such a presence that some Pueblo Indians capitulated upon sight of them. Not so the Querechos. They greeted and questioned the newcomers, seemingly as interested in the strangers as the strangers were in them.

Jaramillo, another member of Coronado's expedition, also commented on the Querechos.

> We found Indians among these first cows, who were, on this account, called Querechos by those in the flat-roof houses [the pueblos]. They do not live in houses, but have some sets of poles which they carry with them to make some huts at the places where they stop, which serve them for houses. They tie these poles together at the top and stick the bottoms into the ground, covering them with some cowskins which they carry around, and which, as I have said, serve them for houses. From what was learned of these Indians, all their human needs are supplied by these cows, for they are fed and clothed and shod from these. (Jaramillo in Winship 1964:376)

Most of the natives of the New World that had been encountered previously by the Spaniards lived in houses that were enough like European houses to appear sensible and familiar. But those who lived in tipis could only be likened to some of the Arabs with whom the Spanish had become familiar through being conquered by Arabic-speaking peoples and through the travels of some Spanish into northern Africa. Even so, Querechan homes and their total dependence upon the buffalo were novel practices to be commented upon at length. Another account from the Coronado expedition states,

> Four days from this village [Cicuye or Pecos] . . . [is] a country as level as the sea, and in these plains there was such a multitude of cows that they are numberless . . . Having proceeded many days through these plains . . . came to a settlement of about 200 inhabited houses. The houses were made of the skins of the cows, tanned white, like pavilions or army tents. The maintenance or sustenance of these Indians comes entirely from the cows, because they neither sow nor reap corn. With the skins they make their houses, with the skins they clothe and shoe themselves, of the skins they make rope, and also of the wool; from the sinews they make thread, with which they sew their clothes and also their houses; from the bones they make awls; the dung serves them for wood, because there is nothing else in that country; the stomachs serve them for pitchers and vessels from which they drink; they live on the flesh; they sometimes eat it half roasted and warmed over the dung, at

other times raw . . . they drink the blood just as it leaves the cows . . .
they have no other means of livelihood. These people have dogs like
those in this country, except that they are somewhat larger, and they
load these dogs like beasts of burden, and make saddles for them like
our pack saddles, and they fasten them with their leather thongs, and
these make their backs sore on the withers like pack animals. When they
go hunting, they load these with their necessities, and when they
move—for these Indians are not settled in one place, since they travel
wherever the cows move, to support themselves—these dogs carry their
houses, and they have the sticks of their houses dragging along tied on
to the pack-saddles [making a travois], besides the load which they
carry on top, and the load may be, according to the dog, from 35 to 50
pounds. (Winship 1964:346–49)

The strange people who moved after the buffalo, rather than leading a sedentary existence and planting crops, as both the Pueblo Indians
and the Spanish did, were a fascination to the explorers. While some
comparisons could be made with Arabs, these people were new and different from those the Spaniards had previously seen in Mexico or the
lands to the north of the primary Spanish Mexican settlements. The
people were not only different, they were fearless and were described as
being intelligent, an adjective the Spanish saved for special occasions. No
less a fascination was the land itself.

The country is so level that men became lost when they went off half a
league. One horseman was lost, who never reappeared, and two horses,
all saddled and bridled, which they never saw again. No track was left
of where they went, and on this account it was necessary to mark the
road by which they went with cow dung, so as to return, since there
were no stones or anything else. (Winship 1964:349)

Traveling through the region today by car, or flying over it in an
airplane, is no less spectacular. Today the grasses are not so high and,
especially from the air, the lines made by wagons and later roads are
clearly visible. But it is still awe inspiring and difficult to describe. The
explorers, using everyday analogies, rendered well the feelings of those
traversing the land for the first time.

In traversing 250 leagues, the other mountain range was not seen, nor
a hill nor a hillock which was three times as high as a man. Several lakes
were found at intervals; they were round as plates [sinkholes], . . . The

country is like a bowl, so that when a man sits down, the horizon sur-
rounds him all around at the distance of a musket shot. (Winship
1964:279)

Several facts emerge from these accounts of the Coronado expedition: the people Puebloan Indians called Querechos inhabited the buffalo plains east of the Rocky Mountains in present-day New Mexico during the spring and summer; they wintered in or near certain pueblos,
probably coming there sometime in the late fall; they relied totally upon
the buffalo as a kind of lumbering supermarket; they brought buffalo
skins, and probably jerked meat as well, back with them to their winter
encampments; and they were exemplary people whose intelligence and
physiques impressed the Spaniards. Unfortunately for all, the picture
changed radically and rapidly as more Spaniards entered the area and as
interactions quickened between the groups. All too soon the curiosity
represented by the Querechos was replaced with hatred and fear.

For their part, Apaches of today have stories told by the "grandfathers," a term used to mean ancestors, of meeting the Spanish on the
buffalo plains, of being frightened of—yet curious about—them, for they
initially appeared to be a combination of man and beast. Soon it became
evident that they were simply men who had wondrous animals at their
command, animals the Apaches coveted. Apaches tell stories of the Foolish People, those who, upon first receiving horses, did not know how to
ride them, which way to face, how to make them go or stop. Yet riding,
too, was soon demystified, and horses became the property of Apaches
once again—for their folklore also tells them they once had the horse,
only to lose it through their disobedience to the Creator. They tell jokes
of the Spanish performing essential services for Apaches, such as breeding
horses and then bringing them to the Apaches, where they were available
for the clever to take. And take them they did, rapidly becoming a horse
people who could accumulate more possessions, since the horse could
carry much more than a dog. They could stay in one place longer with
the hunters taking to horse to slaughter buffalo rather than having an
entire camp move each time the buffalo moved. But as the relationship
between Apaches and horses became closer, that between Apaches and
the Spanish became more distant and difficult.

The Llano Estacado, the staked plains as they are sometimes
called, was not an area the Spanish coveted. It was too vast, too formi-

dable, with too few resources to command attention. Rather, the Spanish explorers, and later the conquistadores and colonizers, stayed close to rivers and streams—commodities largely missing on the Llano. But by preferring riverine sites, they usurped lands of the sedentary, and largely nonhostile, Pueblo peoples. At first, the Querechos were a mere curiosity, an adjunct to the pueblos. Later, as the Spanish began to venture out from the rivers and streams, the Querechos and their descendants, usually now termed Apaches, became more of a problem. They were no longer viewed as friendly, intelligent, exemplary people but came to be viewed as hostile, crafty, belligerent people. They did not sit still, as did the Pueblos, nor did they cooperate in their own eventual enslavement. The term "enemy, heathen Apache" became almost a litany in the Spanish chronicles.

In the eighteenth century clear distinctions began to be made between western and eastern Apachean people, with the western people said to be those who planted and the eastern people still being associated with a more nomadic, buffalo-following lifestyle. It was also during this time that first mention is made of the Mescaleros as a separate, identifiable people of the eastern division. By the mid-1700s more and more letters were being sent by Spaniard administrators on the Indian frontier to both Viceroy and King requesting additional troops, more material, and in general greater support to combat the Apaches. Apache attacks on both settlers and soldiers became increasingly brazen, beginning to take place in broad daylight rather than under cover of night. Nonetheless, the Mescaleros were considered to be more trustworthy than many of the other bands of Apaches (Moorhead 1968:47–48), although the general feeling was that Apaches were to be avoided whenever possible.

But trust was not a commodity in high regard on the frontier of the eighteenth century, as Moorhead makes clear in his discussion of Ugarte's attempts to pacify the Indians. Ugarte, a Spanish employed governor, consciously set out to pit one group of Apaches against another, to promise peace while waging war, in short to do whatever was necessary in order to secure the northern frontier of New Spain (Moorhead 1968:120, 125, 131). Time and again peace was promised to the Mescalero, who ranged between southcentral New Mexico and northern Mexico as well as east past the Llano Estacado into the area of central Texas. And time and time again the promises went unfulfilled. Political machinations among the various Spaniards vying for favor from the same, distant viceregent did not help matters. By the last two decades of the eighteenth century, the Mescalero were once again ensconced in the mountains of northern Mexico and southern New Mexico, from which they raided in all directions. Yet in 1790 Ugarte was able to boast of having secured peace with three thousand Mescaleros, as well as other Apaches (Griffen 1988b:57; Moorhead 1968:277).

Despite continuing hostilities on an official level, there is evidence of cooperation between Apaches and some settlers. Several settlers on the frontier reported being warned of impending Apache attacks by arrows tied with bits of red (the color associated with men, warfare, hunting, and killing) cloth planted along trails. Dunn (1911:205) reports that prior to attacking a Coahuila (Mexico)-to-San Antonio (Texas) supply train, in which mules were stolen and the train's drivers killed, Apaches planted red-tied arrows in the ground. From this sign settlers knew to keep off the trails until the arrows were removed. Thus, there seems to have been selective slaughter against the Spanish government, and its representatives, rather than against people in general. The stated policy of the Spaniards was "to use the Apaches as a bulwark against the French and their Indian allies" (Dunn 1911:209), who were impinging on Spanish territory from the east. It seems the Apaches were unwilling to be placed in this position, to be used as buffers.

The Apaches were not without duplicity, however. As Moorhead, Thomas, and Dunn each note, when it was expedient, the Apaches sued for peace, requested priests, and sought education for their children. When the Apaches felt threatened, usually by the Comanches and later the Utes, they formed alliances with the Spanish governmental representatives; when they felt safe, they attacked the Spanish, or Mexicans, in general, often bypassing particular individuals.

Trade in slaves complicated all relationships. The Pawnees, who were allied with the French to the east of Spanish territory, raided Apaches taking their women and children who were then sold into slavery among the French. In turn, the Apaches sold captured Pawnees to the Spanish in New Mexico (Thomas 1935:20). The Spanish sold Apachean women and children as slaves from Taos in the north to Chihuahua City in the south (Bailey 1966:19). Mescalero Apaches today relate stories of capturing Spanish/Mexicans in the south to sell as slaves in the east or capturing non-Apachean Indians in the north to sell in the south.

One Mescalero family today keeps the memory of a French

woman with red, curly hair who was purchased (or stolen) from the Pawnees in the eighteenth century; the Pawnees had purchased (or stolen) her
from around present-day St. Louis, Missouri. Her legacy can be seen
today in that family—especially in the summertime, when red glints are
evident in hair that is wavy without benefit of perms. In contrast to the
practices of most other Indians of the time, when Mescaleros captured or
bought women, they were properly married into the tribe; while such
women were never considered full members of the tribe, their children
were. In other words, the women could, and did, establish matrilineages.

According to Bailey (1966:197), the slave trade between Indians
and Mexicans did not reach its height until the mid-nineteenth century.
Slavery and debt peonage were so severe after the Southwestern area became a part of the United States through the Treaty of Guadalupe Hi-
dalgo (1848) and the Gadsden Purchase (1853) that the United States
Congress enacted legislation in 1867 to abolish peonage in New Mexico
(see Ellis 1975:55). However, it seems the problem persisted, since in
1868 Lt. Gen. William T. Sherman was given power by Congress to end
bondage in New Mexico (Bailey 1966:186). Many familiar with the
New Mexican practices judged the situation of debt peonage and slavery
in New Mexico to be much less humane than that of black slavery in the
American South (Beck 1962:146), not itself a model of enlightened
treatment.

Spanish imperialism suffered a decline as the influence and power
of the nascent United States of America were on the rise. In 1821 Spain
officially lost control of her new world to Mexico. But Mexico was to
control the American Southwest for only twenty-five years; in 1846 the
United States formally took control through General Stephen Watts
Kearny. With the treaties of 1848 and 1853, the Apache problem became
the United States' problem. When the United States became heir to the
Apache problem, they took over the attitudes of the Mexicans and the
Spanish before them without questioning the reasons for the behavior of
the Indians. Thus the enemy, heathen Apache of the Mexicans and Spanish became the enemy, heathen Apache of the United States. Before the
Apaches were subdued, the United States government would spend mil-
lions of dollars and both sides would suffer grievous losses. Had there
been an enlightened soul such as Benavides (see Forrestal 1954) or had
the United States government paid attention to the history of the region
and the accounts of travelers within it, perhaps some of the subsequent

bloodshed could have been avoided. Unfortunately for all concerned, the information that did exist—in archives, letters, diaries, official and family histories—was ignored.

Fear of Apaches multiplied in the nineteenth century, despite the popularity of Josiah Gregg's account of his 1831 trip from Independence, Missouri to Santa Fe and his subsequent trips over the Santa Fe Trail and down the Rio Grande into Mexico. Gregg's account of his trips, *Commerce of the Prairies,* was first published in 1844; it achieved great popularity and was republished several times. In his book, Gregg included a chapter on "The Wild Tribes of New Mexico," several pages of which were devoted to the Apaches. His writing style has a special character that makes it worth quoting at length.

> . . . Apaches, the most extensive and powerful, yet the most vagrant of all the savage nations that inhabit the interior of Northern Mexico. They are supposed to number some fifteen thousand souls, although they are subdivided into various petty bands, and scattered over an immense tract of country. Those that are found east of the Rio del Norte [Rio Grande] are generally known as Mezcaleros, on account of an article of food much in use among them, called mezcal [an agave and a carbohydrate source, not the hallucinogenic mescaline] . . . They never construct houses, but live in the ordinary wigwam, or tent of skins and blankets. They manufacture nothing—cultivate nothing . . . but depend almost entirely upon pillage for the support of their immense population, some two or three thousand of which are warriors . . . [they] rely chiefly upon the flesh of the cattle and sheep they can steal from the Mexican rancheros and haciendas [the buffalo were already a vanishing species, nor was the land still available on which to hunt them] . . . The depredations of the Apaches have been of such long duration, that, beyond the immediate purlieus of the towns, the whole country from New Mexico to the borders of Durango [in Mexico] is almost entirely depopulated . . . To such a pitch has the temerity of those savages reached, that small bands of three or four warriors have been known to make their appearance within a mile of the city of Chihuahua in open day, killing the laborers and driving off whole herds of mules and horses without the slightest opposition. Occasionally a detachment of troops is sent in pursuit of the marauders. (Gregg 1974:201–3)

Gregg goes on to describe, in very negative terms, the efforts of the Mexican army to attempt to bring the Apaches to justice. But he also cites reasons why the Apaches preyed on the Mexicans rather than on the Anglo settlers, as he relates incidents of perfidy on the part of the Mexicans against the Apache. One such incident involved Juan Jose, an Apache leader who had been educated in Chihuahua and who could read and write Spanish as well as speak it. The Mexican government, by proclamation, gave permission for anything taken from Apaches to be the legal property of those who stole it. Shortly after this proclamation, a group of Mexicans with an American, James Johnson, as their leader took out after Apaches. Gregg continues the narrative:

> In a few days they reached a rancheria of about fifty warriors with their families, among them was the famous Juan Jose himself, and three other principal chiefs. On seeing the Americans advance, the former at once gave them to understand, that, if they had come to fight, they were ready to accommodate them; but on being assured by the leader, that they were merely bent on a trading expedition, a friendly interview was immediately established between the parties. The American captain having determined to put these obnoxious chiefs to death under any circumstances, soon caused a little fieldpiece which had been concealed from the Indians to be loaded with chain and canister shot . . . The warriors were then invited to the camp to receive a present of flour, which was placed within range of the cannon. While they were occupied in dividing the contents of the bag, they were fired upon and a considerable number of their party killed on the spot! The remainder were then attacked with small arms, and about twenty slain, including Juan Jose and the other chiefs. Those who escaped became afterwards their own avengers in a manner which proved terribly disastrous to another party of Americans, who happened at the time to be trapping on Rio Gila not far distant. The enraged savages resolved to take summary vengeance upon those unfortunate trappers; and falling upon them, massacred them every one! They were in all, including several Mexicans, about fifteen in number. (Gregg 1974:204–5)

In a footnote Gregg states that prior to this event the Apaches had committed "but few depredations upon foreigners" (ibid.:206n.15). He then relates another incident when a Mexican commandant, pretending to free some Apaches from jail, trapped approximately twenty Apache warriors in the jail and then gave the order for them to be killed; several of the Mexicans were killed as well before they could dispatch all of the Apaches. Gregg also notes that New Mexico had seen little of the Apachean menace that plagued the Mexicans to the south. His documentation of the Apaches only attacking those Anglo settlers who had mistreated them was not heeded in the panic against Apaches that was soon to follow.

Yet again the fears were unrealized; the Apache attacked governmental representatives rather than individuals, unless they had specific quarrels with the individuals. As an example, in 1846–47 Susan Shelby Magoffin accompanied her husband on the Santa Fe Trail and into Mexican territory; from a spot near present-day Las Cruces, New Mexico—and thus in the Mescalero area—she wrote that the Apaches "a few nights since . . . came into this town and drove off twenty yoke of oxen belonging to the government" (Magoffin 1962:20). They harmed no one, taking only food.

Or consider the 1849 writing of William Henry Chase Whiting who kept a journal of a trip from San Antonio to El Paso del Norte (present-day Juarez, Mexico and El Paso, Texas), a distance of over five hundred miles, much of it through Apache territory. Upon reaching his destination he wrote,

> For fourteen days we had toiled among the wild mountains of the Apache . . . Few will ever know . . . that march of this little party, regarded by those behind as moving to certain destruction. No hour of no day but we listened for the yell of the Apache. At no time was any man's rifle out of his reach. (Whiting in Bieber 1938:306)

Yet they experienced no difficulty, even while traveling through the bastion of the Apaches.

It was politically expedient for the United States government, as it had been for the Mexican and Spanish ones before it, to perpetuate the image of the free ranging, fierce, bloodthirsty, enemy, heathen Apache.

By the 1860s and 1870s, the worst fears had been realized. Apaches were being tortured by both Anglos and Mexicans while the latter two groups were tortured by Apaches. The Apaches were getting the worst of it, however; their population was decimated, yet they were still feared by all and sundry. In 1870 William Frederick Milton Arny, a "dedicated and idealistic" American (Murphy in Arny 1967:8), was named Special Agent for the Indians of New Mexico. He was charged with taking a census of Indians in every village as well as with paying attention to the needs of the Indians. Eight months later, as he completed his charge, he ended his journal by noting that he had traveled over 3,100 miles in New Mexico. His census of all the Apaches in New Mexico indicated 1,237 warriors out of a total population of 4,502; for the Mescalero he recorded 760 people, of whom 160 were warriors and 280 adult women. Even those numbers were to shrink as the Geronimo wars increased in intensity and ferocity.

The Civil War of the United States, although primarily fought far to the east, impinged on the Indians and settlers of the southwestern territories. For a period of time, Confederate troops were in nominal control of the area around El Paso, Texas and thus in close proximity to Apaches. Skirmishes were common with the Confederate troops as they had been with the Mexican and Spanish troops before them and as they were to be with the troops of the Union.

Yet again, promises made went unkept. Mescalero raiding of settlers for food and horses quickened. Such raids brought complaints to the Army and to the distant Washington, D.C. government after Union troops had again established their claim to the area. Problems were compounded because the United States government did not realize that, although Apaches would follow a particular man to war and perhaps another one on the hunt and even a third for other specific tasks, no one person could speak for a tribe. Indeed, there was no feeling on the part of Apaches of being a tribe. They recognized loyalty to family, kin, and band. Usually each band had a headman who led the group; but such a person held his office only by consensus of the group—not through heredity or by election (Basehart 1970). An agreement concluded with a headman might or might not be followed by those usually in association with him. This lack of formalized leadership was a concept the Americans either did not heed or could not understand.

In the 1850s various leaders of the Eastern Apaches had persuaded their followers to sue for peace with the recently arrived Americans. Food in the mountains was becoming scarce as the increasing populations of non-Indians fenced ranges and plowed meadows. Then, too, whites on their way to the gold fields in California were passing through the territory, further stressing the minimally adequate resources. The buffalo were gone. If the Apaches did not raid, they did not eat. And often raids made by others, especially along the San Antonio road, were attributed to the Mescalero.

By 1855 war was declared against the Mescaleros by the governor of the territory. After winter battles, during which the Apaches were defeated, they were confined to Fort Stanton, an area near the present eastern border of their reservation where the Ruidoso and Bonito rivers meet. The treaty that placed them on this land was never ratified. There were no provisions for them; they were destitute, hungry, and incarcerated. Gradually the able bodied men slipped away into the mountains where they could find food for their families.

Dr. Michael Steck, an eastern physician, was their Agent during this time. The Mescalero trusted him and he did his best for them (see Sonnichsen 1973 for an excellent summary of this period). Through Steck's efforts some farming was started; it is an occupation for which most Mescalero have no great love, but they did try it. "Steck was sure that a firm policy, along with adequate subsistence and good leadership in helping the Indians to make a living for themselves, was the only possible course to follow" (Sonnichsen 1973:92). Under Steck's leadership, the situation was stabilized for a few years. However, the American Civil War moved priorities east and the Indian problems in the West again ensued.

In 1862 the United States' attention was again turned to the Indian problem through General James Carleton, an avowed Indian hater. With the help of the New Mexico Territory governor at the time, Governor Connelly, and by commanding the militia under Colonel Kit Carson, Carleton set out to round up the Mescaleros and place them in custody at Fort Stanton. Other troops were ordered to move against the Mescalero from the south. Soon the Mescalero surrendered themselves to Carson at Fort Stanton, but Carleton wanted more (Sonnichsen 1973:112–13). Fort Sumner, at the Bosque Redondo on the Pecos River in eastern New Mexico, was established and in 1863 most of the Mescalero were moved there. Those who chose fighting to incarceration gradually disappeared from their Army jailers and went to join relatives to the west.

But in 1863 and 1864, still operating under Carleton's orders, Carson began moving Navajos into the Bosque Redondo, after having burned them out of their homes. Rations were not sufficient for both groups and, additionally, the Navajos and Mescaleros had not been on friendly terms for a good number of years. The Navajos vastly outnumbered the Mescalero; in addition to being the minority, the Mescalero felt their labor improving the Army's property was more of an advantage to the Navajo than to themselves or the Army. Crops failed due to adverse weather; disease was rampant in the overcrowded conditions. "Bad water, disease, crop failure—and the end was not yet in sight. Just finding wood to cook with was an increasingly serious problem, and before the period was finished, some of the Indians were going as far as eighteen miles for something to burn and carrying it home on their backs" (Sonnichsen 1973:117).

Carleton forbade the Indians leaving the Fort to hunt while the meat they were being fed was from animals that had died of disease. The situation continued to deteriorate while Carleton continued to pontificate, listening neither to Steck, or others who had a long history of success with Indians, nor listening to public opinion that had turned against him.

By 1864 more and more Mescalero were leaving whenever the opportunity presented itself. Many of them retreated to the rugged Sacramento Mountains where there are caves and other hiding places that their descendants identify today as places where they hid from the troops Carleton sent to pursue them. Mescalero pressures against the Pueblos and settlers increased as some began raiding in earnest the communities along the Rio Grande, as well as the scattered settlements to the east and west of the river. Raiding into Mexico was also common during this time, as were raids on any unescorted travelers.

Congress addressed the issue of the situation at Fort Sumner in both 1864 and 1865. However, graft and corruption persisted and the Indians seldom received what Congress voted them. Sonnichsen (1973: 132−33) relates succinctly what happened next:

> Everything came to a head in the summer of 1865. It was the worst year New Mexico had known for generations. Frost, hail, blight, drought, destroying insects . . . Supplies had long since run out, and on account of the wartime conditions in the East, none could be obtained. Carleton ordered the bread ration cut to three-quarters of a pound per day, and the meat ration to one pound per head . . . A little later he was forced to reduce the ration still farther . . . for some time the head men counseled patience. If a few left the reservation, they would be followed and killed. If everybody left at once, the whole tribe might get away . . . Just before winter set in, in 1865, they were ready. On the third of November, during the night, every Apache who could travel arose and vanished. In the morning only the sick and the crippled were left, and within a few days they vanished also. They were not pursued. How could the soldiers chase a whole tribe at once, and in all directions?

The Mescalero disappeared: some went to their old lands on the Llano Estacado; others went into the Sacramento Mountains; a group went west to the Rio Grande and across it; a contingent went south into Mexico—even today at Mescalero there are stories of "our relatives living in the mountains of Mexico." It was not until May of 1873 that a permanent reservation was established for the Mescaleros, and then they still had to deal with squatters who had taken up their lands. Even today in the middle of the reservation there is land that is deeded to non-Indians. Whenever this land becomes available, the tribe buys it—but almost 120 years later they still do not have all the land that is supposedly inside their reservation boundaries. It took years before the Mescalero were truly safe and self sufficient within their reservation, and in the meantime their "cousins" were engaged in war with the Americans to the west of the Mescalero territory.

Jason Betzinez was a Warm Springs Apache, some of whom joined with Geronimo and some of whom lived with the Mescalero during the turbulent 1870s and 1880s. Betzinez was born in the summer of 1860 and was a cousin of Geronimo, a Chiricahua Apache from Arizona. Betzinez's life story provides interesting information on a volatile period in New Mexican history. In later life he was converted to Christianity and married an Anglo missionary. If one ignores statements such as, "In my time the Apaches had not yet reached the same degree of civilization as the white man" (Betzinez 1959:27) and others of an apologetic nature, there are much data in Betzinez's narrative that present the Indian view of a difficult time.

Betzinez notes the Warm Springs Apaches were kin to both Mescalero and Chiricahua Apaches. They were also located on land between the two groups. Sometimes, he states, the Mescalero drove stolen stock into his group (ibid.:43), while other times he hints that the Chiricahua, being more war-like than his own people, caused trouble for the Warm Springs (ibid.:39, 43). He confirms earlier reports of the Eastern Apaches having "many virtues such as honesty, endurance, loyalty, love of children, and sense of humor . . . also . . . at least two serious faults . . . drunkeness [sic] and . . . fighting among themselves" (ibid.:38). The Apachean perception of their reputation for hostility was that they fought only when pushed off their land, or when they were unfairly treated, or when they were taking justifiable revenge (ibid.:49). He confirms Apache pride in disguising themselves and covering their tracks or leaving signs so as to appear to be a different people (ibid.:55). He was taught that

Mexicans were treacherous because they offered peace, only to slaughter Apaches when the offer was accepted (ibid.:80), a belief for which there is ample documentary evidence as well. Stealing was something that the Apache did to escape, as with horses, or to keep from starving, as with sheep and cattle, or to supply other needs, as with taking dry goods from pack trains.

Yet Betzinez also fought with Geronimo, a fight he perceived to be essential to survival. Of Geronimo's first surrender to General Crook in Mexico in 1883, Betzinez states, "I am sure that this was one of the happiest days of the year for General Crook . . . We Apaches felt the same way about it. It was a great relief to give up to superior authority, to have someone take charge. No more worries, no more sleepless nights, fearing attack by an enemy" (ibid.:116). In the 1883 surrender, Geronimo, thinking so many extra people to feed would be a burden to Crook, brought with him a herd of stolen Mexican cattle to be used as food and could not understand why Crook did not appreciate the gesture. But soon Geronimo was on the warpath again, having found not all Anglo soldiers could be trusted as easily as could Crook. Geronimo had a genuine high regard for Crook (ibid.:135) and was upset when he was removed by Washington, because of one of Geronimo's escapes.

Geronimo's final surrender in 1886 was preceded by broken promises and killings on both sides. The settlers in the territories of New Mexico and Arizona were exerting pressure on the Army and government to rid the area of what was commonly called "the Apache menace." With that final surrender, Geronimo's worst fear was realized: he and his people were imprisoned far from their own homeland in the desert Southwest. They lived as prisoners of war in Florida, Alabama, and Oklahoma until their kinsmen at Mescalero extended an invitation to join them on their reservation in 1911. By 1912 the arrangements had been made, and in 1913 those survivors who so chose were allowed to journey to Mescalero. Here their descendants still live, all enrolled as members of the Mescalero Apache Tribe, although with notes on their tribal census records as to whether they are actually Mescalero or Chiricahua (or Lipan) and how much of each. Many of them, however, elected to remain in Oklahoma, where they are known today as the Fort Sill Apaches. Neither Geronimo nor his descendants nor the descendants of his followers were ever again to live on lands west of the Rio Grande.

THE PRESENT

In 1904 and 1905, several years before the Chiricahua Apaches joined the Mescalero, the remnants of the Lipan Apaches moved to Mescalero. Today, even while living on the Mescalero reservation, they maintain ethnicity through language and kinship as well as through details of clothing and decoration. These details are kept current through a vital oral tradition. As Betzinez (1959:136) states, "The Indians had wonderful memories." They still do, and they carry complex webs of interrelationship in their minds. They are one people now, but are still loyal to former bands and groups which they keep alive through memory and telling of relationships of cousins and grandparents—sometimes more than six generations removed and once, in my hearing, for nine generations. And while some linguists claim there is no extant Lipan Apache language, I recorded two men, one in his late sixties and the other in his mid-thirties, conversing in Lipan in 1984; others speak the language as well. People are proud of being Lipan or Chiricahua or Mescalero; they often volunteer the differences between how they say a word and how it is said by the other ethnic groups. They point to a turned-up toe on moccasins as a sign of Chiricahua ethnicity and note that the Mescalero have plain toes on their moccasins. They speak of particular color combinations as being Chiricahua or Mescalero. Lipan speakers speak "more slowly," it is said, while both Mescalero and Chiricahua not only use different words for the same items or phenomena but also divide the body differently when speaking of anatomy. It is important, still, who one's ancestors were and who one's parents are.

Ethnicity is traced through the mother. If a person's mother is Mescalero, then that person is also Mescalero. The relatives of one's father are important, too, but they are secondary in establishing one's primary ethnicity, as when a person speaks of a mother's brother as being a "blood uncle" and of a father's brother as being simply an "uncle." Mescalero people will often attribute a bit of their knowledge or a particular practice to "my Chiricahua grandfather/grandmother." Chiricahua and Lipan do the same for each other's groups and the Mescalero. People report feeling closer to their relatives through their mother than they do to their relatives through their father. But grandparents, from whichever side, are extremely important. A properly raised person is one who has had the opportunity of learning from the grandparents.

While one's mother and her family constitute one's primary descent and kin, there are, nonetheless, those who choose to emphasize a father's rather than a mother's line. Usually this choice is made on the basis of prestige or access to tangible and intangible resources. For instance, a person descended through the father from a famous warrior of the nineteenth century might well choose the opportunity to emphasize that relationship if the mother's side of the family can boast of no such famous people. People also choose to emphasize their father's line, if their mother is Indian but not Apache. Children can be enrolled members of only one tribe, in most instances. Since the Mescalero have a more than twenty-five year history of astute management of tribal funds and enterprises, it is often an economic advantage to be Mescalero. A father's line may be emphasized as well if the mother is non-Indian. In such an instance, the children can be enrolled members of the Mescalero tribe only if their father is one-half or more Apache of Mescalero, Chiricahua, or Lipan ethnicity, as demonstrated by blood relationship and tribal census records.[1] The norm is for people to follow their mother's line in establishing their Mescalero identity; however, there are other strategies available to cover common cases where it is more advantageous to be allied with the father's family.

Nonetheless, the Mescalero claim they are "closer" to their mother's kin than to their father's. Indeed, if a Mescalero woman marries a non-Mescalero man or a non-Indian man, the children of such a marriage are regarded as somehow more Mescalero than those of a Mescalero father and a non-Mescalero or non-Indian mother. This is so even when the blood level (i.e., $\frac{1}{4}$ or $\frac{5}{8}$ or whatever) is quantified the same on the tribal records. The actual everyday practices are flexible, but in general the Mescalero (including Lipan and Chiricahua) are a matrilineal people. It is essential to remember, however, that what is listed on the tribal census records and what strategic choices an individual makes may well vary throughout that individual's lifetime. Also, it is important to remember that when initially presenting themselves to outsiders, people have a tendency to state that they are Apaches from Mescalero; when it is considered appropriate to give more information, they then state their ethnicity as Mescalero, Chiricahua, or Lipan. In general to outsiders, those who live at Mescalero are Mescaleros; that does not mean that all the people consider themselves as Mescalero, however. It is, instead, analogous to stating one is an American on initially meeting a foreigner rather than stating my mother is, for example, Italian-American with a little French and my father was Irish- and English-American.

When approaching the reservation from any of the roads that serve it, at the reservation line there is a large sign stating, "Welcome to the Homelands of The Mescalero Apache Tribe," with an indication of the number of miles to the Tribal and Administrative Center. This sign is arresting, with its bright yellow background and larger than life representation of a Mountain God dancer.

The Tribal and Administrative Center is located at Agency, so named for the fact that it was the site of the home and office of the Indian Agent in times past. Agency is about fourteen miles east of Tularosa and about twelve miles west of Ruidoso on Highway 70. The canyon in which Agency is located is narrowed to the east by mesas and a moraine. On the mesas are the sites of the girls' puberty ceremonial arena and the rodeo grounds. St. Joseph's Catholic Mission, with its magnificent mini–Gothic church, constructed under the direction of Father Braun, tops the moraine. Below the moraine and to the south is a national fish hatchery. On the north side of the canyon are terraces that support the original Agency buildings, now used for other tribal purposes, the Bureau of Indian Affairs (BIA) building, the Cattle Growers Association building, Indian Health Service and BIA housing, the hospital, elderly housing, and baseball fields. Across the canyon, facing the north terraces, is the current tribal center, as well as the law enforcement building and offices, a greenhouse nursery run by the tribal conservation people, and, climbing up the canyon wall, housing. Also on the south canyon wall is a mesa with the elementary school, the Bent-Mescalero School, which has had both teachers and a principal who were Mescalero Apaches. The school is administratively attached to the Tularosa Independent School District. Tularosa Creek runs through Agency, and, as it moves to the west, it skirts the land that was deeded to others prior to the establishment of the reservation—land that the tribe buys whenever it becomes available.

At the lowest level of Agency Canyon, hard by the creek, there is a small shopping center with a few small businesses—that, like their counterparts throughout the country, come and go with frequency. This area currently has a gas station, post office, Tribal Store, Tribal Museum, and a laundry. Across the road to the west is the Tribal Center, which houses the administrative offices, an Olympic-size indoor (almost a necessity at the 6,600 foot altitude) swimming pool, a bowling alley, a library, conference rooms, a cafeteria, a child care center, the Head Start program, and a large auditorium used for tribal meetings, as well as for basketball, small powwows, dances, wrestling, movies, concerts, or whatever is of an appropriate community nature.

Upon entering the double glass doors of the Administrative and Tribal Center, there is a replica of the 1873 Executive Order establishing the Mescalero Apache Reservation on the left wall and a scale model of the reservation ahead and to the right. The scale model indicates the approximate size of the reservation (somewhat over 460,000 acres) and shows in relief the mountainous terrain. The reservation's lowest point is 3,400 feet, while the highest, Sierra Blanca, is just over 12,000 feet. Most of the land is mountainous, with the primary living areas clustering between 6,600 and 6,800 feet.

Looking at the housing gives graphic presence to history. In the 1890s the government forced the people to build and live in log cabins. However, the people had no experience with this type of structure—in terms of building or living—and found them to be exceedingly uncomfortable. In the 1920s Old Ladies Village was built with the idea of separating the generations. The predominant governmental philosophy was one of assimilation, and it was felt that, by separating the grandparents from the children and grandchildren, the goal of assimilation could be reached more quickly. It did not work, despite the fact that families were forcibly separated. There is a moral imperative at Mescalero, and among Apaches in general, to honor and take care of elderly people; it is only when one is older that one has lived long enough "to know things" and to be a cultural resource. No proper family would send its old members off to live by themselves. So, as quickly as possible, a daughter or granddaughter would show up, often with her children, to live in Old Ladies Village with the grandparents. The government policy failed.

During the 1930s there was a critical shortage of housing; many people were living in totally inadequate structures. The situation continued into the 1940s. In the 1950s an unscrupulous contractor built for the tribe cinderblock housing that was unsealed and totally uninsulated. By the 1960s the tribe had taken over its own housing plans and built A and B Sections, properly built cinderblock houses on two adjacent mesas. Also at this time, the houses from the Old Ladies Village of the 1920s were renovated, with bathrooms added and insulation and heating added or upgraded. The 1970s saw the construction of California ranch style houses. And the end of that decade saw a repeat of the 1920s fiasco; this time, in a well-intentioned plan to move the elderly people closer to the hospital and medical facilities, elderly housing was built on the north terrace of Agency. These are small homes (under nine hundred square feet), adequate for an aged couple but totally inadequate for the population they quickly held. I recall seeing a swing set installed before curtains were in one house, for a proper family had moved in with their aged relatives in order to care for them. Thus, in a house designed to hold two, there were four adults and three children.

The 1980s saw a continuation of housing built by the tribe in several styles, for one of the stated goals of the tribe has been to provide adequate housing for each family. Additionally, there are a few privately financed and constructed homes on the reservation as well as some mobile homes that are individually owned.

While the Agency section appears to be the area of most tribal activity, that is a misconception. A significant portion of tribal income is from tourism. There are camp areas, fishing lakes, and the crown jewel, the Inn of the Mountain Gods. Opened in 1975, the Inn has since experienced expansion. It is a luxury resort with swimming, golfing, horseback riding, skeet shooting, canoeing, tennis, fishing, boating, and skiing—in season—readily available. There are convention facilities as well. Many people come to the Inn for the ski season, skiing Sierra Blanca on a tribally owned and managed ski area. Others come for the summer racing season in Ruidoso, a few miles to the southeast of the Inn. Increasingly, people come for conventions, but there are still those who come simply to relax in the spectacular surroundings and the luxury of the resort.[2]

The tribe reserves for tourists a small number of purchased permits for hunting antelope, deer, bear, and elk. Each person whose number and name is drawn in the lottery for these permits must have an Apache conservation officer/guide along on the hunting trip.

In addition, the tribe maintains a sustained yield timber cutting program and operates a small sawmill on the reservation. Several tribal members are employed at each of these enterprises as well as in the forestry and conservation programs. There is seasonal employment in fire towers and stations; fires caused by lightning or careless tourists are fairly frequent, but careful monitoring during fire season of all the lands has prevented major fires on the reservation. There is also employment for some as cowboys, managing the polled Hereford herd that is pastured and marketed communally; those Apaches who wish to do so may buy stock in the livestock operation. Finally, there are a few small businesses on the reservation that provide modest employment.

While most areas of the reservation are accessible to tourists, even if it is necessary to have guides for some areas, there is one place closed to all but tribal members: the Tribal Lounge. Mescalero shares an alcohol problem with most other Indian reservations in this country. During the course of my year's sustained stay at Mescalero, over 80 percent of the deaths were alcohol related; of these, many were car accidents involving drunken drivers. Partly to mitigate this problem and partly to keep those who will drink at home rather than in the surrounding, not always friendly communities, the tribe built and manages a bar, lounge, and package store for Indians only.

Highway 70, the major road on the reservation, was widened to four lanes and straightened in the late 1980s as it goes through the reservation. In support of this project, there was a rock crushing operation on the reservation. While many are distressed at the widening of the highway, fearing that it will cause too much incursion from tourists, most feel that the increased safety for both residents and tourists is worth the inconvenience. Until very recently, parents had to send their children to junior high school and high school on a narrow, winding, often ice covered, seventeen mile long road in the winter. In the past ten years, moving eastward from Tularosa, the road has been gradually widened and straightened so that eventually a four lane highway will run through the entirety of the reservation, from Tularosa on the west to Ruidoso on the east.

Some individuals on the reservation have secured Small Business Administration loans in order to open and operate a variety of independent businesses. These have ranged from a ceramics shop to a restaurant, from a credit union to a crafts outlet. The success and failure rates of these businesses are consistent with those of the country at large.

Despite the variety of jobs available on the reservation, there is still not a sufficient number to employ every tribal member who wishes to work. Thus, many people leave the reservation daily to commute to jobs in Ruidoso, Tularosa, Alamogordo, or Holloman Air Force Base. Others choose to follow a career path and live where they must; this is particularly true of those who have advanced degrees, or even four-year college degrees, or those who are in the military—the closest thing to a warrior life available in our times. Nurses and teachers can usually return to the reservation and find work; computer operators and programmers can likewise be employed easily on the reservation, as can business administration majors. However, there is little opportunity for an attorney on the reservation; similar situations exist in other professions. Thus, the reservation experiences what many developing countries do as well: a brain drain, with the best minds and most highly educated people unable to find work in their areas of specialization at home.

Being forced to work away from home does not mean alienation from home, however, as people make concerted efforts to return for the annual July girls' puberty ceremony. Having contact with home and kin is vitally important today, as it was in the past, for the more than twenty-five hundred people who call themselves the Mescalero Apache.

Almost as important is a sophisticated sense of the law. The Mescalero have been very successful indeed in prosecuting cases against the United States government and the State of New Mexico in order to have affirmed their rights under the 1873 proclamation. Current concerns revolve around water rights, an issue that is both sensitive and emotional in the arid southwestern portions of the United States.

So, Mescalero fights continue to this day, but the venue has moved from the vast Llano Estacado, from the mountains and plains of the American Southwest, from the canyons and riversides to the no less significant courtrooms of Santa Fe and Washington, D.C. Those once known for their intelligence on the Llano Estacado are now known for their astuteness in business and the law. They have changed through time, in lifestyle and in a myriad of other ways as well. But they still are here, a vital presence, a presence to be attended to with respect rather than fear. And, it seems to me, that is all they have ever wanted: to be respected for who and what they are, a desire they share with all other human beings.

NOTES

NOTES FOR CHAPTER 1: INTRODUCTION

1. Throughout this work "Mescalero Apache" is used in a generic sense. The Mescalero Apache Reservation has, as enrolled members of the Mescalero Apache Tribe, people with varying Apachean ethnicity: Mescalero, Chiricahua (or Fort Sill), Lipan, Warm Springs, Tularosa, Mimbreño, and others. Most of my learning experience (in ethnoastronomy, values, religion, and philosophy) was from Bernard Second, a Mescalero who represented the Mescalero viewpoint, sometimes in concert with the Chiricahua one, for he was trained by singers with both tribal identities. (See the Appendix for a fuller description of Eastern Apachean history, including ethnicity.)

2. I first used the terms "blue archaeoastronomy or ethnoastronomy" in an unpublished 1986 letter to the editor of *Sky and Telescope* magazine as a response to an article by Aveni (1986). Blue archaeoastronomy has since gained currency in the interdiscipline and was used in the title of a paper for the Third Oxford Conference on archaeoastronomy, held in St. Andrews, Scotland in September 1990. The term is also discussed in Williamson and Farrer 1992.

3. Throughout the book, an en dash [–] in quoted speech equals approximately one second of silence. Ellipses (. . .) are used to indicate that material has been omitted. Aside comments by speakers are in parentheses, while my comments appear in brackets. No corrections of grammar have been made; the speech quoted is conversational with the false starts and convolutions we all use.

4. Upon being queried on her rationale, my mother said that when she entered nurses' training she found that she had an advantage in that she already had a well-used framework for observation and mnemonics for memorization. Hers was an immigrant family; she did not learn English until she went to grammar school. But her family was well educated, albeit in Italian. She had been admonished as a child to watch the Americans and imitate them. Her mother taught her some of the memory aids she taught us, although my mother's nurses' training gave her an impetus to invent additional techniques that she subse-

quently taught her children—and, I should add, that my sister and I have taught to our children. I now teach these techniques in field ethnography courses.

After this book was completed, Tom Curtin of Waveland Press alerted me to a similar instance of primary enculturation including memory training for Nancy O. Lurie; see Lurie 1972:155–56.

5. The fictive relationship was offered by Bernard Second's extended family as a means of legitimizing the amount of time he and I were spending together. There were two choices: we could marry or become relatives. Bernard was already married, so we became relatives—I became as a sister to Bernard and his siblings, while my daughter was niece to many and cousin to many more. The relationship, once inaugurated, is for life. I still visit my Mescalero family, usually yearly, and we talk on the phone or exchange letters much more often than that. Truth be told, I was disappointed that the "adoption" was only verbal; I had looked forward to a Hollywood-type initiation procedure. Instead, one day I was poor by Apachean cultural standards, in that I had no relatives, "no one to look out for you and stand up for you," and the next day I was rich in brothers, sisters, nieces, nephews, and cousins, as well as enmeshed in a new set of reciprocal arrangements to learn and within which to function.

NOTES FOR CHAPTER 2: CREATING THE UNIVERSE

1. I have used a modification of Dennis Tedlock's (1983) notation system for rendering oral narrative in alphabetic format. The placement of the words on the page is designed to simulate the spoken words. Each space indented from the left margin, which itself is indented two spaces to indicate direct quoting from Bernard, approximates a second of time. New lines at the two-space-indent margin indicate a slight pause or change in voice tone. Double spacing between segments indicates longer pauses and corresponds to verses or paragraphs. Words that are emphasized are in italics; uppercase words indicate especially strong, and usually louder, emphasis. Asides are rendered in parentheses, and my ammendations are in brackets. Capital letters are used for the quintessential or to indicate specific personages rather than generalities: e.g., "Buffalo" means the Spirit Animal Buffalo, the prototype, while "buffalo" means any buffalo available to be hunted; or "twins" refers to the fact of a multiple birth while "Twins" refers specifically to the Twin Warrior Gods.

This narrative's first eleven lines were previously published (Farrer and Second 1981), but were there rendered in prose.

2. This was a teasing statement. Bernard was staying with me in Washington, D.C., where I worked at the time, while he took advantage of a fellowship from the National Endowment for the Arts to work on Apachean material in the Smithsonian Archives and later to learn conservation and preservation of feathers and fibers at the National Park Service Preparation Center in Harpers Ferry, West Virginia. Books were very much on both our minds. Oftentimes, when he or I turned on the tape recorder, he would say, "Chapter One!" or "Chapter Ten!" after I'd done the on-tape identification of time, date, and place of recording. Although he was not interested in my publishing at that time, he had a clear vision that the material would one day be published. Also, at that time I was writing my dissertation in spare moments sandwiched between a time-intensive job with the Arts Endowment and being a mother to my teenage daughter. The

dissertation drafts were spread out all over the study in my apartment; Bernard, when he had nothing better to do, read chapters and commented on them.

On this particular occasion, we had just "joked" each other: me for my Anglo ways and him for his very un-Apache stance that I must tape record and write down what he was telling me.

3. Pronouns in Mescalero Apache indicate whether one refers to first, second, dual second, third, or honorific fourth person; there is no ascription of gender in pronouns. One knows from context whether a male or a female person is being referenced; should context be insufficient, then description about the person referenced will allow auditors to know if a male or female person is meant. The Apache pronoun that Bernard uses when referring to Creator, or the Great Spirit, God, is the honorific fourth person pronoun, *gu*. It is impossible to link Creator (*Bik ʔégudiⁿdé* [According To Whom There Is People/Life]) with maleness in Apache, nor would it make any sense to do so. However, Bernard was here speaking in English. After a four second pause on the tape, he chose to use the word "He" to refer to Creator, since it is proper in English to refer to God as "He." Subsequent conversation confirmed that Creator is viewed as being beyond the ken of people; to the Apache way of thinking, conventional sexuality is inappropriate in reference to that Power. Creator, for Apaches, is both male and female; at the same time, Creator is neither male nor female. Sexuality is present in Creator for it to have been present in Creation, but it is of no consequence for Creator other than as an empowering force. Thus, all references to "He" in the dialogues must be read with the knowledge that Bernard did not intend to imply maleness. The use of the gender-specific pronoun was a convention demanded by the use of the English language.

4. The appended syllabic *n* nominalizes what is essentially a descriptive verb phrase. The names appear to change due to the way in which Bernard refers to them. Killer of Enemies, in Apache as well as in English, has a slightly different connotation than Monster Slayer, although they refer to the same person. Here the terms mean He Killed on Earth and Killer of Enemies, both referring to the First Born Twin, who did indeed kill the enemies—many of whom were monsters—of the People, the Apaches, *ⁿdé*. The elevated *n* is a syllabic *n* with a high tone; it is a distinct phoneme in Mescalero. Nominalizations are also formed with syllabic *a* or *i*; these letters are always indicated by an en dash (–) following the word to which they are inalienably attached.

5. This dialogue was recorded with pen and notebook in shorthand at Bernard's house after we (Bernard, David Carmichael, and I) had been running errands around the reservation. I did not have my tape recorder with me.

David Carmichael is an archaeologist who was trained at the University of Illinois and who took my ethnographic theory and method course there. At the time of this dialogue, he had recently begun working with Bernard on ethnobotany and hunting information.

6. If the Athabaskan speakers originated on the Asian steppes, as some scholars aver, then it is quite possible, indeed probable, that they did have the horse and lost it, as some of their stories relate. Most scholars place the Athabaskan languages in the macro stock of Tibeto-Burman. If they are correct, then it lends credence to the idea that Apachean ancestors were affiliated at one time with the people we today term Mongols, who, of course, are renowned horsemen and have been for millennia.

7. This is not to be interpreted to mean that Apache women are seen as

passive and noninvolved; far from it! Apache women, through the strength rendered by matrilineage principles and all they entail, are sources of great strength. They are perceived as being naturally wise. An ideal woman is generous and nurturing, but she is both from a position of strength. In contrast, men are viewed as being less emotionally stable, more apt to lose control, to become angry and to fight. Men must be taught to be generous, rather than naturally being so; men are naturally prideful, but it is a pride predicated on physical strength. A man's active, strong, life force must be channeled in order to be brought to society's use.

8. I do not choose to enter into the arguments over what is "truly" traditional and what is Christian influenced. I firmly believe that the word "traditional" is a relative term, in that the time period must be very carefully specified. What was traditional for Apaches in the 1300s undoubtedly differs from what was traditional in the 900s or the 1700s and from what is traditional today. As will become apparent in subsequent chapters, Apaches borrow from those they encounter and with whom they interact. They surely borrowed from Western Europeans during the more than four hundred years of contact and interaction. Nonetheless, the narratives they present are what Apaches maintain is their tradition—and that is sufficient for me, even though they do not specify to which time period their use of tradition refers.

NOTES FOR CHAPTER 3: PAYING ATTENTION

1. This chapter has had many incarnations. The 1983 version was prepared for and read at the First International Conference on Ethnoastronomy, held at the Einstein Planetarium of the Smithsonian Institution in Washington, D.C. and jointly sponsored by them and The Center for Archaeoastronomy at the University of Maryland. The title of the paper was "'You're standing on my Indian watch!': Mescalero Apache Ceremonial Timing." It was then revised for publication in *Ethnoastronomy: Indigenous Astronomical and Cosmological Traditions of the World,* selected Conference proceedings; the two-volume edited work has been in press since 1984 and as I write in 1990 has yet to appear. A shorter, revised version was presented in 1987 to the British Traditional Cosmological Society, meeting in St. Andrews, Scotland; this version was jointly published by the Society in *Cosmos 4* and *The Canadian Journal of Native Studies,* as "Star Clocks: Mescalero Apache Ceremonial Timing." Both appeared in Spring 1989, although they bore two other dates (Farrer 1987a; 1988).

An earlier unpublished paper, "'It's the same thing!': Aspects of Mescalero Apache Ethnoaesthetics," was prepared for and read at the Conference on New Directions in Native American Art History, held in 1979 in Albuquerque, New Mexico. Some of the basketry designs in chapter 4 were first presented in this latter paper. Design sets, divorced from their plastic contexts and from body painting, were illustrated and interpreted in "Living the Sky: Aspects of Mescalero Apache Ethnoastronomy" (Farrer and Second 1981). That version had been read at the 1979 Conference on Archaeoastronomy in the Americas, held in Santa Fe, New Mexico.

This chapter includes material borrowed from each of these sources; it is nonetheless different from all of them. In other words, I have been thinking about the material for a very long time.

Graphics for this book were professionally produced, with very little lead time, by Laura Kling, director, Instructional Media Center, California State University, Chico. It is a pleasure to acknowledge such fine work.

2. I use "power" here to mean authority in the family that is derived from matrilineal kinship and economic might from owning children as well as the home and its contents. Other kinds of power are recognized at Mescalero as well. There is political power, such as is wielded, with greater or lesser degrees of success, by Tribal Council members, some of whom are women. Council power is not a major force in the lives of the Apaches; it is of considerable concern to non-Apache Indian and Anglo outsiders on the reservation, however. There is also Power from the supernaturals.

3. Most of the evidence for these statements is still in archives, such as those maintained by the Documentary Relations of the Southwest section of the Arizona State Museum at the University of Arizona in Tucson. Lately, however, some of the evidence has been published; see, for example, Griffen (1988a,b).

4. Virginia Klinekole was Tribal Council President for a brief time in the early 1960s, in between terms of Wendell Chino. Both Mrs. Klinekole and Mrs. Evelyn Breuninger have consistently been elected to the Tribal Council during the past three decades.

5. Morris Opler has published extensively on Apachean folklore, as a perusal of most library card catalogs will attest. A good portion of his Mescalero and Chiricahua data came from the work of Regina Flannery, as he acknowledges in his publications. Dr. Flannery (now Herzfeld) was a member of Ruth Benedict's 1931 Field Training Project at Mescalero, as was Opler. Flannery was assigned folklore collecting and the roles of women as her primary responsibilities; she collected most of her material from old women. In those days, tribes were "given" to particular people; Opler received Apaches, largely because he had evinced the primary interest in them by writing a master's thesis (at the University of Chicago) on their kinship. Thus, all the students on the Rockefeller sponsored Field Project (Sol Tax, Jules Blumensohn Henry, Frank Gillin, Regina Flannery, and Lawrence Frank) turned their summer's materials over to Opler, who added them to his own. This information is from private communication with Flannery-Herzfeld, Frank, Opler, and Tax, as well as from the files of the Field Project housed in the Library of the Laboratory of Anthropology, Museum of New Mexico, Santa Fe. My thanks to Laura Holt, Librarian, and Curtis Schaafsma, State Archaeologist, for their assistance in alerting me to the files (Schaafsma) and making them consistently available (Holt.) See also my commentary (Farrer 1987b; 1987c), and Opler's (1987) responses, on this Project.

6. Complex religious and healing ceremonies are most often sung, rather than recited, among the Apache as among the Navajo. Thus, one who conducts such ceremonies is referred to as a singer. Singers are roughly analogous to a combination of priest/minister and physician.

7. When I speak of "the Apache language" here, it is to be understood in a generic sense. There are two mutually intelligible languages spoken with great frequency at Mescalero: Mescalero Apache and Chiricahua Apache. Lipan Apache is spoken by fewer than two dozen people and did not figure into either my own linguistic training or that of the children in the Bent-Mescalero School.

While the two primary languages are quite similar, there are lexical and tonal differences, as well as differences in referent as when the particular part of the arm referred to by *"gu gan"* differs depending upon whether the speaker is Mescalero or Chiricahua.

8. Bernard was familiar with both terms from his reading and, I believe, from an introductory anthropology course he had taken. It was he who proposed that I teach him introductory linguistics in exchange for his teaching me about his language. He had in mind eventual literacy classes for his people in general and not just for those associated with the Title programs in the school. His goal was realized in 1977 when, as a result of our work together and with a syllabus we jointly constructed, he taught adult literacy classes on the reservation. In our initial work, I used Elaine Clark's orthography as our basis for writing the language with the exception that I used "ł" for the fricative "l," rather than the "lh" that she preferred. The "ł" and all the other symbols I used were those approved by the elders' language committee in 1975. Unfortunately, that standard has not been followed by all who wish to write the language; there are several idiosyncratic and competing systems in operation on the reservation today.

9. To Bernard's everlasting frustration, I speak Apache with a Navajo accent. In graduate school, while preparing for fieldwork with the Mescalero, I attempted to learn the language from the only printed material available, *Chiricahua and Mescalero Apache Texts* (Hoijer 1938). The texts are bilingual and there are extensive grammatical notes. However, I still did not know how to pronounce what I had learned to read minimally. Despite the fact that the texts were in a standard phonetic alphabet, there was no indication of any differences between, for example, glottalized consonants and glottal stops or of precisely what was meant by a high tone or a low one, let alone rising or falling ones. Therefore, I used the University of Texas-Austin Language Laboratory's tapes that accompany Goossen's (1967) introduction to spoken Navajo, *Navajo Made Easier*. From those tapes, I acquired my lingering Navajo accent. When not frustrated with my pronunciation, Bernard thought it humorous that I had neither a New York (the place of my birth) nor a Texas (the place of my recent schooling) accent, but rather sounded like a Western Navajo. He placed this whole business of my inadequate, Navajo-accented pronunciation in the category of just one more inexplicable aspect of some whites, while reminding me that Kenneth Hale (a superb linguist from the Massachusetts Institute of Technology, whom he had met and with whom he had worked briefly) spoke Apache impeccably and, Bernard maintained, with no accent. This latter fact also served to support his insistence that men are more gifted linguistically than are women, one of his prejudices that I found disquieting.

10. Having my notes open to the people has had an unexpected benefit. In off-reservation times when working with my field notes, I flagged questions or places where I required additional data with a metal tab or, in recent years, Post-it notes. Bernard especially would take my field notebook, open it to one of the flags, and either provide the additional data or direct me to a specific person or event to fill in the spaces in the data. After my year long stay at Mescalero, it seemed there was seldom sufficient time to think or to put my notes in proper order during my brief visits. Thus I found that each year after leaving, there were still questions to be asked. I always seem to be playing catch-up with field notes.

11. Ceremonies are sung in virtually every part of the reservation. This

public July ceremonial, however, has since the 1930s been held on a series of mesas to the north of Highway 70, just east of Agency proper and St. Joseph's Catholic Mission. On the lowest mesa, closest to the road, there are now a few homes. It is also used as a camp area during ceremonial times and is often referred to as Cricket City, for reasons that should be obvious. The middle mesa is now a parking lot during ceremonial time; it was on this middle mesa that I first observed the ceremonial. The current ceremonial mesa is a little higher (more northerly) than the previous two mesas that were used. Above this current mesa, there are camps of the various families who attend the ceremonial.

12. See Farrer and Ammarell (in press) for a detailed explanation of how this timing is accomplished. In brief, any given star will transit any two tipi poles in very close to ninety minutes. Thus, by fixing on a star sighted between Holy Lodge poles and monitoring its progress periodically, it is possible to have a ninety-minute clock. This assumes that the Holy Lodge, or ceremonial tipi, has been constructed properly, with its twelve poles equidistantly spaced around the east-opening. However, not all singers are equally skilled in tipi construction, so some years it may take any given star closer to two hours to transit between two poles. Finer adjustments, of course, are also possible simply by knowing that a song set takes the amount of time for the given star to move from point A to point B, while *n* song sets require the complete transit between two poles. By the time the Big Dipper has "set," or "fallen into the north ridge," it is time to have finished all the night songs and be ready to declare a break before beginning the morning star watch to the east.

Also, it must be remembered that times given are Mountain Daylight Time (MDT). MDT is one hour ahead of local astronomical time, or six hours *behind* Greenwich Mean Time.

13. There is a story of two sisters in love with the same man; they vowed to share him through eternity. They went together (died at the same time), and all three ascended into the sky, where they remain together to this day as The Three Who Went Together.

14. This is measured by standing at the east end of the ceremonial arena and stretching one's arms out in front of the body at eye level. With thumbs tucked in and palms toward the face, one blocks off approximately twenty degrees of the horizon. If *suus biné* is more than two palms' width above the horizon, then full sunlight will come too early for all that must still occur. The same posture using only one arm and palm will yield a 10° measure, about one hour of Anglo clock time. In a similar manner, one half hour of Anglo clock time equals 5° or one half hand. That is, with the hand held at arm's length, wrist bent, and palm toward the ground, thumb and plane of fingers yields a 5° measure.

By noting the position of stars and planets against a horizon backdrop, say at the beginning of singing, and then noting where one was in the song sets when the position had changed 10°, time and singing can be correlated. By so doing, a singer moves his singing out of the realm of ordinary people and into the realm of Power and Creation. It is through such attention to integration of this world with the world of Power that the universe is re-created during each singing of the girls' puberty ceremonial.

15. Bernard's knowledge of the sky was phenomenal. Not only was he capable of using the stars to provide a clock for Mescalero ceremonials, but also he used them to guide his travel, to find how far he was from home, and to time

ceremonials that he sang for other Apaches (especially Western and Jicarilla) in several locations on their reservations.

16. From the house where my daughter and I lived in 1974–75, we could watch the sun "rise" over a forty minute period. Our house was at Agency on the north side of the east-west running canyon. First the sun strikes a house sitting isolated on a high mesa on the west end of the canyon. Then it quickly runs down the southwest side of the canyon, lighting features as it goes, and finally illuminates St. Joseph's Mission, the Catholic church that sits on a moraine at the east end of the canyon. The Mission snuggles against East Mountain that effectively blocks the sun's rays until it is quite high in the sky. Thus sunrise (or daily initial sunshine, to be more precise) occurs at different times, depending upon where one happens to be at Agency, or, for that matter, anywhere else on the mountainous reservation.

17. This requirement—for long hours and years outside at night in order to learn thoroughly the celestial regularities and use them in a culturally appropriate way—is in danger of being lost because of the necessity of Mescalero children having to be educated in the whiteman's way in order to succeed in the modern world. A child cannot walk around for a goodly portion of the night with a singer and still be expected to function in school the next day. Learning the summer sky, as can be done when school is not in session, is insufficient for a singer of ceremonies. He must also know the sky of the other seasons, since, for example, Capella is morning star only during the summer. There is, though, an apparent primacy to the summer sky: for example, the names of stars are usually descriptive of their summer positions; the year is said to begin at the summer solstice, *sha? sizi* [sun standing still]; and the middle of the year is the winter solstice, *hai?łdi* [winter center/middle]. Bernard speculated (to Gene Ammarell in July 1984) that this might have come about when they were still a northern people who did not do celebrations in the winter. Consequently, he suggested, they had no need for precise timing in the winter, when they were usually huddled inside hoping their food would last until the spring.

NOTES FOR CHAPTER 4: SEEING THE PATTERN

1. During my first months on the reservation in 1974, I helped prepare food for a benefit for the reservation girl scout troop, of which my daughter was a member. There was to be a chili lunch to raise money for activities for the girls, and I volunteered to bring some chili stew as well as some sandwiches. While my sandwiches went quickly, my chili stew was the last to be served; it was brought out only when there was no more chili stew, save mine. The first person to be served from my pot was a man who bellowed, "Who is the white lady who put carrots in chili stew?" The man was one I knew rather well, so his public teasing of me was accepted and we all laughed; I blushed, too. I had eaten several cooks' chili stew by that time, I had never found anything in it except meat, chili, potatoes or posole, and occasionally squash. Nonetheless, stew, in my subcultural upbringing, meant carrots—so carrots it was, at least for that one time. I no longer put carrots in chili stew, but "doing a carrots" became, for a while, a way some of us referred to making a cultural mistake.

2. In 1990, a portion of the Bent-Mescalero School burned, an arson fire. It will be interesting to see how the school is reconstructed.

3. Should no consensus be reached, the item(s) under discussion would be tabled for another time, unless such topic(s) required immediate resolution. When that was the case, the president or vice-president of the council would state the position the tribe as a whole would put forth. Those still in opposition, if any, could still voice their beliefs. I did not ever see such an impasse, but only learned of the extended procedure in discussions of what-if scenarios.

4. Such public disagreements among the members of a matrilineally extended family were rare in my experience. Usually families would work out their differences prior to a tribal meeting and thus present a united front at the meeting.

5. There are many narratives concerning White Painted Woman, or Changing Woman, as she is sometimes called. In essence, she provided the proper model for both women and life. When first she came to The People, she was a young woman; some say she came from the east, while others say because she was young she was associated with the east. Regardless, she lived among The People, aging as do we all. When she was a very old woman, she disappeared into the west, the direction associated with death. However, the next day she reappeared in the east, once again a young woman. Her changes were literal in that she aged and metaphoric when her rejuvenation is considered. She is also credited with being present at the beginningtime in some narratives or with bringing some accoutrements of a proper life to The People in other narratives. Essentially, however, she presents a changing but ever-renewing quality.

6. The way in which people spoke during formal speech events in the tribal meeting could also be seen in everyday speech deemed to be of particular importance, whether to make a point, relate a narrative, quote those in authority, or lend credence to one's idiosyncratic experience. It is the formal speech in the tribal meeting, however, that I have chosen as illustration for the structure of important talk.

7. These are my etic terms and have no emic realization to my knowledge. While Apaches agree on the proper speech making style, I have never heard names for the segments that constitute that proper style.

8. On one occasion, when a middle-aged woman rose and tried to shush her elderly father's rambling speech, she was hissed into silence and returned, obviously chagrined, to her seat. She had violated two canons of decorum by interrupting an older person and by calling attention to the lack of unanimity in the matrilineage. The hisses directed at her were first in shock at her behavior and then as disapproval of it.

9. See Witherspoon (1977) for an elegant, if somewhat controversial, discussion of a related concept among the Navajo.

10. My research for this section of the book was made possible through the efforts of many people, to each of whom I am grateful. W. W. Newcomb, Jr., formerly director of the Texas Memorial Museum in Austin, not only taught me museology but also allowed me access to collections in order to begin my study of basketry when I was a raw neophyte. The Research Board of the University of Illinois, Urbana/Champaign provided summer grant funds allowing Bernard and me to work in the collections of the Laboratory of Anthropology (Museum of New Mexico, Santa Fe), The Indian Arts Collection (School of American Re-

search, Santa Fe), and the Wheelwright Museum (Santa Fe). We benefited from courtesies extended by Curtis Schaafsma while he was director of the Laboratory of Anthropology and by members of his staff—especially Nancy Fox, Laura Holt, Barbara Mauldin, and Marina Ochoa. Douglas W. Schwartz, president of the School of American Research, and Barbara Stanislawski, formerly curator of The Indian Arts Fund collections, were most helpful in making the School's material available at our convenience. Richard Lang, formerly director of the Wheelwright Museum, along with Rain Parrish, also formerly with the museum, provided access to their collections during a time when they were quite busy with other concerns. Donald Rundstrom of Santa Fe took some of the basketry photographs, as did I, while others were provided by the School of American Research. These photographs were the basis of the drawings done by James R. Yingst while he was my graduate assistant at the University of Illinois.

In March 1982 I read my preliminary foray in this area ("Signs of Self and Other in Mescalero Apache Basketry") at the Native American Art History Conference held in Ames, Iowa.

11. I neither measured the baskets illustrated in this chapter nor counted their stitches; for this information I rely on Whiteford (1988: passim).

12. An example of the difficulties of assigning items to a particular group on the basis of place of purchase can be seen in an article by Dutton (1980) reporting on and describing a pair of "Mescalero" moccasins. She notes she bought these moccasins at The Summit on the Mescalero Apache Indian Reservation in 1956. The Summit was, at that time, a restaurant and gift shop fronting tourist cabins and a camping area on Highway 70, between Agency and Ruidoso. The moccasins described and depicted in the article, however, are Chiricahua Apache, not Mescalero Apache, as I am sure she would have been told had the proper question been asked. The distinctive feature is the "toe guard," as Apaches call it in English—that portion of the front of the moccasin that is turned up perpendicular to the sole. This turned-up toe is the distinguishing difference between Chiricahua and Mescalero style moccasins. Only one whose mother was Chiricahua is also Chiricahua; and only the Chiricahua people wear moccasins with a toe guard. Mescalero moccasins are plain in the front and follow the conformation of the foot. Apaches, both Mescalero and Chiricahua, say that the Chiricahua needed protection from the cactus, because they used to live in an area in Arizona that was more desert than is the Mescalero Apache Reservation in New Mexico. The Chiricahua maintain that, throughout their imprisonment in Florida, Alabama, and Oklahoma, they kept this mark of their ethnicity, as they did after they moved to Mescalero. Whatever the reasons for the toe guard, it is one very important way people publicly demonstrate their ethnicity on the reservation today, as they did in 1956. Unfortunately, Dutton assumed a purchase *at* Mescalero meant the item was Mescalero. The danger of this kind of thinking is equally present in making such an assumption for manufacture of basketry based upon place of purchase or gift.

13. Bernard frequently noted that his maternal grandmother "made her living" between 1910 and 1946 by making baskets, often on consignment, for the tourist trade.

14. I am indebted to Peter Furst and David H. Snow for independently suggesting this reference and the Goodell article. Both read the first draft of this chapter and both referred me to Wilbert and Goodell.

NOTES FOR CHAPTER 5: CLOWNING AND CHIASM

1. This chapter, like chapter 3, has had many incarnations. Different versions were read at meetings of the American Anthropological Association and The Association for the Study of Play; it has been given as a lecture in various and sundry places. I am grateful to audience members in each venue whose comments helped me hone my argument. In particular, I appreciate the detailed critical commentary of Don Handelman whose understanding of clowning is without peer and whose questions led to my clarifying and rewriting several segments of this chapter. In addition, I appreciate the careful and thoughtful readings given by Beverly J. Stoeltje, Barbara Tedlock, Claire Sanderson, and Janice Wygant, each of whom provided cogent criticism of written versions.

2. Later, Schechner (1982:71) used a similar model in discussing rehearsal and performance.

3. There are alternative explanations for the "out" mentioned here. The first, that Bernard preferred, was that it meant that *Libayé* was the first of the second set of Holy Beings to emerge from the Earth. Both *Libayé* and his consorts, the Mountain Gods, arrived on the Earth's surface after Father Sky, Mother Earth, White Painted Woman, and the Twin Warrior Gods. The Mountain Gods and *Libayé* were not placed on Earth by Creator, as were the first Holy Beings; rather, they emerged from a cave. The second explanation is a tacit recognition of history in that both *Libayé* and the Mountain Gods are a latter addition to Mescalero cosmogony—a fact Bernard acknowledged. Most people aver that these figures were added to Mescalero belief and ceremonial only after Apaches arrived in the Southwest from their northern wanderings. This second view accords "out" a meaning of liberated, brought out, from a Puebloan context and appended to a Mescalero one. Gifford (1940:186) states that the Mountain God complex was secured "ca. 100 years ago."

4. Anthropologists have been describing time for a long time now but, for the most part, have yet to address times. Hall's (1967, 1969, 1977, 1983) work is the outstanding exception. Hall has long been concerned with the differential perceptions of time and cultural values placed upon it, as well as on its analogue: space.

5. A chiasm is many other things as well, things not discussed here. Suffice it to say that a chiasm can be animate (such as a singer, see-er, clown, shaman, medicine person, or owl) or inanimate: a ritual event (such as a girls' puberty ceremonial or a funeral); a part of the physical landscape (such as a cave or a mountain); or an action (such as a formulaic prayer or a song). All are phenomena capable of existing simultaneously in The Two Worlds and in multiple times.

6. Austin's (1975) perceptive work has largely been ignored by those who have adopted the performance perspective from folkloristics. However, his use of the term "performative" is one well worth reiterating. A performative is that which accomplishes its referent through the utterance, such as when a member of the clergy says the words, "I now pronounce you husband and wife." Prior to that statement, the couple is unmarried; upon the utterance of the statement, the couple is one, a married pair. All too often the term "performative" has been used to mean "performance" or "the act of performing," rather than being used in its technical sense as established by Austin.

7. In order, from front to back of the dancing line, the Mountain God dancers's names are as follows: *Gąʔhidziłihitlin, Gąʔhidziłigan, Gąʔhidziłitsulin,* and *Gąʔhidziłchilin,* followed by *Łibayé.* Collectively, and colloquially, the set is called *Gąʔhé,* a term that is also sometimes applied to an individual dancer, although *Gąʔhi* is more correct. The first part of each name (*Gąʔhi-*) refers to the Holy Being; the second term (*-dził-*) means mountain, while the remainder of each word describes particular characteristics, including a symbolic color, of each individual figure. *Łibayé* is either called by that term or is called clown.

8. This maker prefers to remain anonymous. The quotation is from a tape recording made in the Mescalero Museum in 1975 in the presence of the then director of the Museum and one of the men who sings along with the particular maker during performances by the Mountain Gods. All three preferred anonymity.

9. I am aware that the Mescalero clown has not always been so perceived. For example, Opler (1938:77) states that the "masked dancers perform for the amusement of the people . . . [while] the clown acts in the capacity of funmaker . . . [or] is often asked by the parents of an unruly child to single out the miscreant and frighten him." While amusement and fright may well have been the primary functions of Mountain God dancers and clowns in 1931–35, when Opler did his fieldwork, (ibid.:75), contemporary Apaches maintain the Mountain Gods dance to heal and bless while the clown's power is for very serious purposes, not the social control of children. I have never seen little girls approach the clowns, but little boys do so, usually running up to a clown dancer to snatch at the dangling cowbell and then to retreat quickly in mock horror—often accompanied by screams and giggles. I have never heard a parent, or child caretaker, threaten a child with action by a clown. Nor do the Mountain Gods, or clowns ensure the success of the social dancers as they did in the 1930s (ibid.:78). Perhaps even more remarkable is that now clowns are boys, while in the 1930s they were men (ibid.:76). Opler's data did include Mountain Gods' curing and times when the clown was extremely important (ibid.:78–79), but he maintained that "The activities of the masked dancers at the four day girl's puberty rite are not of a serious nature, in the main" (ibid.:78). Obviously, these are examples of culture change.

10. I became aware of this when, at the Ruidoso horse race track one summer, I was being a "proper" parent trying to teach my daughter the evils of gambling. An Apache gambler met us, "the first ones I saw from home," after having won a bet. He insisted upon giving us 10 percent of his winnings, even though I protested we were not Apaches. He maintained the medicine man he saw told him to "give the money to the first one you see from home." We were living on the reservation at that time and, therefore, qualified in his mind. He later told us his action was confirmed as correct, because he continued his winning streak. I, however, lost all heuristic value in regard to the senselessness of gambling for my daughter.

NOTES FOR CHAPTER 6: SINGING FOR LIFE

1. The title of this chapter was initially used for a 1978 Advanced Seminar at the School of American Research in Santa Fe and in 1980 was published jointly

by the University of New Mexico Press and the School of American Research in *Southwestern Indian Ritual Drama,* edited by Charlotte J. Frisbie, the organizer of the seminar. An abridged version was printed in *Betwixt & Between: Patterns of Masculine and Feminine Initiation,* edited by Mahdi, Foster and Little and published by Open Court. The Frisbie volume was reissued in 1989 by Waveland Press with minor changes to my chapter. The subject, the girls' puberty ceremony, remains the same, although the version presented here differs greatly in emphasis from the others.

2. Bernard's tenure as Head Singer began on a controversial note in that he changed some of the procedures and songs. He always maintained that one former singer, Old Man Comanche, had introduced Christian elements that Bernard's grandfathers, who had taught Bernard, deplored. Bernard said that personal dreams and visions, as well as direct instruction from his grandfathers, mandated that he purge the Christian elements and restore the pre-Christian ones. This he did with a vengeance. As becomes apparent later in this chapter, changes within the ceremonial are more frequent than might at first be expected; they always engender controversy—whether or not they are permanent.

3. As an example, once, when Bernard came to do some guest lectures at the University of Illinois, Champaign/Urbana where I was teaching, he was visibly embarrassed by the sorry state of his tennis shoes, his only footwear save for his favorites of moccasins or cowboy boots. He and I went to a shopping mall, where I bought him a pair of new tennis shoes. There was no thank-you. Rather, he showed off his new footwear to people and said I'd gotten them for him, "just like a sister is supposed to do." He used the incident in lectures to students to illustrate giving and receiving with no loss of face; such a loss of face, he maintained, was a common aspect of all Anglo giving. He also used the incident to illustrate how resources in a family are communal: he needed shoes but had no money; I had money, so he had shoes. All proper families are supposed to work in this manner.

4. Again, I avoid a discussion of alcoholism that increasingly intrudes even into the ceremonial. When I first observed the ceremonial in 1964, being drunk in public was a rarity and was virtually absent on the ceremonial grounds. By the mid-1970s, fights and general disorderliness due to drunkenness were, unfortunately, common events even at the ceremonial. Despite the tribe's best efforts, people continue to abuse alcohol, and in ever increasing numbers.

There is a cultural conflict in operation as well. A proper Apache does not interfere with another's life; simultaneously, there is a concerted tribal effort to reduce alcoholism. This conflict places Apachean health care delivery people in an impossible double bind.

5. I find the implications of this statement intriguing. Although this may seem to be an accommodation to the Western system, it seems equally logical to assume there were twelve moons in the aboriginal lunar year. Apaches do not like uneven numbers and take great pains to avoid them or justify as being even what may appear to others to be odd. In traditional times, the summer solstice not only began the new year but also was time-out-of-time when the public girls' puberty ceremonial was held. I suspect that the moon of the summer solstice was unnamed and simply marked as the beginning of the year. The next lunar month was, then, the first one after the solstice, with the others following in numerical order. At the end of the twelfth lunar month of counting in this fashion, one would arrive back at the summer solstice.

6. The color sequence is multivocalic and subject to change depending upon the context and the singer. Sometimes, for example, in certain specific contexts Bernard said yellow was a masculine color associated with the east; in other contexts yellow could be associated with the west. In order to know the symbolic significance of color, it is important to specify context. Colors and their symbolic loads are complex at Mescalero. There is no one-to-one correspondence between a color and a direction, or a color and its meaning, that holds for all situations and occasions, although as a general rule the lighter colors are in the east and north while the darker ones are in the west and south.

7. They have sometimes incorrectly been labeled devil dancers. I suspect this has occurred because their torsos are usually painted black. The association of black and devil is an Anglo one, however; the Apaches do not have this association, nor do they have a devil in their religion. Neither are the dancers in any way devilish; the misnomer is widespread and unfortunate.

8. The completed film, "Geronimo's Children"—a particularly inappropriate title, I argued to no avail—was produced and directed by Michael Barnes for the BBC's Horizon series. It was first aired in London in April 1976 and subsequently on some PBS stations in this country as a part of the NOVA series in 1976 and 1977.

9. This practice of fire making with yucca wood, dry grasses, and friction was reinstated when Bernard was Head Singer. The girls make fire in this way, without matches, on the afternoon of the second or third day. In a rare bit of sheer luck, I was able to confirm that indeed the making of fire used to be a part of the ceremonial. In the 1931 Rockefeller sponsored field training project at Mescalero led by Dr. Ruth Benedict, one of the participants, and the only woman among the students, was Regina Flannery, now Dr. Regina Flannery-Herzfeld. During an interview with Dr. Flannery- Herzfeld in her Washington, D.C. apartment in 1983, she asked me if the girls still knew how to make fire with wood, friction, and dried materials. It had, at that time, been only a couple of years since the practice was reintroduced. When we discussed the way in which the fire making was accomplished, it was evident that the verbal re-tellings had been sufficient to reintroduce the practice as she remembered it having been done. An event that had ceased a full decade or more prior to his birth had been placed and kept in Bernard's memory and nurtured there until the time was right to reintroduce it. That the memories of singers are highly trained and developed is well illustrated by the renewal of the fire making ritual. This return to the old ways is consistent with others that are also occurring now. At the same time, there are changes being incorporated into the ceremonial that were never a part of tradition.

10. The practice of beginning a new day only at sunrise can lead to disjunction for Anglos as when days are de facto canceled. On occasion I have seen days canceled, due to rain or overcast conditions, during the ceremonial. At these times, reservation people return to their jobs in the midst of the ceremonial. When the weather is right again, they return to the ceremonial grounds to resume the ritual events. The girls, however, are supposed to remain at the ceremonial grounds throughout, regardless of the weather. The decision of whether or not to cancel days is left to the Head Singer who usually, out of politeness, consults with the other singers and the families of the girls. Technically, however, there is nothing to cancel; rather, things go on the equivalent of hold. If there is no sunrise, there is no new day; without a sunrise and consequent new day, people must still

be experiencing the previous day. It makes logical sense, even if it plays havoc with the cognitive necessities of having to switch back and forth between Indian and Anglo time.

11. Re-setting of the universe, when it happened at the summer solstice, provided "free" days that allowed a 12 month lunar calendar to be kept in synchrony with the 365¼ (approx.) day solar year. See also note 5, this chapter.

12. It is midnight in sky time but about 1 A.M. MDT.

13. Clans are a relatively new, although well entrenched, phenomenon for the Navajo and the Western Apache, those the Mescalero Apache consider to be their "cousins." Since Southern Athabaskans all speak mutually intelligible languages and share common stories of having once been a conjoined people—albeit stories with differing rationales for their no longer being so—these peoples recognize their essential unity, a unity Anglo scholars predicate on linguistic, archaeological, and sociocultural analyses added to historical data for the latter period of time. For Eastern Apaches, especially the Mescalero and the Lipan, there was never any evidence of a clan organization within their band structure, while clans seem to have become a part of the Western Athabaskans as a result of their proximity to Puebloan people.

Basehart (1967; 1970) is especially illuminating in this regard.

NOTES FOR CHAPTER 7: CRYING FOR DEATH

1. This chapter benefited from a graduate seminar on the rituals and ceremonies of death and dying that I taught at California State University, Chico in the Spring semester of 1989, immediately after Bernard Second's death and that of Joan Montgomery, one of our graduate students. I shall always be grateful to the students in that seminar, who not only helped me to be able to write this chapter, but who also assisted me in my own adjustment to two very painful losses: Cheryl Adams, Kathlynn Beranek, Joyce Graff, Blossom Hamusek, Amanda Johnson, John McMillan, Antoinette Martinez, Frederick Newton, Patricia Rafter, Lisa Swillinger, Deborah Tibbetts, Barbara Wheeler, Martha Whitaker, Anne Marie White, and Virginia Wolf.

2. The Land of Ever Summer is the poetic name for The Real World.

3. A proverb is used to explain why very personal items are usually buried with their owner: "Guchi–i shijaáe najiałdał" [You will return to the place where your things are]. Since objects have the potential of calling one back, and since the dead are not ones most people would choose to call back, it is better to be on the safe side and eliminate potential attractions by seeing that particularly personal items of the deceased remain with the deceased.

NOTE FOR APPENDIX: A BRIEF HISTORY OF MESCALERO APACHES

1. In contemporary times the term "Chiricahua" subsumes the former Warm Springs, or Ojo Caliente, band as well as those Apaches who used to live in Arizona and who followed Geronimo, Nana, Cochise, Naiche, and Mangus

Colorado. "Mescalero" includes those who were once called Sierra Blanca, or White Mountain, Apaches in New Mexico and Mexico. They were also called Faraones, Querechos, Vaqueros, and Tularosa Apaches, among others. Names, which are in vast confusion and profusion through time, could well be a separate treatise.

2. Since this section was written, the tribe has also added gambling, Bingo, slot machines, and other gambling games.

References

Arny, W. F. M.
    1967   *Indian Agent in New Mexico: The Journal of Special Agent W. F. M. Arny, 1870.* Introduction and notes by Lawrence R. Murphy. Santa Fe, NM: Stagecoach Press.

Austin, J. L.
    1975   *How to Do Things with Words.* 2d ed. Cambridge: Harvard University Press.

Aveni, Anthony F.
    1986   Archaeoastronomy: Past, Present, and Future. *Sky and Telescope* 75(5):456–60.

    1989   Introduction: Whither Archaeoastronomy? In *World Archaeoastronomy.* A. F. Aveni, ed. Cambridge: Cambridge University: 3–12.

Babcock, Barbara A.
    1978a Introduction. In *The Reversible World: Symbolic Inversion in Art and Society.* Barbara A. Babcock, ed. Ithaca: Cornell University Press: 13–36.

    1978b "Liberty's a Whore": Inversions, Marginalia, and Picaresque Narrative. In *The Reversible World*: 95–116. See Babcock 1978a.

Bailey, Lynn R.
    1966   *Indian Slave Trade in the Southwest.* Los Angeles: Westernlore Press.

Basehart, Harry W.
    1967   The Resource Holding Corporation among the Mescalero

Apache. *Southwestern Journal of Anthropology* 23:277–91.

1970   Mescalero Apache Band Organization and Leadership. *Southwestern Journal of Anthropology* 26:87–106.

Bass, Thomas
1985   *The Eudemonic Pie.* Boston: Houghton Mifflin.

Basso, Keith H.
1979   *Portraits of "The Whiteman": Linguistic Play and Cultural Symbols among the Western Apache.* Cambridge: Cambridge University Press.

Bauman, Richard
1984   *Verbal Art as Performance.* Prospect Heights, IL: Waveland Press reissue. First published 1977.
1986   *Story, Performance, and Event: Contextual Studies of Oral Narrative.* Cambridge: Cambridge University Press.

Beck, Warren A.
1962   *New Mexico: A History of Four Centuries.* Norman: University of Oklahoma Press.

Begley, Sharon, John Carey, and Ronald Kahn
1983   Finding the Order in Chaos. *Newsweek,* July 18: 53.

Betzinez, Jason with Wilbur Sturtevant Nye
1959   *I Fought with Geronimo.* Harrisburg, PA: The Stackpole Company.

Bieber, Ralph P., ed.
1938   *Exploring Southwestern Trains 1846–1854: Journals by Philip St. George Cooke, William Henry Chase Whiting, & Francois Xavier Aubry.* Glendale, CA: The Arthur H. Clark Company.

Billard, Jules B., ed.
1974   *The World of the American Indian.* Washington, DC: National Geographic Society.

Broda, Johanna
1982   Astronomy, Cosmovision, and Ideology in Pre-Hispanic Meso-America. In *Ethnoastronomy and Archaeoastronomy in the American Tropics.* Anthony F. Aveni and Gary Urton, eds. *Annals of the New York Academy of Sciences* 385:81–110.

Bunzel, Ruth
1932   Zuni Katcinas: An Analytical Study. In *Annual Report of the Bureau of American Ethnology* 47:837–1108. Washington, DC: Smithsonian Institution.

Chabot, Maria
1936   Basket Making among the Indians of the Southwest. *Indians at Work* 3(20):22–27.

Chamberlain, Von Del
1982 *When Stars Came Down to Earth: Cosmology of the Skidi Pawnee Indians of North America.* Los Altos, CA: Ballena Press; College Park, MD: The Center for Archaeo-astronomy.

Clifford, James and George E. Marcus, eds.
1986 *Writing Culture: The Poetics and Politics of Ethnography.* School of American Research Advanced Seminar series. Berkeley: University of California Press.

Douglas, Frederic H.
1934 *Apache Indian Coiled Basketry.* Leaflet 64. Denver, CO: Denver Art Museum.
1935 Apache Basketry. *Indians at Work* 2:16, 21–23.

Dunn, William Edward
1911 Apache Relations in Texas, 1718–1750. *Texas Historical Association Quarterly* 14:198–274.

Dutton, Bertha P.
1980 Cultural Gaps and a Construct. *Collected Papers in Honor of Helen Green Blumenschein.* Albuquerque: Papers of the Archaeological Society of New Mexico, vol. 5.

Ellis, Richard N., ed.
1975 *New Mexico Historic Documents.* Albuquerque: University of New Mexico Press.

Espinosa, J. Manuel, ed.
1940 *First Expedition of Vargas into New Mexico, 1692.* Albuquerque: University of New Mexico Press.

Evans, Glen L. and T. N. Campbell
1970 *Indian Baskets of the Paul T. Seashore Collection,* 2d ed. Museum Notes no. 11. Austin: Texas Memorial Museum.

Farrer, Claire R.
1973 The Performances of Mescalero Apache Clowns. *Folklore Annual* 4 & 5:135–51.
1978 Mescalero Ritual Dance: A Four Part Fugue. *Discovery 1978*: pp. 1–13. School of American Research Bulletin.
1979 "Libayé, the Playful Paradox: Aspects of the Mescalero Apache Ritual Clown." Paper read at American Anthropological Association annual meeting, Cincinnati.
1980a "Play and Chiasm: The Ritual Clown." Paper read at the Association for the Anthropological Study of Play annual meeting, Henniker, NH.
1980a "Play and Chiasm: The Ritual Clown." Paper read at the

Association for the Anthropological Study of Play annual meeting, Henniker, NH.

1980b   Singing for Life: The Mescalero Apache Girls' Puberty Ceremony. In *Southwestern Indian Ritual Drama*. Charlotte J. Frisbie, ed. Advanced Seminar series. Albuquerque and Santa Fe: University of New Mexico Press and the School of American Research: 125–59.

1981   Contesting. In *Play and Culture*. Alyce T. Cheska, ed. West Point, NY: Leisure Press: 195–208.

1983   Libayé: Chiasm and Continuity. Paper read at 11th International Congress of Anthropological and Ethnological Sciences, August; Vancouver, BC, Canada.

1985   Review of *Diné Bahane?: The Navajo Creation Story*, by Paul G. Zolbrod. *Parabola* 10(3):121–25.

1987a   Star Clocks: Mescalero Apache Ceremonial Timing. *The Canadian Journal of Native Studies* 7:223–36. (Cf. 1988a.)

1987b   Amplification: The Death of Henrietta Schmerler. *Anthropology Newsletter* 28(1):3–4.

1987c   The 1931 Mescalero Apache Field Project: Review and Response in Reconstructing the Past. *Anthropology Newsletter* 28(5):3.

1987d   On Parables, Questions, and Predictions. *Western Folklore* 46:281–93.

1988   Star Clocks: Mescalero Apache Ceremonial Timing. *Cosmos* 4:223–36. (Cf. 1987a.)

1990   *Play and Interethic Communication: A Practical Ethnography of the Mescalero Apache*. New York: Garland Publishing. (The Evolution of North American Indian series, David Hurst Thomas, general editor.)

In press   Mescalero Apache Ceremonial Timing. *Ethnoastronomy: Indigenous Astronomical and Cosmological Traditions of the World*. Von Del Chamberlain, M. Jane Young, and John B. Carlson, eds. Los Altos and Thousand Oaks, CA: Slo'w Press.

Farrer, Claire R. and Gene Ammarell
In press   Mescalero Apache Ethnoastronomy: Problems and Praxis. *Archaeoastronomy*.

Farrer, Claire R. and Bernard Second
1981   Living the Sky: Aspects of Mescalero Apache Ethnoastronomy. In *Archaeoastronomy in the Americas*, Ray A. Williamson, ed. Los Altos, CA: Ballena Press: 137–50. (Anthropological Papers, no. 22.)

1986   Looking through the Mirror of Life. *Parabola* 11(2):70–73.

Farrer, Claire R. and Ray A. Williamson
1991   Epilogue: Blue Archaeoastronomy. In *Earth and Sky: Vi-*

sions of the Cosmos in Native North American Folklore. Ray A. Williamson and Claire R. Farrer, eds. Albuquerque: University of New Mexico Press.

Feigenbaum, Mitchell
    1981   Universal Behavior in NonLinear Systems. *Los Alamos Science* 1:4–27.

Flannery, Regina
    1932   The Position of Women among the Mescalero Apache. *Primitive Man* 5(1):26–32.

Forrestal, Peter P., trans.
    1954   *Benavides' Memorial of 1630.* Washington, DC: Academy of American Franciscan History.

Gifford, Edward Winslow
    1940   *Culture Element Distribution: XII—Apache-Pueblo. University of California Publications in Anthropological Records* 4:1–208. Berkeley: University of California Press.

Gill, Sam D.
    1987   *Mother Earth: An American Story.* Chicago: University of Chicago Press.

Gleick, James
    1987   *Chaos: Making a New Science.* New York: Viking.

Goodell, Grace
    1969   A Study of Andean Spinning in the Cuzco Region. *Textile Museum Journal* 2(3):2–8.

Goossen, Irvy
    1967   *Navajo Made Easier.* Flagstaff, AZ: Northland Press.

Gregg, Josiah
    1974   *Commerce of the Prairies.* Max L. Moorhead, ed. Norman: University of Oklahoma Press.

Greimas, A. J. and F. Rastier
    1971   The Interaction of Semiotic Constraints. In *Game, Play, Literature.* Jacques Ehrmann, ed.: 86–105. Boston: Beacon Press.

Griffen, William B.
    1988a *Utmost Good Faith: Patterns of Apache-Mexican Hostilities in Northern Chihuahua Border Warfare, 1821–1848.* Albuquerque: University of New Mexico Press.

    1988b *Apaches at War and Peace: The Janos Presidio, 1750–1858.* Albuquerque: University of New Mexico Press.

Hall, Edward T.
    1967   *The Silent Language.* Greenwich, CT: Fawcett. First published 1959.

    1969   *The Hidden Dimension.* Garden City, NY: Anchor Books/Doubleday. First published 1966.

1977 *Beyond Culture.* Garden City, NY: Anchor Books/Double-day.

1983 *The Dance of Life: The Other Dimension of Time.* Garden City, NY: Anchor Press/Doubleday.

Handelman, Don
1981 The Ritual-Clown: Attributes and Affinities. *Anthropos* 76:321–70.

Handelman, Don and Bruce Kapferer
1980 Symbolic Types, Mediation, and the Transformation of Ritual Context: Sinhalese Demons and Tewa Clowns. *Semiotica* 30:41–47.

Hieb, Louis A.
1972 Meaning and Mismeaning: Toward an Understanding of the Ritual Clown. In *New Perspectives on the Pueblos.* Alfonso Ortiz, ed. 163–95. Albuquerque: University of New Mexico Press.

1979 The Ritual Clown: Humor and Ethics. In *Forms of Play of Native North Americans.* Edward Norbeck and Claire R. Farrer, eds. 171–88. 1977 Proceedings of the American Ethnological Society. St. Paul, MN: West Publishing Company.

Hoijer, Harry
1938 *Chiricahua and Mescalero Apache Texts.* Chicago: University of Chicago. Publications in Anthropology, Linguistic Series.

Honigmann, John J.
1942 An Interpretation of the Social-Psychological Functions of the Ritual Clown. *Character and Personality* 10:220–26.

James, George Wharton
1972 *Indian Basketry.* New York: Dover Publications. First published 1909.

Josephy, Alvin M. Jr.
1973 *The Indian Heritage of America.* New York: Bantam Books. First published 1968.

Kirshenblatt-Gimblett, Barbara
1975 A Parable in Context: A Social Interactional Analysis of Storytelling Performance. In *Folklore: Performance and Communication.* Dan Ben-Amos and Kenneth S. Goldstein, eds. 105–30. The Hague: Mouton & Co.

Laski, Vera
1959 *Seeking Life.* Memoir no. 50. Philadelphia: American Folklore Society.

Leach, Edmund
1965 *Political Systems of Highland Burma.* Boston: Beacon Press. First published 1954.

Lee, Dorothy
    1950   Codifications of Reality: Lineal and Nonlineal. *Psycho-somatic Medicine* 12:89–97.

Lorenz, Edward
    1963a Deterministic Nonperiodic Flow. *Journal of Atmospheric Sciences* 20:130–41.
    1963b The Mechanics of Vacillation. *Journal of Atmospheric Sciences* 20:448–64.
    1964   The Problem of Deducing the Climate from Governing Equations. *Tellus* 16:1–11.

Lurie, Nancy Oestreich
    1972   Two Dollars. In *Crossing Cultural Boundaries: The Anthropological Experience.* Solon T. Kimball and James B. Watson, eds. San Francisco: Chandler Publishing Company: 151–63.

Lyon, William H.
    1989   Gladys Reichard at the Frontiers of Navajo Culture. *Native American Quarterly* 13:137–63.

MacCannell, Dean
    1980   A Community Without Definite Limits. *Semiotica* 3: 87–98.

Magoffin, Susan Shelby
    1962   *Down the Santa Fe Trail and into Mexico, Diary of 1846–1847.* New Haven: Yale University Press.

Makarius, Laura
    1970   Ritual Clowns and Symbolical Behavior. *Diogenes* 69: 44–73.

Mandelbrot, Benoit
    1977   *The Fractal Geometry of Nature.* New York: Freeman.

Marcus, George E., and Michael M. J. Fischer, eds.
    1986   *Anthropology as Cultural Critique: An Experimental Moment in the Human Sciences.* Chicago: University of Chicago Press.

Mason, Otis T.
    1904   Aboriginal American Basketry. *Annual Report—1902. United States National Museum,* 171–545. Washington, DC: Smithsonian Institution.

Miller, Stephen Nachmanovitch
    1974   The Playful, the Crazy, and the Nature of Pretense. In *The Anthropological Study of Human Play.* Edward Norbeck, ed. Special issue of *Rice University Studies* 60(3):31–51.

Moorhead, Max L.
    1968   *The Apache Frontier: Jacobo Ugarte and Spanish-Indian Relations in Northern New Spain, 1769–1791.* Norman: University of Oklahoma Press.

Opler, Morris E.
    1938   The Sacred Clowns of the Chiricahua and Mescalero Indians. *El Palacio* 44:75–79.
    1965   *An Apache Life-Way.* New York: Cooper Square Publishers. First published 1941.
    1969   *Apache Odyssey: A Journey between Two Worlds.* New York: Holt, Rinehart, and Winston.
    1987   Response to Dr. Farrer. In "Past Is Present" column entitled "Further Amplification on Apache Fieldwork and the Schmerler Death." *Anthropology Newsletter* 28(3):3.

Ortiz, Alfonso
    1969   *The Tewa World.* Chicago: University of Chicago Press.

Parsons, Elsie Clews and Ralph L. Beals
    1934   The Sacred Clowns of the Pueblo and Mayo-Yaqui Indians. *American Anthropologist* 36:491–514.

Peacock, James L.
    1978   Symbolic Reversal and Social History: Transvestites and Clowns of Java. In *The Reversible World: Symbolic Inversion in Art and Society.* Barbara A. Babcock, ed. Ithaca: Cornell University Press, 209–24.

Pinxten, Rik and Ingrid van Dooren
    1992   Some Notes on Navajo Earth and Sky and the Celestial Life Force. In *Earth and Sky: Visions of the Cosmos in Native North American Folklore.* Ray A. Williamson and Claire R. Farrer, eds. Albuquerque: University of New Mexico Press.

Prigogine, Ilya
    1984   *Order out of Chaos: Man's New Dialogue with Nature.* New York: Bantam.

Ray, Verne F.
    1945   The Contrary Behavior Pattern in American Indian Ceremonialism. *Southwestern Journal of Anthropology* 1:75–113.

Ruby, Jay, ed.
    1982   *A Crack in the Mirror: Reflexive Perspectives in Anthropology.* Philadelphia: University of Pennsylvania Press.

Schechner, Richard
    1982   Collective Reflexivity: Restoration of Behavior. In *A Crack in the Mirror*: 39–81. See Ruby 1982.

Smale, Stephen
    1980   *The Mathematics of Time: Essays on Dynamical Systems, Economic Processes, and Related Topics.* New York: Springer-Verlag.

Sonnichsen, Charles L.
    1973   *The Mescalero Apaches.* 2d ed. Norman: University of Oklahoma Press.

Sparrow, Colin
  1982   *The Lorenz Equations, Bifurcations, Chaos, and Strange Attractors*. New York: Springer-Verlag.
Steward, Julian H.
  1930   The Ceremonial Buffoon of the American Indian. *Michigan Academy of Science, Arts, and Letters* 14:187–207.
Tanner, Clara Lee
  1968   *American Indian Craft Arts*. Tucson: University of Arizona Press.
  1982   *Apache Indian Baskets*. Tucson: University of Arizona Press.
Tedlock, Dennis
  1983   *The Spoken Word and the Work of Interpretation*. Philadelphia: University of Pennsylvania Press.
Thomas, Alfred Barnaby, trans. and ed.
  1935   *After Coronado: Spanish Exploration Northeast of Mexico, 1696–1721—Documents from the Archives of Spain, Mexico, and New Mexico*. Norman: University of Oklahoma Press.
Toelken, Barre
  1979   *The Dynamics of Folklore*. Boston: Houghton Mifflin.
Toelken, Barre, and Tacheeni Scott
  1981   Poetic Retranslation and the "Pretty Languages" of Yellowman. In *Traditional American Literatures: Texts and Interpretations*. Karl Kroeber, ed. Lincoln: University of Nebraska Press: 65–116.
Turnbaugh, Sarah Peabody, and William A.
  1986   *Indian Baskets*. West Chester, PA: Schiffer Publishing.
Turner, Victor
  1967   *The Forest of Symbols: Aspects of Ndembu Ritual*. Ithaca: Cornell University Press.
  1969   *The Ritual Process*. Chicago: Aldine.
  1975   Ritual As Communication and Potency: An Ndembu Case Study. In *Symbols and Society: Essays on Belief Systems in Action*. Carole E. Hill, ed. Athens, GA: University of Georgia Press: 58–81.
van Gennep, Arnold
  1960   *The Rites of Passage*. Trans. Monika B. Vizedom and Gabrielle L. Caffe. Chicago: University of Chicago Press. First published in 1908 as *Les Rites de Passage*.
Vansina, Jan
  1985   *Oral Tradition as History*. Madison: University of Wisconsin Press.
Whiteford, Andrew Hunter
  1970   *North American Indian Arts*. New York: Golden Press.
  1988   *Southwestern Indian Baskets: Their History and Their*

Makers. Santa Fe, NM: School of American Research Press.

Wilbert, Johannes

1974 *The Thread of Life: Symbolism of Miniature Art from Ecuador.* Studies in Pre-Columbian Art and Archaeology no. 12. Washington, DC: Dumbarton Oaks.

Williamson, Ray A. and Claire R. Farrer, eds.

1992 *Earth and Sky: Visions of the Cosmos in Native North American Folklore.* Albuquerque: University of New Mexico Press.

Winship, George Parker, ed.

1964 *The Coronado Expedition, 1540–1542.* Reissue. Chicago: Rio Grande Press. First published in 1896 as the *Annual Report of the Bureau of American Ethnology, 1892–1893.* Washington, DC: Smithsonian Institution.

Witherspoon, Gary

1977 *Language and Art in the Navajo Universe.* Ann Arbor: University of Michigan Press.

Zolbrod, Paul G.

1984 *Diné Bahane': The Navajo Creation Story.* Albuquerque: University of New Mexico Press.

Glossary and Pronunciation Guide

The orthography used throughout the text is that agreed upon by the Mescalero Apache Tribal Language Committee as of 1975. The committee had representatives for each of the Apachean languages (Mescalero, Chiricahua, and Lipan) spoken on the Mescalero Apache Indian Reservation. Since Apache languages contain sounds not found in English, their approximate English equivalents are given. Note that vowels can have high tone marks [´] as well as be nasalized [̨] or be both high in tone and nasalized [e.g., ą́]; there are no English equivalents for these sounds.

     Apache has four tones: low (unmarked), high (marked as above), and rising or falling—the latter two are not marked by agreement among the Language Committee members. There is no glottal stop [ʔ] in most dialects of English; however, pronunciating "bottle" Brooklynese-style, with a catch in the breath between the two "t"s, approximates the glottal stop [i.e., bot [catch breath] le. The ⁿ is an "n" but with a high tone; again, there is no English equivalent. Similarly the fricative l [ɫ] is not found in English but approximates the sound of the initial double l in Welsh; it is pronounced by putting the tip of the tongue against the upper central front incisors and saying English "l" but forcing the sound out the sides of the mouth. In each of the following examples, pronunciation should be in standard American English, that spoken by most national network news anchors.

a	as in father	nd	as in and
aa	as in ah	[o]	as in go; this sound is rarely encountered in the Eastern Apachean languages
b	as in bat		
ch	as in church		
ch꞉	no English equivalent; similar to church with a sharp intake of breath between the ch and the u	s	as in see
		sh	as in she
		t	as in top
d	as in doll	t꞉	no American English equivalent (but see note above)
dl	as in candle		
dz	no English equivalent; similar to ladies or cards	tl	as in standard American English bottle; in some dialects of Apache this is pronounced like dl
e	as in met (short a sound)		
ee	as in cane or brain		
g	as in go	tl꞉	no American English equivalent; similar to Yiddish yentle
gh	no English equivalent; similar to goat but rolled high against the palate		
		tł	no American English equivalent
		tł꞉	even worse for a native speaker of English
h	as in hat		
i	as in he	ts	as in cats
ii	as in bee	ts꞉	no American English equivalent
j	as in jail	u	as in boot
k	as in cake	uu	as in gooey
l	as in lean	y	as in yes
ł	as in Welsh Llewellyn	z	as in zoo or his
m	as in me	zh	as in vision
n	as in nice	꞉	glottal stop; no standard American English equivalent
n̄	no English equivalent; similar to English n but with a high tone		

This glossary is intended for the nonspecialist. Thus, some words are paraphrased, some are a direct translation, and some are a transliteration. In each instance I chose to render the Apache into the kind of English that came closest to the flavor of the Apache.

Capital letters are used where they are appropriate in English. The alphabetization follows English as closely as was possible with the special Apachean characters being treated as variations of their closest English equivalents. An asterisk after a word indicates that it is in the ritual language used for ceremonies and other religious events or narratives about rituals, ceremonies, and religious matters.

Singular and plural forms are the same in Apache. One knows the number intended from the context. Similarly, there is no gender ascription in nouns or pronouns; again, context serves to define what is handled with separate words in English.

ʔanaaguʔłiin   one who makes them; maker.

au   yes; affirmative; agreement; sure.

Bikʔégubijedidii*   According To Whom There Are The Four Legged; Third Grandfather Pole.

Bikʔégudindé*   According To Whom There Are People, or sometimes According To Whom There Is Life; Creator. Fourth Grandfather Pole.

Bikʔéguindan-n*   Life-Giver.

Bikʔéguʔiyaa*   According To Whom There Are Sky Elements And Sky Beings. First Grandfather Pole.

Bikʔégunaagishnaatʔa*   According To Whom There Are Flying And Crawling Beings. Second Grandfather Pole.

chʼenetłʔu   corral; runway.

daabaaʔiłhénsi   I am grateful for it; profound thanks.

daaiinaa   here it ends; it is finished.

deishehí   process of giving birth.

dii jidigha   four-traveling continuously; endless cycling of the life course.

diindá   four-stages-of-life.

Diizii   Fourth Standing; Fourth Grandfather Pole.

dził   mountain.

dził luzi   mountain cross.

ʔełtsesizi*   First Standing; First Grandfather Pole.

Gąʔhe   colloquial term for the Mountain God dancers.

Gąʔhi   single Mountain God dancer.

Gąʔhidziłchilin*   last Mountain God dancer in the line.

Gąʔhidziłigan*   second (from the front) Mountain God dancer.

Gąʔhidziłihiitlin*   lead (first in line) Mountain God dancer.

Gąʔhidziłitsulin*   third Mountain God dancer in the line.

gu gan   someone's arm.

gushkʔish   mud.

gutąął   singer (of ceremonies); one who sings.

guzhuguja*   that which is in order and balance; perfect harmony; that which is exquisitely ordered.

haighạ   pulling the sun. (Fast speech form.)

ha ʔiɫdi   winter's center or middle; winter solstice; mid-year in the aboriginal year.

Hanyaadigha ʔsizi*   Going Down Standing; Third Grandfather Pole.

hⁿzhúne   good; proper; harmonious; beautiful; balanced.

huskane   "Indian bananas"; fruit of *Yucca baccata*.

ʔich ʔayuat ʔé   oppositeness; contrariness.

ʔijish   between; space-filler.

ʔiɫchibighạ*   Home of Wind.

ʔin ʔch ʔindi   communication without words or speech.

ʔindidé sạạ ʔigish*   Old Man Thunder and Little Boy Lightning.

intin   road; pathway; trail.

ʔis ʔa ʔanebikugh ʔạ*   Old Age Home; Holy Lodge; Ceremonial Tipi.

ʔisdzanatɫ ʔeesh*   White Painted Woman.

ʔiyane   buffalo; bison.

ʔizha ʔshnant ʔạ*   Bird of Authority; eagle.

juuɫgu*   being encircled; circularity.

kughạ   home; house; tipi.

kughạ ʔbikine*   Home of Winter/Ice; northland.

Ɫibayé*   Dust- or Gray- or Dirt-Colored One; Clown. The last figure in
a line of Mountain God dancers.

ɫį́į́   horse [contemporary term]. See also neɫį́į́yé.

ɫika   sweet; good taste.

má   mother; mama; mom.

naabik ʔaash-n*   one of two dance steps used by girls during puberty
ceremonial dancing in the Holy Lodge.

naaikish*   godmother; female director of a girl undergoing her puberty
ceremonial; female ritual specialist during the girls' puberty ceremonial.

naaisha   I have done/completed this.

Naakisizi*   Second Standing; Second Grandfather Pole.

naant ʔạ-ạ   slave; one who is ordered about/around by others.

Naayéⁿeskạne*   He Killed on Earth; Killer of Enemies. Elder of the
Twin Warrior Gods.

nahakus   that which pivots around itself, falling; the Big Dipper.

nahakus biyaa ʔ   from under the Big Dipper; that is, the north land or,
poetically, winter.

ⁿdaʔi bijuuł sią̃ʔ* ⊕; life's living circle; life's/creation's circleness/completion sits/exists there.

ⁿdé The People; Apaches.

ⁿdé binaantʔą-ą that one who people order about/around.

Níaguchilááda* When The World Was Being Made; in the beginningtime.

Ninaayéⁿskąn-n* Killer of Enemies; also called He Killed On Earth. Elder of the Twin Warrior Gods.

nishjaa owl.

niųʔyé* Land of Sorrow/Hardship.

neł̨įyé burden bearer; horse or dog (depending upon time period being referenced).

nųʔbił whirling; whirlwind; dust devil; chaos.

sha ʔ sun.

Shaʔihiyaiyusi* Standing Winter. Fourth Grandfather Pole. See also Diisizi and Bikʔégudiⁿde.

shaʔighą* pulling the sun [proper term]. See also haighą.

shąʔsizi sun standing still; summer solstice; beginning of the aboriginal year.

shi first person singular pronoun.

shił first person singular reflexive pronoun.

shimá my mother.

Shi Tsuye Tłendił* My Grandfathers Spiraled Together; Holy Lodge tetrapod.

sizi standing (with the connotation of still).

sųųs star.

sųųs biné morning star (Capella in the summertime).

Taasizi* Third Standing; Third Grandfather Pole.

Taanashkaʔda Three Who Went Together (constellation of Capella, auriga Eta, auriga Iota).

teł cattail; tules (*Typha latifolia*).

tiswin corn beer.

tsął cradle; cradleboard.

tsełʔlighą-i* bald eagle.

tsełʔłitsu* golden eagle.

tse nųʔbił rock spinning; whirling rock.

tu water

Tubaaʔjishʔchʔinné*   Born of/for Water; Water's Child; Younger of the Twin Warrior Gods.

Tubaʔjishʔdiné*   He Was Born For Water; Water's Child; Younger of the Twin Warrior Gods.

Tuduubitsʔałidaa*   Water That One Cannot See Over.

yeijish   one of two dance steps used by girls during dancing in the Holy Lodge during the girls' puberty ceremonial.

Index

This Index was prepared with the assistance of Alison Davies through a grant from the California State University Graduate School.